The Archaeological Heritage of Oman

THE FIRST PEOPLES OF OMAN
Palaeolithic Archaeology of the Nejd Plateau

JEFFREY I. ROSE, YAMANDÚ H. HILBERT
ANTHONY E. MARKS & VITALY I. USIK

Sultanate of Oman
Ministry of Heritage and Culture

ARCHAEOPRESS PUBLISHING LTD
Summertown Pavilion
18-24 Middle Way
Summertown
Oxford OX2 7LG
www.archaeopress.com

The First Peoples of Oman. Palaeolithic Archaeology of the Nejd Plateau
(Includes bibliographical references and index).

1. Arabia. 2. Oman. 3. Dhofar. 4. Nejd Plateau. 5. Palaeolithic. 6. Stone tools.

This edition is published by Archaeopress Publishing Ltd in association with the Ministry of Heritage and Culture, Sultanate of Oman.

Printed in England

ISBN 978-1-78969-284-6
ISBN 978-1-78969-285-3 (e-Pdf)

Ministry of Heritage and Culture
Sultanate of Oman, Muscat
P.O. Box 668 P.C. 100
Khuwair, Muscat
Phone: +968 24 64 13 00
Fax: +968 24 64 13 31
Email: info@mhc.gov.om
Web Site: www.mhc.gov.om

Cover image: A stone workshop site in Wadi Haluf, central Dhofar (photograph by the Dhofar Archeological Project).

Contents

List of illustrations

5.7. Schematic representation of multi-occupation site formation processes showing 178
hypothetical retreat of the scarp doe to erosion: (a) Stage 1 shows a typical block section
from the Nejd with chert nodules and slabs eroding within, (b) Stage 2 shows the
advance of scarp erosion that exposes fresh chert nodules, which were used to produce
Lower Palaeolithic stone tools by the initial hominid inhabitants of the Nejd Plateau, (c)
Stage 3 shows continued erosion and retreat of the low scarp, which exposes new chert
nodules, continuing throughout the Palaeolithic and Holocene. During subsequent
stages, successive groups of toolmakers returned to exploit fresh chert nodules eroding
from the edge of the scarp (illustration by Y.H. Hilbert).

TABLES

Acknowledgements

This volume is the product of over fifteen years of research in the Sultanate of Oman, to which we owe our gratitude to several individuals. First and foremost, we thank His Majesty Sultan Qaboos bin Said Al-Said for cultivating and inspiring the scientific curiosity of a nation. We thank His Royal Highness Sayyid Haitham bin Tarik Al-Said, Minister of Heritage and Culture. We are grateful to the Undersecretary for Heritage, H.E. Salim bin Mohammed Al-Mahrooqi, and the Adviser for Heritage sites, H.E. Hassan bin Mohammed Al-Lawati, as well as to Sultan bin Saif Al-Bakri, Director General for Archaeology. We thank Khamis Al-Asmi in his role as both Director of the Department of Excavations and Archaeological Studies and as a team member during our first Dhofar fieldwork campaign in 2004.

We wish to thank each and every colleague who has dedicated their time and energies to the Dhofar Archaeological Project over the years: Jeanne Marie Geiling, Christopher Galletti, Mohammed Jaboob, Said Al-Saqri, Ali Al-Mahrooqi, Yaqoub Al-Busaidi, Amir Beshkani, Adrian Parker, Michael Morley, Ash Parton, Natalia Pankova, Philip Van Peer, Marta Lahr, Robert Foley, Richard 'Bert' Roberts, Kira Westaway, Laine Clark-Balzan, Matthias Blessing, Ignacio Clemente-Conte, Musallam Al-Mahri, Daniel Richter, Diego Angelucci, Teresa Medici, Kathryn Price and Henry de Santis. This volume is the culmination of all their efforts.

The project was funded by a UK Arts and Humanities Research Council Early Career Research grant (AH/G012733/1) and National Geographic Society Waitt grant (W253-12) awarded to J.I. Rose, as well as a Fondation Fyssen grant awarded to Y.H. Hilbert supporting his post-doctoral research and laboratory analyses. We are particularly grateful to the editor of this series, Dennys Frenez, for his steadfast patience and support throughout the occasionally painful process of writing this book.

In its inception nearly two decades ago, the Dhofar Archaeological Project was made possible by the help and encouragement of Juris Zarins, Joy McCorriston, Dan Potts, Mauro Cremaschi, and H.E. Ali Al-Shanfari, as well as those no longer with us: Maurizio Tosi, Serge Cleuziou, Said Al-Mahri and Norman Whalen. It is with our deepest gratitude and in their memory that we dedicate this work.

Preface

The study of prehistory focuses on the archaeological periods that precede the written word. It is not confined to the past of our own species, but seeks to understand cultural expressions of our ancestors and predecessors. According to the late Hans Jürgen Eggers (1986: 14), *"Prehistory is the science of the shovel"*.

This statement may be fitting for the prehistoric archaeology of Europe, where digging into the ground is how information is typically acquired. This is not the case, however, for the arid landscapes of southern Oman. Over the course of five field seasons, the Dhofar Archaeological Project team walked hundreds and drove thousands of kilometers, collecting well over a metric ton of stone tools scattered on the surface. It is a land of total archaeological visibility, with few preserved sediments. Throughout our entire campaign we used just three shovels, but sacrificed countless shoes and punctures to the flint teeth of the rocky desert. In Oman, it would be more accurate to say prehistory is the science of rubber soles and flat tires.

The First Peoples of Oman – Palaeolithic archaeology of the Nejd Plateau presents the results of our archaeological research in the Governorate of Dhofar between 2010 and 2013. Initially, the aim of the project was to test the rapid coastal migration hypothesis of early modern human expansion out of Africa. Dhofar is an ideal candidate to study this specific route of dispersal, due to its seasonal rainfall, plethora of chert outcrops and karstic cavities riddling the mountain escarpment. The continental shelf in Dhofar remained relatively stable throughout the past, whereas in many other places along the Indian Ocean rim, rising sea levels have submerged ancient coastal landscapes that served as hypothetical corridors of early human migration.

During the first few months of the 2010 campaign, our survey focused on the Dhofar mountain seaward slopes and coastal plain. These were the least productive and most discouraging months of the entire project. We did not find a single Middle, Upper, or Late Palaeolithic site. We tirelessly tested rockshelters, caves and terraces for sediments bearing Palaeolithic cultural remains, without producing a single artifact. On the advise of Juris Zarins, with years of archaeological survey experience in Dhofar, we eventually set our sights on the western Nejd Plateau.

It was there, around the village of Mudayy, at last we struck gold (chert, to be precise). On an ancient terrace above Wadi Aybut, we discovered a stone tool industry made by one of the earliest modern human populations on earth. This was a breakthrough in both our understanding of early human dispersal, as well being able to read the Palaeolithic landscapes of Dhofar. In subsequent campaigns, our team mapped hundreds of prehistoric sites across the region, some multi-occupation sites with evidence of successive habitation for over a million years.

This volume summarizes these findings in five chapters. We begin with an overview of geography and palaeoenvironments, describing the diverse landscapes and fluctuating palaeoenvironmental record of Dhofar. The next three chapters present our discoveries from the Lower, Middle and Upper-Late Palaeolithic archaeological periods. Each chapter begins with a short overview of the major cultural and biological milestones from a global and regional perspective, before describing a sample of findings from the Dhofar Archaeological Project. The final chapter synthesizes these data and considers prospects for future Palaeolithic research in southern Oman.

Chapter 1

Geography and palaeoenvironments

The earth's climate and environments are in a perpetual state of flux. Our planet orbits the sun along an eccentric elliptical path, which alters the amounts of average annual solar radiation we receive over 100,000-year cycles. In addition, the earth wobbles and tilts as it spins on its axis, influencing climatic fluctuations over 41,000 and 26,000-year periods (Milanković 1920). Evidence of these fluctuations are embedded within the landscape, called environmental proxy signals, which are among the most important sources of information for researchers studying early human prehistory and ecology. In and around Oman, such environmental proxy signals include ancient lake sediments in the desert, dust deposits on the sea floor, stalactites dripping from cave ceilings, even the dunes themselves.

With the development of innovative dating techniques in the last few decades that reach beyond the 40,000 year limit of traditional radiocarbon dating, scientists are able to measure the age of calcium carbonate rock, volcanic ash, or the time elapsed since a grain of sand has been exposed to light. Harnessing these various methods for measuring the age of stratified deposits, it is possible to reconstruct the chronology and impact of climate change on the prehistoric landscapes of Oman.

One particularly effective environmental proxy signal comes from deep-sea cores, which store an archive of climate change reaching back several million years. By observing variations over time in the chemical composition of plankton deposited in the seabed, scientists have recorded cyclical fluctuations in the ratio between different oxygen isotopes. These cycles, in turn, are a function of how much of the earth's water is trapped in glaciers. During glacial periods, rainfall rich in ^{16}O was frozen in continental ice sheets that extended down into North America and Europe, skewing the marine isotope ratios toward higher amounts of ^{18}O versus ^{16}O. Conversely, warm periods caused widespread glacial melting that released ^{16}O-rich water into the oceans, all of which are recorded within the calcareous shells of planktonic foraminifera. These cold and warm intervals are referred to as Marine Isotope Stages (MIS), beginning with the most recent MIS 1 and counting backward in time. Odd-numbered isotope stages indicate interglacial periods, when warm and humid conditions prevailed, while even-numbered isotope stages denote glacial periods, when cold and dry climatic conditions enveloped the globe.

Isotope stages can be further divided into sub-stages, such as MIS 5.1, 5.2, 5.3, etc. Sub-stages are either brief periods of a warmer climatic regime during glacial periods (i.e., interstadials) or an episode of global cooling during an interglacial (i.e., stadials) (Anderson *et al.* 2007; Lisiecki and Raymo 2005; Waelbroeck *et al.* 2002).

These glacial-interglacial cycles, known as the ice ages, began 2.58 million years ago at the start of the Quaternary geological period and Pleistocene geological epoch (Gibbard *et al.* 2010). More than 100 marine isotope stages have been identified within the Pleistocene, which lasted for over 2.5 million years. The Pleistocene was characterized by climatic instability and oscillations between warm and cold global temperatures. Fluctuations between warm interglacial and cold glacial periods became increasingly extreme in the latter half of the Pleistocene. The period between 132,000 and 112,000 years ago is referred to as the Last Interglacial (MIS 5.5), dominated by an unusually warm and wet climate across most of the earth (Otvos 2015; Shackleton *et al.* 2003).

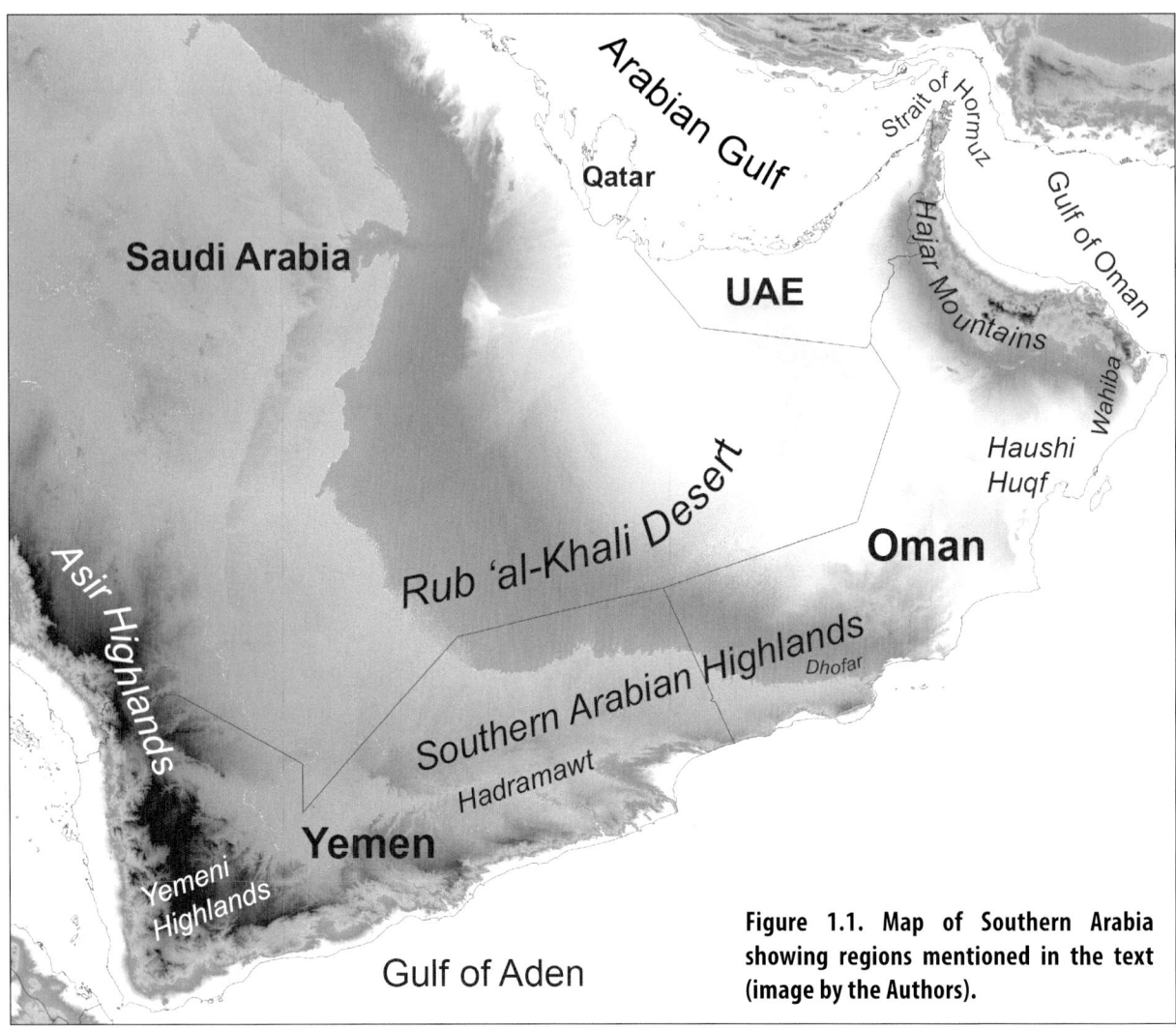

Figure 1.1. Map of Southern Arabia showing regions mentioned in the text (image by the Authors).

Increasingly cold and dry conditions culminated around 20,000 years ago during MIS 2, the Last Glacial Maximum, at which time ice sheets advanced far south into Europe and sea levels dropped 120 meters below current levels.

The Pleistocene is followed by our current geological epoch known as the Holocene, beginning 11,700 years ago (Walker *et al.* 2012). In Oman, the period between approximately 10,000 and 8,000 years ago is also referred to as the Holocene Climatic Optimum, given the generally warm and wet conditions that prevailed (Parker *et al.* 2004). This wet period was followed by a general drying trend that was punctuated by recurring century-scale megadroughts between 8,000 and 6,000 years ago, during the Middle Holocene (Preston *et al.* 2015)

The Palaeoclimatic Record and Research Paradigms

The evidence from speleothem, sedimentary and marine environmental proxy signals found throughout Oman show a number of climatic fluctuations over the course of the Quaternary period, corresponding with recurring glacial-interglacial cycles. Wet periods, triggered by the northward migration of the Inter Tropical Convergent Zone (ITCZ), activated the interior draining *wadi* systems and filled the inland playa lake basins. Studies of speleothem and lacustrine deposits suggest the onset of pluvial conditions was rapid, followed by a gradual decline in rainfall over several millennia as the ITCZ slowly returned southward.

Hence, the southern highlands encompassing Dhofar, Hadramawt and southwestern Yemen, remained under the delayed influence of a heightened rainfall regime for a longer time than inland regions (Fleitmann *et al.* 2007; Lézine *et al.* 2017).

Using these palaeoenvironmental data, researchers are able to build a framework of climate change with which to model prehistoric occupations. Massive alluvial deposits in northern Oman indicate that the climate of the early Quaternary, from two million to half a million years ago, was generally warmer and wetter than today (Blechschmidt *et al.* 2009). Oman became increasingly more arid after that, with evidence for heightened rainfall around the following times: 1) 410,000 BP, 2) 330,000-300,000 BP, 3) 220,000-200,000 BP, 4) 130,000-115,000 BP, 5) 105,000-100,000 BP, 6) 82,000-78,000 BP, 7) 60,000-40,000 BP, and 8) 10,000-8,000 BP. While the MIS 5 pluvial periods are thoroughly represented in the terrestrial and marine archives throughout all of Arabia, the evidence between 60,000 and 40,000 BP (early MIS 3) suggests only brief and ephemeral wet periods that were insufficient to trigger speleothem growth, or to fill the interior lake basins for any sustained length of time (Matter *et al.* 2015; Preusser 2009).

During pluvial periods, sea levels around the Arabian Peninsula were roughly equivalent to today, in some cases exceeding current levels by up to three meters (Macumber 2011). For the remainder of human prehistory, sea levels were reduced between 40 and 120 m (Lambeck 1996). There was an inverse correlation between the amount of annual precipitation and shoreline configuration, which is fundamental to understanding human prehistory in the Arabian Peninsula. This dynamic created a pushing and pulling mechanism from the interior grasslands to the emergent continental shelf, as these zones repeatedly cycled between habitable and uninhabitable over the course of the Pleistocene.

Figure 1.2. The Al-Hajar Mountains near Wadi Al-Ain (photograph by the authors).

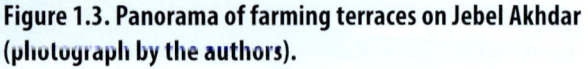

Figure 1.3. Panorama of farming terraces on Jebel Akhdar (photograph by the authors).

Two different research paradigms have developed among scholars seeking to model early human demographics in the Arabian Peninsula. The first, called "*tabula rasa*", envisions that populations could only settle in the Peninsula during pluvials and were subsequently displaced when cyclical climatic downturns caused widespread desertification (Drechsler 2007; Rose 2006; Uerpmann *et al.* 2009).

A second paradigm argues for the presence of demographic refugia, which were stable habitats around which human groups coalesced when rainfall became scarce (Bailey *et al.*, 2015; Rose, 2007, 2010). Genetic studies of modern Arabian populations point to the latter possibility, with a major ice age refugium located in South Arabia (Al-Abri *et al.* 2012; Černý *et al.* 2011; Gandini *et al.* 2016; Platt *et al.* 2017; Yang and Fu 2018).

Geographic Scope of the Dhofar Archaeological Project

Virtually the entire Pleistocene archaeological record of Oman is comprised of chipped stone waste and stone tools (lithics). The countless lithic scatters found across South Arabia are vestiges of the many successive prehistoric groups that inhabited the region. Although most artifacts found on these deflated surfaces cannot be directly dated, arid landscapes such as the Nejd Plateau provide nearly total archaeological visibility, enabling researchers to track early human tool-making activities and tool usage across the whole terrain. In this section, we present the different landscapes of southern Oman with specific attention to the Nejd Plateau. We discuss the geology of these landscapes and when various ecological niches in southern Oman would have been available to sustain human habitation during the Pleistocene.

The Sultanate of Oman

Nestled in the southeastern corner of the Arabian Peninsula, the Sultanate of Oman (Figure 1.1) is delimited by the Rub Al-Khali desert to the west, the Arabian Sea and Sea of Oman to the south and east, the Musandam Peninsula to the northwest and a land border separating Dhofar from Mahra in the southwest of Oman. The country is naturally divided into three geological zones: the Al-Hajar Mountains in northern Oman, the central plateau and the Huqf depression in the interior and the Dhofar Mountains in the southwest (Platel *et al.* 1992). The Al-Hajar Mountains form a continuous mountain range from the northern tip of the Musandam Peninsula, at the Strait of Hormuz, to its easternmost point terminating near Al-Ashkharah in the northern Ash Sharqiyah region (Figure 1.2). The Al-Hajar Mountains extends for over 700 km and rises up to 3000 m above sea level, reaching its highest points around Saih Hatat and Jebel Akhdar (Figure 1.3). A narrow coastal plain made up of alluvial and aeolian deposits intermingled with khabra deposits bounds the Al-Hajar to the northeast, while massive alluvial fans are found to the south and west.

Numerous wadis dissect the plateau, which once flowed with ancient rivers draining into the Umm as Samim and Huqf depressions (Glennie 2005). During MIS 5 and the Early Holocene Optimum, basins within the Huqf, Ash Sharqiyah and southern Rub Al-Khali were filled with perennial lakes (Matter *et al.* 2015; Radies *et al.* 2005; Rosenberg *et al.* 2012). Within the Huqf depression, there are extensive sabkha deposits created by high groundwater that form an evaporitic crust. In this region, sabkhas, palaeolake marls and stabilized dune fields are all that remain of a once productive landscape (Jagher and Pümpin 2010).

Figure 1.4. Archaeological survey near Adam in central Oman (photograph by the authors).

The Governorate of Dhofar

In the south of Oman is the Governorate of Dhofar, which is partitioned into six distinct ecological zones: 1) coastal plain, 2) seaward slopes and southern draining *wadis*, 3) summit grasslands, 4) northern mountain slopes and rain shadow, 5) plateau and canyon lands, and 6) southern Rub Al-Khali basin (Miller and Morris 1988; Raffaelli and Tardelli 2006).

Flat open desert dominates the northern part of the region, which is comprised of gravel plains, sabkhas and increasingly higher dunes as one travels deeper into the Rub Al-Khali sand sea. Vegetation across the open desert consists of generally sparse shrub communities including *Calligonum crinitum*, *Cornulaca arabica* and *Haloxylon persicum* (Mandaville 1990). The dry Nejd Plateau is rocky and hilly, increasing in elevation to the south where it abuts the Dhofar Mountains. The mountains, escarpment and interior plateau are comprised of shallow marine sediments that overlay the crystalline basement of the Arabian shelf. The horizontally bedded limestone that composes the escarpment and plateau belong to the Hadramawt geological group, which extends all the way from central Yemen. Over the course of successive Quaternary pluvial phases, the northward draining *wadis* across the Nejd have carved long, meandering river valleys through the Tertiary limestone plateau, debouching toward the Rub Al-Khali basin in the north. Stands of shrubs, acacia and ghaf trees are found along *wadi* beds, where surface runoff collects during storms. Since the introduction of center pivot irrigation in the last decade, numerous farms have sprung up in the fertile zone at the interface of the Nejd.

Figure 1.5. Salalah coastal plain with the Dhofar Mountains on the right (photograph by the authors).

The summit grasslands and seaward slopes form an orographic barrier between the monsoon-affected areas to the south and the dry plateau to the north. The grasses in this region belong to an endemic plant community of *Themeda quadrivalvis*, which is a palaeorelict outlier of the East African savannah (Patzelt 2011). The seaward slopes house woodlands and shrublands that form part of the southern Arabian cloud forest; vegetation fed by the dense moisture brought by the annual monsoon (Hildebrandt and Eltahir 2006). Arboreal species include the endemic *Anogeissus dhofarica* and *Commiphora* spp.

The coastal plain is a 50-kilometer long crescent shaped landmass stretching form Ras Raysut to Mirbat, ranging from ten to fifteen kilometers wide (Figure 1.5). It is composed of Quaternary conglomerates and alluvial fans dipping toward the coast, which are cut by short *wadis* draining into the sea. Vegetation on the coastal plain tends to be primarily composed of neophytes such as date palms, coconut palms and bananas grown on irrigated fields near the major *wadi* outlets (Platel *et al.* 1992).

On the plain stretching between Taqa and Mirbat, there a series of major faults within the Upper and Lower Hadhramawt limestone formation, which are responsible for the irregular relief of this region. Among the tertiary limestone deposits encountered in this area, the Rus formation is of considerable importance. An outcrop of this facies is found east of Taqa, within a recrystallized collapsed breccia containing chert nodules. Tectonic uplift, however, has caused the chert nodules to shatter, rendering them undesirable for knapping. East of Mirbat, the exposed crystalline basement is composed of metamorphic and plutonic rocks (Figure 1.6). Intrusive dolerite and rhyolite dykes occasionally slice across this landscape.

Figure 1.6. Landscape east of Mirbat showing rhyolite dykes (photograph by the authors).

The 1200 m high Dhofar Mountain escarpment traps moisture brought by the Indian Ocean monsoon, enveloping southern Oman in fog and rain annually between June and September. During the monsoon season, called the khareef, the southward draining *wadis* are filled with running fresh water (Figure 1.7). The major southern drainage systems include Wadis Jarzis, Arbat, Arzat, Haskeem, Darbat and Hinna. Recent to sub recent travertine deposits are found within the *wadi* valleys (Platel *et al.* 1992).

During the khareef, interdunal and coastal estuaries form along the plain. These are protected by sand barriers and typically do not connect to the ocean. Fresh water flowing from springs and major coastal *wadis* create these lagoon estuarine ecosystems, called *khawrs* (Hoorn and Cremaschi 2004). Moisture and vegetation have produced layers of soil rich in clay, covering the slopes and uplands. In addition to *Anogeissus dhofarica* woodlands found along the seaward slopes, there is a single stand of baobab trees (Figure 1.8), which may have been planted by the nearby occupants of the late Iron Age port city of Sumhuram (Aronson *et al.* 2017).

The Nejd Plateau

Given its wealth of prehistoric archaeology, our survey focused on the bare desert scabland and incised canyons that comprise the Nejd Plateau. This distinct geomorphic zone begins with small *wadis* dissecting the barren tableland at its southern extent (Figure 1.9).

In the central Nejd, the *wadis* conjoin to form wider and deeper canyons. The landscape becomes more homogeneous as the plateau dips northward, giving way to a gently undulating plain across the northern extent. Here the major catchment systems converge at the interface of the Rub Al-Khali, flowing northeastward into the basin.

The DAP survey partitioned the Nejd into eastern and western halves, with the gravel plain transecting Thumrayt serving as the boundary between the two. Each side was then divided into southern, central and northern sectors. In the south, low table mountains (mesas) and inselbergs between 5 and 20 m in elevation rise above a terrain of gravel plains and *wadi* channels (Figure 1.10).

Two main geological groups are found in the southern Nejd: 1) the Lower Hadramawt group consisting of the Umm er Radhuma and Rus formations, and 2) the Upper Hadramawt group made of the Dammam and Aydim formations. The Umm er Radhuma formation is a thick, shallow marine unit that comprises the main tertiary carbonate sequence. This grey to whitish limestone is full of large, high quality chert nodules – a prominent source of raw material for the production of stone tools throughout human prehistory.

The Rus formation is also significant for its frequent and high quality chert outcrops (Figure 1.11). Throughout the southern Nejd, the Rus formation is divided into two members; the lower chalky *Aybut* member and the upper marly-carbonated Gahit member (Platel *et al.* 1992). The *Aybut* member is a 3-5 m thick brecciated dolomitic limestone with thin yellow-orange chert nodules at the bottom. The quality and size of these nodules are highly variable. *Aybut* chert plaquettes are often highly fractured and range in size and quality. The Gahit member consists of thinly bedded, bioclastic layers of banded grey chert nodules and slabs.

Figure 1.7. Wadi Darbat during the monsoon season (photograph by the authors).

Figure 1.9. View from the Dhofar orographic barrier facing north towards the Nejd Plateau (photograph by the authors).

Figure 1.8. Vegetation on the flanks of the Dhofar Mountains (photograph by the authors).

Figure 1.10. Scablands on the southern Nejd Plateau in the vicinity of Wadi Haluf (photograph by the authors).

In the region around Thumrayt, the central Nejd forms a gravel plain with patches of aeolian sediments and sparse inselbergs that are remnants of the upper Hadramawt group. These low, isolated hills often have chert slabs and nodules eroding from the scarps. The Nejd's northward draining *wadis* carry reworked aeolian and alluvial sediments downstream as they downcut during sporadic activation (Figure 1.12).

The northern Nejd is a desolate gravel plain covered by a thin veneer of aeolian sands (Figure 1.13). Prominent landscape features are ancient alluvial fans, rare travertine deposits and calcareous palaeosoils interstratified within Miocene limestone beds. Sometime in the Late Pleistocene, minor tectonic folding occurred along an east-west band in the northern Nejd, diverting stream flow and creating fracture springs (Zarins 2001). Beyond the Nejd, the Rub Al-Khali stretches to the central Arabian Peninsula, with sand dunes reaching over 200 m of height (figure 1.14). Pleistocene river systems once flowed across this interior depression, draining northeastward toward the Gulf (McClure 1976; Zarins 2001).

Summary

The fluctuating climate caused by glacial-interglacial cycles has profoundly affected the landscapes of Arabia and, consequently, early human habitation. Interglacial periods pulled the ITCZ northward, depositing rains across the interior and activating *wadis* and lake basins. Conversely, glacial phases pushed the ITCZ southward, depriving the interior of moisture. Examples of pluvial events are well documented from terrestrial and marine archives during the Last Interglacial (MIS 5.5) and to a lesser degree during MIS 5.3 and 5.1.

Figure 1.11. Raw material outcrops found across Dhofar (above); dense carpet of chert artifacts above Wadi Ghadun close to Mutahafah (below); chert nodules outcropping from the limestone bedrock of the Nejd (photographs by the authors).

Figure 1.12. Panorama over Wadi Aybut on the west-central Nejd (photograph by the authors).

Figure 1.13. The northern Nejd Plateau near Shisr Farms (photograph by J.M. Geiling).

Figure 1.14. Sand dunes north of Al-Hashman in the southern Rub Al-Khali (photograph by the authors).

The ITCZ returned northward again during the Holocene Climatic Optimum between approximately 10,000 and 8,000 years ago. These pluvial periods replenished subterranean springs, activated perennial rivers, filled lake basins and facilitated the expansion of tall-grass savannahs. With the grasslands came large herbivores including extinct giant bison, extinct straight-tusked elephants, aurochs, oryx, gazelle and wild camels (Hadjouis 2007; Rachad 2007; Stewart *et al.* 2017). These mammals, in turn, attracted apex predators such as leopards, cheetahs and humans.

While researchers believe that the onset of pluvial conditions in South Arabia was relatively abrupt, the southward migration of the ITCZ and subsequent environmental desiccation was gradual (Fleitmann *et al.* 2007; Lézine 2009; Lézine *et al.* 2017). As the ITCZ drifted southward, desertification advanced. Groundwater levels sunk, while aeolian transportation and sporadic runoff across dry terrain eroded the topsoil. The widespread savannah grasslands constricted into the Dhofar highlands (Patzelt 2011) and the large mammals that once roamed the plains dwindled and disappeared by the Middle Holocene.

Chapter 2

The Lower Palaeolithic in Dhofar

The Lower Palaeolithic falls chronologically between 2.5 million years (ma) and 300,000 years ago, beginning with the appearance of the first constructed stone tools. This period is broadly partitioned into the Oldowan and the Acheulean cultural complexes. The latter complex is further subdivided into the Lower Acheulean, Middle Acheulean and Upper Acheulean. The makers of the Lower Palaeolithic industries were early species of the genus *Homo*. This chapter focuses on Lower Palaeolithic material discovered by the Dhofar Archaeological Project (DAP). We briefly review Oldowan and Acheulean lithic technologies, as well as the Lower Palaeolithic record throughout the rest of the Arabian Peninsula.

The Oldowan

Indirect evidence for stone tool usage has been documented as far back as 3.4 ma BP (McPherron *et al.* 2010). Researchers identified cut marks on bones that are consistent with butchering marks produced by stone tools. At Lomekwi 3, located close to the western shores of Lake Turkana, researchers excavated rudimentary stone tools from Pliocene layers dated to 3.3 million years ago. The assemblage is composed of diverse pounding tools and flaked artifacts produced by block on block percussion. This material is thought to represent a technological phase between the use of unmodified stones and fully developed free-hand percussion to create stone tools (Harmand *et al.* 2015).

The Oldowan is the oldest known lithic cultural complex exhibiting direct percussion. Artifacts of this type are found from approximately 2.5 ma to 1.5 ma BP. Oldowan stone tools include diverse choppers and chopping tools, discoid cores, polyhedrons, stone anvils, perforators and retouched pieces. Researchers group Oldowan artifacts into four categories following a basic categorization defined by Olduvai Bed I and II assemblages (Leakey 1971): manuports, hammer stones, cores forms and flakes. Manuports are unmodified pieces deliberately brought to the site, while hammer stones show active and/or passive traces of repeated percussion. Core forms are pebbles, chunks, or other pieces of conchoidally fractured raw material from which flakes have been intentionally removed. These are further divided into cores for the deliberate production of flakes and core tools, which have been shaped to perform a specific task. Tool types are classified based on the manner in which they have been retouched, size and shape. The Oldowan is notable for its lack of (detectable) assemblage variability over an immense chronological span.

Throughout its million-year duration, the Oldowan industry shows minor technological variation (Klein 2009). This variability has been attributed to differences in raw material availability and physical properties of the raw material. For instance, Oldowan toolmakers at Gona and Koobi Fora had access to fine-grained obsidian cobbles and pebbles, allowing the toolmakers to produce more elaborately flaked cores and large flake tools (Leakey and Harris 1978; Semaw 2000; Toth 1985).

At the lower Omo Valley, in contrast, quartz pebbles were the only available raw material and Oldowan lithic assemblages there are composed of small, irregular flakes and shattered quartz pebbles and cobbles. Studies show that some Oldowan toolmakers selected specific types of raw materials, suggesting deliberate choice in raw material procurement strategies (Braun *et al.* 2009; Stout *et al.* 2005).

Some distinct techno-typological trends began to appear toward the end of the Oldowan stage. In the Karari industry, a *facies* of the Oldowan, ovoid bifacial forms are present (Harris and Isaac 1976). Within Bed I at Olduvai, there are occasional chopping tools with crudely shaped points, classified as protobifaces (Leakey 1971). This bifacial prototype was fully realized by the beginning of the Acheulean technocomplex around 1.8 ma, which developed from the Oldowan in Africa. The transition from Oldowan to Lower Acheulean lithic technologies was a gradual, non-linear process that began as early as 2.6 million years ago (Semaw *et al.* 2009; Stout *et al.* 2010).

The makers of Oldowan artifacts are thought to be *Homo rudolfensis* and *Homo habilis*, who coexisted with archaic Australopithecine species during this period. Here we face the problem of associating lithic artifacts and biological species. Given that there were different hominids present in East Africa, the toolmakers' taxonomy remains in question. The larger brain capacity of *Homo habilis* and *Homo rudolfensis* is used to infer their association with the Oldowan toolmakers.

Whether Oldowan toolmakers hunted, scavenged, or both is debated. The association of stone tools and bone fragments at numerous Oldowan sites may be related to post depositional disturbance such as secondary transport, carnivore kill sites, scavenger hoards, or even porcupines actively leave traces on faunal assemblages. Equally debatable is the use of fire by the early representatives of the genus *Homo*, where evidence of burning at Oldowan sites is more likely to be the result of post depositional conflagration.

While burnt sediment patches have been noted at an Oldowan locality at Koobi Fora (Bellomo 1994) and burnt clay fragments associated with Oldowan artifacts have been reported at Chesowanja (Gowlett *et al.* 1981), there are no clear links between these burnt sediments and the use of controlled fire by either *Homo habilis* or *Homo rudolfensis*. Given these limitations, questions of Oldowan hominid behavior are difficult to answer. Regardless of meat intake, there is little doubt that gathering plant resources played a greater role in early hominid subsistence than is archaeologically visible.

The Acheulean

The Acheulean lasted between 1.8 ma and 300,000 years ago and is primarily recognized by a tool type known as the handaxe. Acheulean handaxes are found throughout Africa and Eurasia for over a million years, associated with *Homo erectus, Homo ergaster, Homo heidelbergensis*, archaic *Homo sapiens* and *Homo neandertalensis* (Klein 2009; Tomsky 1982). Handaxes are bifacially retouched implements of various sizes and shapes (Bordes 1988). Acheulean assemblages display greater variability than the preceding Oldowan and demonstrate the use of other organic materials such as wood to craft spears and digging sticks.

Evidence for the controlled use of fire becomes increasingly common during the Acheulean, first seen at Koobi Fora and Gadeb in East Africa and Wonderwerk and Swartkrans Caves in South Africa. In the Near East, researchers report evidence for habitual fire usage at Gesher Benot Ya'aqov and in Europe at Sima de los Huesos and Pirro Nord (Attwell *et al.* 2015). Fire was used for cooking, hardening wooden implements like spears and lances and creating light and heat. This last property was perhaps the most important, enabling hominid groups to flourish in cold temperate latitudes.

It is thought that both *Homo erectus* and *Homo ergaster* were capable of tracking, killing and butchering small, medium and even large prey. Over the course of the Middle Pleistocene, researchers observe increasing complexity in tool manufacture and indirect evidence for hunting large fauna becomes more substantial. Noteworthy are the wooden spears discovered at Schöningen in eastern Germany dated to 400,000 years ago (Thieme 2007).

It is likely that such wooden javelins were part of the repertoire of Acheulean hunters, which begs the question: if organic preservation were better, how varied would the material culture of this period be?

The Lower Acheulean is bracketed between 1.8 ma and 800,000 years ago. It is characterized by thick elongated handaxe forms with untrimmed cortical butts for gripping (hence the name). The Middle Acheulean roughly dates between 800,000 and 400,000 years ago, however, is not easily distinguished by any one typological feature or technological change other than a trend toward more finely shaped handaxes. In Africa and the Indian subcontinent, researchers have documented specific techniques for the production of large flakes, which were subsequently shaped into cleavers. The Upper Acheulean falls between approximately 400,000 and 250,000 years ago. As with the Middle Acheulean, this technocomplex shows a wide distribution and significant regional diversification. This is particularly evident comparing Upper Acheulean assemblages from Africa, the Near East and Eurasia. During the Upper Acheulean, we see the introduction of prepared core technologies and a gradual shift from thicker handaxes to thinner bifacial knives, as well as the use of simple blade technologies in some regions.

The Lower Palaeolithic Archaeological Record in Arabia

As the geographic bridge between Africa and Asia, the Lower Palaeolithic archaeological record in Arabia provides important clues for tracking the evolution and dispersals of hominid species through a major corridor of migration. This section explores Lower Palaeolithic evidence from through the Arabian Peninsula in order to contextualize the Early and Middle Pleistocene findings in Dhofar.

Oldowan in Arabia?

Researchers working in Saudi Arabia and Yemen have reported lithic assemblages with Oldowan characteristics (Figure 2.1). Whalen and Schatte (1997) discovered 37 Lower Palaeolithic localities in southwestern Yemen at the interface of the Tihama coast and Yemeni highlands, where they surveyed escarpments and terraces with exposed Pleistocene sediments. Most of these are multi-occupation workshop sites, where artifacts belonging to different chronological phases were found widely dispersed across the surface of the escarpment overlooking Wadi Shahar. These artifacts include a large number of choppers (n=321), polyhedrons (n=11), small retouched tools (n=28) and scrapers (n=78). Handaxes are rare and cleavers are absent (Whalen and Schatte 1997: table 1). The assemblages were predominantly manufactured on quartzite, with a few examples made on volcanic materials including basalt, andesite and rhyolite. The authors report 16 sites exhibiting Mode 1 core technologies. They note, however, that given the absence of absolute dates for any of the material, the Mode 1 assemblages found in their survey area are not necessarily contemporary with the Africa Oldowan technocomplex.

The Joint Yemeni-Soviet expedition conducted in central and eastern Yemen in the 1980s report five sites attributed to the Oldowan. These are Al-Guza cave, Sharkhabil cave, Al-Amira rockshelter, Djidfira and Al-Garb 6 (Amirkhanov 2006). The first three are described by the author as in situ stratified occurrences, while Djidfira and Al-Garb 6 are surface sites where artifacts were collected over a large and diffuse area. Of these sites, Al-Guza is the largest and best studied sample, with a total of 973 artifacts excavated from five archaeological layers. Possible fireplaces were documented in two different levels, one at three meters and the other at nine meters below the surface.

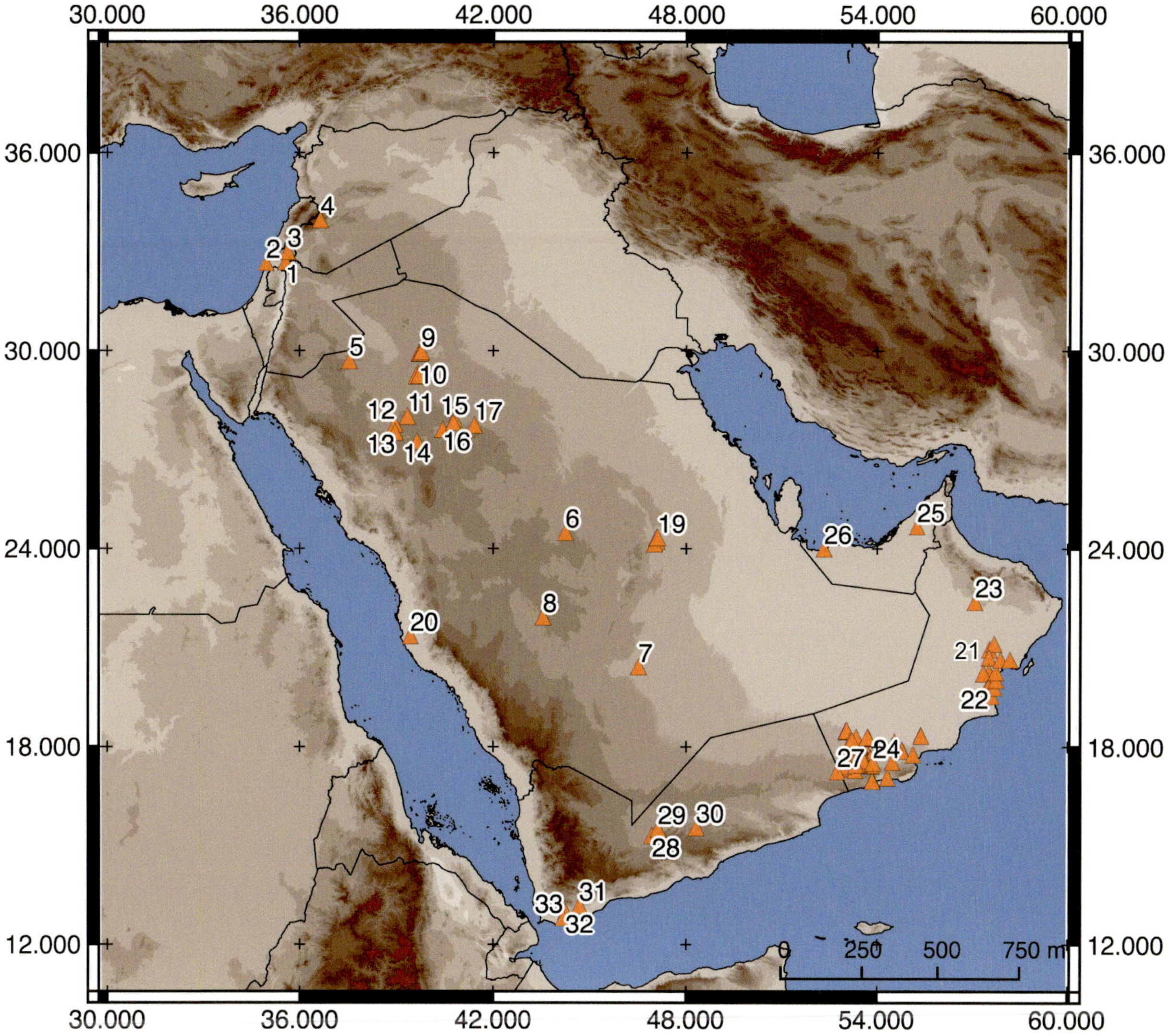

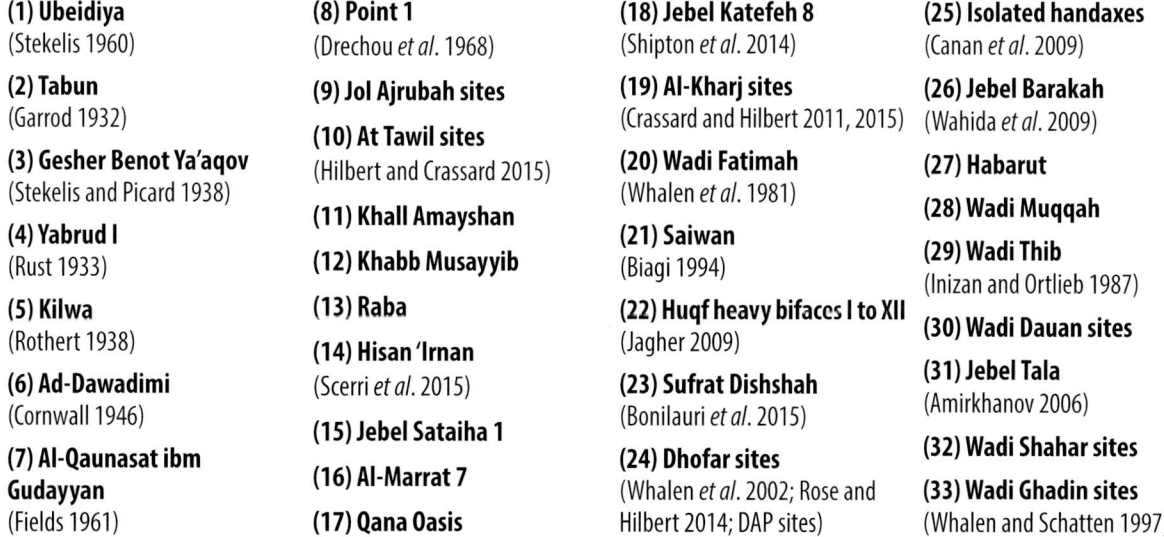

(1) Ubeidiya
(Stekelis 1960)

(2) Tabun
(Garrod 1932)

(3) Gesher Benot Ya'aqov
(Stekelis and Picard 1938)

(4) Yabrud I
(Rust 1933)

(5) Kilwa
(Rothert 1938)

(6) Ad-Dawadimi
(Cornwall 1946)

(7) Al-Qaunasat ibm Gudayyan
(Fields 1961)

(8) Point 1
(Drechou *et al*. 1968)

(9) Jol Ajrubah sites

(10) At Tawil sites
(Hilbert and Crassard 2015)

(11) Khall Amayshan

(12) Khabb Musayyib

(13) Raba

(14) Hisan 'Irnan
(Scerri *et al*. 2015)

(15) Jebel Sataiha 1

(16) Al-Marrat 7

(17) Qana Oasis

(18) Jebel Katefeh 8
(Shipton *et al*. 2014)

(19) Al-Kharj sites
(Crassard and Hilbert 2011, 2015)

(20) Wadi Fatimah
(Whalen *et al*. 1981)

(21) Saiwan
(Biagi 1994)

(22) Huqf heavy bifaces I to XII
(Jagher 2009)

(23) Sufrat Dishshah
(Bonilauri *et al*. 2015)

(24) Dhofar sites
(Whalen *et al*. 2002; Rose and Hilbert 2014; DAP sites)

(25) Isolated handaxes
(Canan *et al*. 2009)

(26) Jebel Barakah
(Wahida *et al*. 2009)

(27) Habarut

(28) Wadi Muqqah

(29) Wadi Thib
(Inizan and Ortlieb 1987)

(30) Wadi Dauan sites

(31) Jebel Tala
(Amirkhanov 2006)

(32) Wadi Shahar sites

(33) Wadi Ghadin sites
(Whalen and Schatten 1997)

Figure 2.1. Map of the Arabian Peninsula showing key Lower Palaeolithic sites (image by the authors).

The industry excavated from Al-Guza cave is described as a "pebble" industry characterized by chopping tools made on cobbles and a notable absence of handaxes. The chopping tools are divided into single-edged, multi-edged and discoidal forms (Amirkhanov 1994). Paleomagnetic dating method was applied to the bottom of layer M at Al-Guza cave, placing the deposit at the Matuyama-Brunhes geomagnetic reversal around 780,000 years ago. The bottom of the sequence, a 1.5 meter thick deposit of pebbles and cobbles within a travertine matrix, is tentatively dated around 1.0 ma BP (Amirkhanov 2006: 605).

In the northern province of Saudi Arabia near Ash-Shuwayhitiyah, Whalen and Pease (1991) report 1517 Oldowan artifacts collected from 16 localities within a four kilometer radius. Grouped under one site number (201-49), the assemblage is characterized by choppers, polyhedrons, discoids, spheroids and a small number of bifaces and cleavers. Based on statistical analysis and comparisons of size clusters with Developed Oldowan assemblages from Oldovai Bed II, the authors infer a cultural relationship between the Developed Oldowan assemblages from Arabia and East Africa, speculating an age for the site between 2.6 and 1.8 ma ago.

Arabian Acheulean

In general terms, Acheulean sites are distinguished by the presence of handaxes, which occur as isolated finds or expansive scatters associated with raw material quarries. Among the earliest discovered Acheulean sites discovered in the Arabian Peninsula are Ad-Dawadimi (Cornwall 1946), Point 1 (Drechou *et al.* 1968) and Kilwa (Rhotert and Böhl 1938) in the Jebel at Tubaiq area of central Saudi Arabia. From a collection made at the Habarut oasis on the Yemeni border in Dhofar, Payne and Hawkins (Payne and Hawkins 1963) were the first to recognize Acheulean handaxes in Oman. Within the last few decades, Acheulean sites have been widely identified across every part of the Peninsula in Saudi Arabia (Inglis *et al.* 2014; Jennings *et al.* 2015; Petraglia *et al.* 2003; Shipton *et al.* 2014; Whalen *et al.* 1981), Oman (Beshkani *et al.* 2017a; Biagi 1994; Bonilauri *et al.* 2015; Jagher and Pümpin 2010; Payne and Hawkins 1963; Rose and Hilbert 2014; Whalen *et al.* 2002; Zarins 2001), the United Arab Emirates (Bretzke *et al.* 2017; Casana *et al.* 2009) and Yemen (Amirkhanov 2006, 1994; Inizan and Ortlieb 1987; Whalen and Schatte 1997).

The Yemeni-Soviet expedition mapped 21 Acheulean localities atop the plateaus and hillsides of the Hadramawt region and deflated plains of Mahra, eastern Yemen. The majority of these findspots are surface sites located in proximity to raw material outcrops. The sites of Meshed 1 to 5 were discovered in stratified contexts within fluvial deposits of Middle Pleistocene age, located in the Wadi Dauan, Hadramawt. Amirkhanov (2006: 606) divides the Acheulean occurrences in Yemen into early and late stages. The earlier material is characterized by ficron handaxes with almond-shaped silhouettes, chopping tools, simple unidirectional blade production from flat cores and large heavy flakes. In terms of handaxe morphology, most prevalent are pointed specimens with untrimmed butts. The "Dauan type" (Figure 2.2) are short handaxes with the tips reduced by two lateral notches. Cross-sections are thick and generally symmetrical in shape. In addition to handaxes, Late Acheulean assemblages exhibit diverse flake tools including side scrapers, as well as semi-prepared cores. The author draws parallels to the Ubeidiya Lower Palaeolithic assemblage from the Levant, dated to around 1.5 ma BP.

In the Huqf depression of central Oman, the Italian Archaeological Mission mapped an extensive scatter of seemingly Lower Palaeolithic artifacts near a chert outcrop (Biagi 1994). The Saiwan lithic assemblage is composed of well-made bifacial tools and fragments, cores with centripetal reduction and a large number of blade blanks and blade cores. The bifaces are thin and range from cordiform to ovate in shape, leading Biagi (1994: 84) to classify the findspot "a late period in the development of the Acheulean Culture."

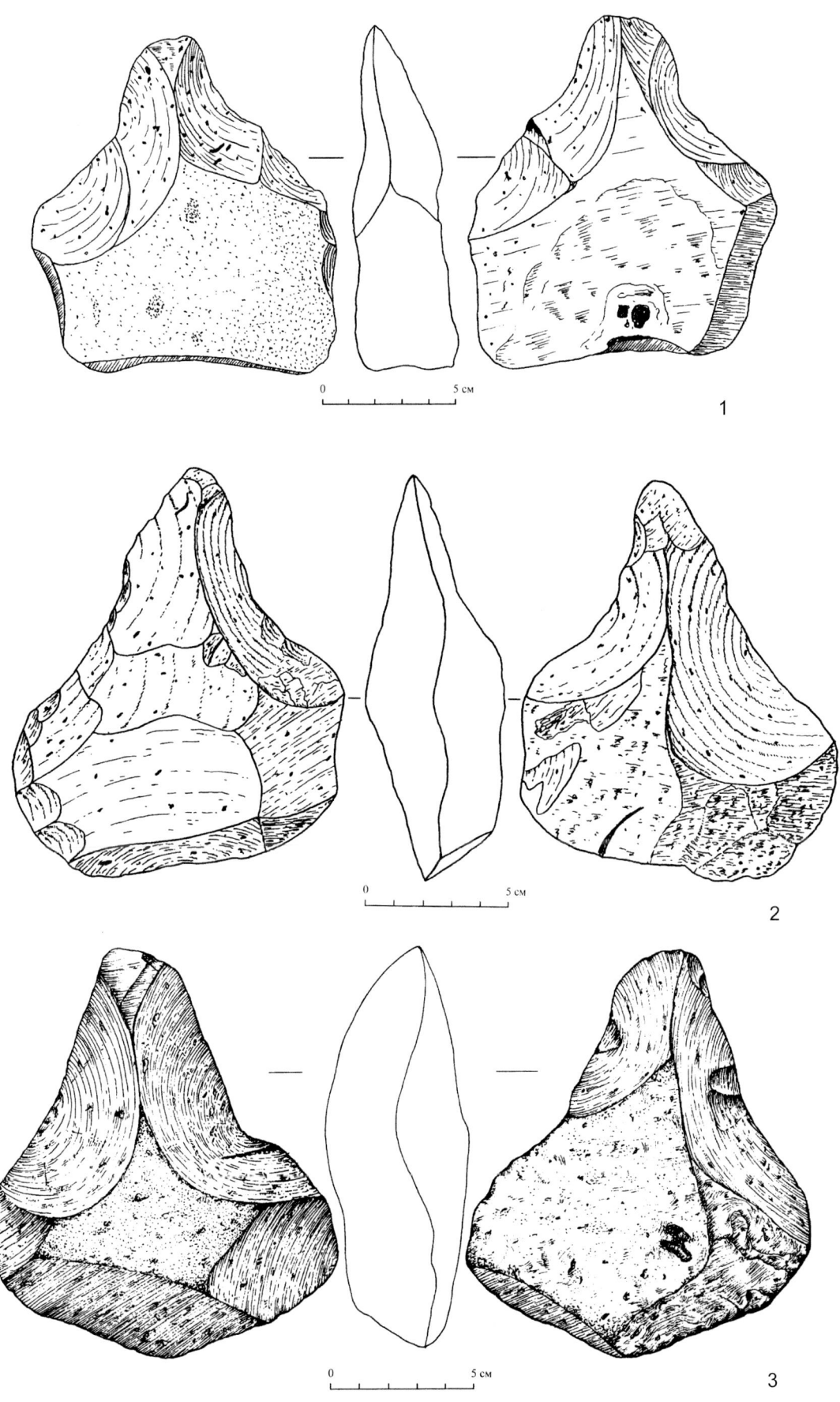

Figure 2.2. Handaxes from (1) Al-Garb VII and (2,3) Djob-Hamid 1 (after Amirkhanov 1987: fig. 8).

Subsequent expeditions to the Huqf have documented hundreds of similar sites, almost all associated with a longitudinal seam of high quality chert found down the length of the depression (Jagher and Pümpin 2010; Rose 2006). Technological analysis of the assemblages collected from sites AD.7-AD.10 in northern Huqf demonstrate a simple, hard hammer, unidirectional technique in which elongated blanks were detached from the narrow side of large, thin chert plaquettes (Rose 2006). Rosenberg *et al.* (Rosenberg *et al.* 2012) report bifacial tools in proximity to an MIS 5.5 palaeolake, speculating that the industry may post-date the Lower Palaeolithic; rather, was associated with a period of lake activation between roughly 130,000 and 100,000 BP.

Other scholars are skeptical of a Lower Palaeolithic date for the Huqf assemblages (Alsharekh 1995; Bretzke *et al.* 2017; Jagher 2009), arguing the sites are palimpsests accumulated over multiple periods of occupation and that the bifacial forms are not typical of the Acheulean. The tools do not have recognizable tips; rather, tend to be convex at both ends. This morphology suggests they were composite hafted tools from a post-Acheulean period. In comparison to the heavily weathered Palaeolithic artifacts from Dhofar, the artifacts from the Huqf exhibit minimal signs of rounding, edge damage, patination, or chemical dissolution. Their techno-typological attributes match those of assemblages from the Neolithic of Dhofar, dating between approximately 8 and 6 ka BP. Given these observations, it seems more likely that the Huqf "Late Acheulean" handaxe and blade assemblages were made in the Middle Holocene (contra Rose 2006, 2007).

Whalen *et al.* (2002) report 67 Acheulean occurrences in Dhofar, noting an absence of Oldowan or other pre-Acheulean industries. Sites are mostly located on lag surfaces and eroded mountain slopes. They observe that Lower Palaeolithic sites are most common in the southwestern quadrant of the Nejd Plateau, close to the Jebel Qara Escarpment. The authors divide the sites into Early and Middle Acheulean based on the composition of the assemblages. Early Acheulean findspots display higher frequencies of choppers and fewer handaxes, while at Middle Acheulean sites handaxes are more prevalent. Like in the Hadramawt region, surveyors note the absence of cleavers. Zarins (2001) comprehensive survey of Wadi Ghadun mapped a large Acheulean scatter on the highest terrace above the river valley, near the modern settlement of Matafah. The assemblage is a flake industry with chopping tools and scrapers manufactured from coarse-grained quartzite cobbles.

DAP Lower Palaeolithic Sites

A total of 92 surface sites were classified as Lower Palaeolithic based on technological, typological and taphonomic observations. Lower Palaeolithic assemblages were recognized by the presence of Acheulean handaxes, choppers, foliates, simple unidirectional cores, discoids and biconical radial cores. These assemblages exhibit a highly advanced state of surface weathering evident in chemical dissolution, patination, rounding and edge damage (Figure 2.3).

Lower Palaeolithic Site Distribution

Most Lower Palaeolithic sites were mapped throughout the western Nejd and southern Rub Al-Khali desert. Of the 92 Lower Palaeolithic localities, 27 are isolated handaxe or bifacial foliate findspots (Figure 2.4). These artifacts were found within *wadi* channels, on hill slopes, or on high terraces; none of which appear to be in primary position.

Figure 2.3. Weathering patterns on a Lower Palaeolithic biface versus a Middle Holocene biface from the same locality (photograph by the authors).

Figure 2.4. Isolated handaxe finds (photographs by the authors).

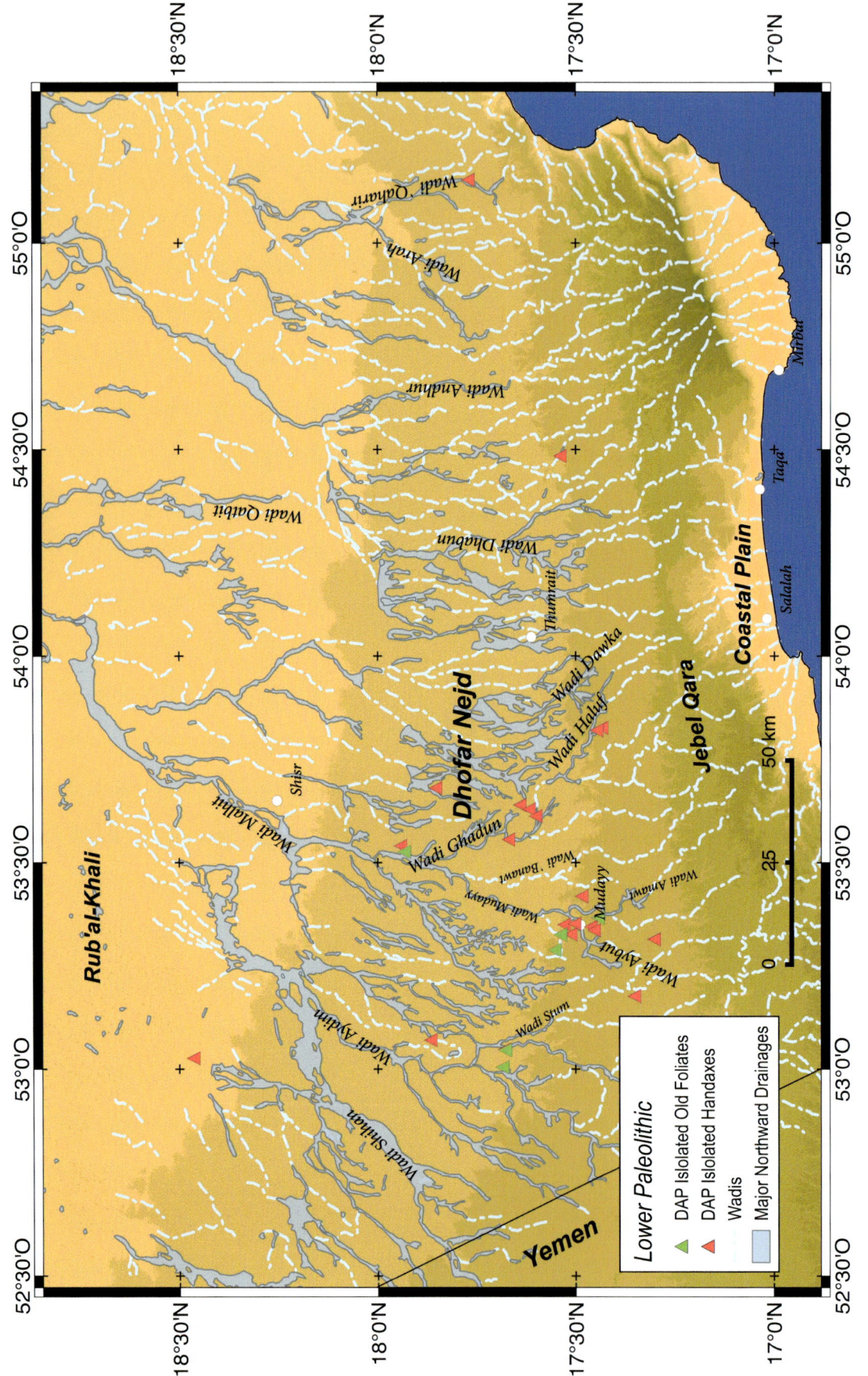

Figure 2.5. Map showing the position of Lower Palaeolithic isolated handaxes and foliate findspots recorded by the DAP (image by the authors).

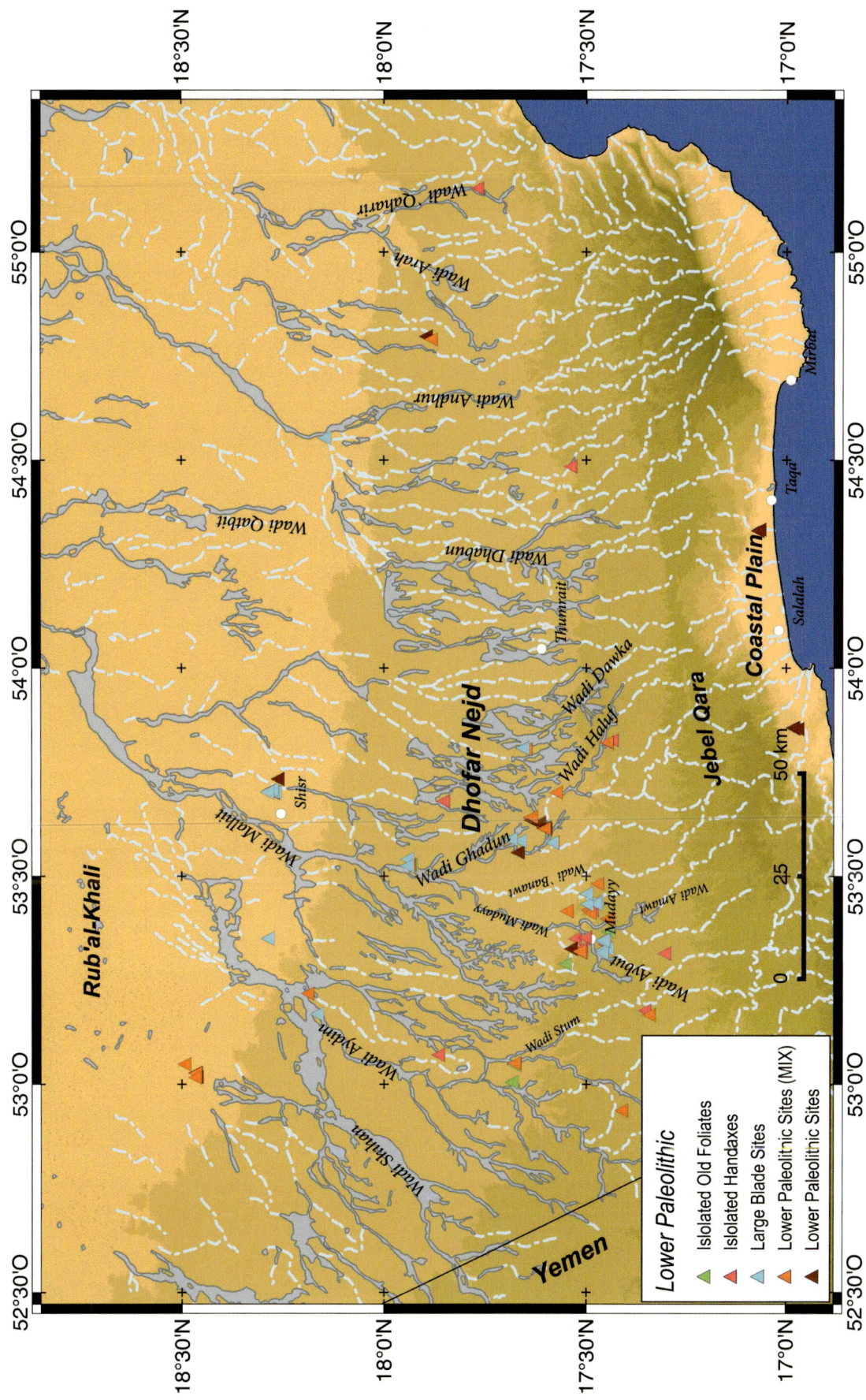

Figure 2.6. Map showing the location of all Lower Palaeolithic findspots recorded by the DAP: isolated handaxes, isolated foliates, late Lower Palaeolithic blade sites and Acheulean sites (image by the authors).

Isolated handaxes and foliates were also found on ancient alluvial fans at the southern edge of the Rub Al-Khali, on fluvial terraces overlooking the major northward draining *wadis*, on prominent landmarks such as inselbergs and mesas and on the high plateaus between the major *wadi* systems (Figure 2.5). At several localities, Acheulean artifacts were but one component of large multi-occupation workshop sites (Figure 2.6).

We did not find any Lower Palaeolithic findspots on the Dhofar mountain slopes or high grasslands. This may be due to low archaeological visibility, as humus deposits cover the mountain landscapes, masking the geological substrate and concealing ancient surfaces. We also noted a disparity between the frequencies of Lower Palaeolithic sites found on the western versus the eastern Nejd. Given the more intensive survey work conducted around Mudayy, there is clear bias in our coverage favoring the western side of the plateau. This may also be influenced by elevation and geomorphology. The Nejd dips gently eastward, leaving the western side a deflated plateau incised by deep canyons, while the eastern landscapes of the Nejd tend to be carpeted in thick layers of reworked aeolian and fluvial sediments. It is noteworthy that both our campaign and previous surveys (Newton and Zarins 2010; Zarins 2001) recorded a concentration of Lower Palaeolithic sites along Wadi Ghadun, which has the largest catchment system on the plateau.

Lower Palaeolithic sites were sub-divided based on the presence of specific typological and technological markers. These include assemblages containing large blades and blade cores, with or without handaxes (represented by turquoise triangles in Figure 3.6), Acheulean assemblages from multi-occupation workshop sites (represented by orange triangles in Figure 3.6) and single phase Acheulean assemblages (represented by brown triangles in Figure 3.6).

Lower Palaeolithic Sample Assemblages

The following section describes significant Lower Palaeolithic assemblages that were collected and analyzed by the DAP. The sites were chosen in order to represent the observed range of technological variability in the Lower Palaeolithic of Dhofar. At most of the sites, due to the diffuse distribution of lithic material, we used an "intensive random" sampling procedure. Intensive random collections sampled a random selection of debitage, cores and tools to acquire a statistically significant (or as many as possible) assemblage. At TH.76 and TH.143, individual artifacts were mapped with a total station to plot and analyze their distribution.

TH.501a

The TH.501 Lower Palaeolithic findspots are located on a widespread chert outcrop that extends across an 8 kilometer strip atop of the western plateau overlooking Wadi Ghadun (Figure 2.7). Two separate occupations were recognized at the site: TH.501a and TH.501b. The former consists of a high-density scatter with Acheulean handaxes, radial cores and associated débitage. TH.501b is comprised of heavily weathered blade cores and débitage attributed to the Lower Palaeolithic based on relative taphonomy – the nearby Middle Palaeolithic artifacts (TH.501c) exhibited far less surface weathering, while the material from TH.501a typically showed more advanced stages of degradation.

The Lower Palaeolithic assemblage collected from TH.501a is composed of 54 artifacts, of which 27 are cores and débitage and 29 are tools. Most tools were handaxes (n=27), with just two choppers. The lithic assemblage from TH.501b is composed of 91 artifacts, of which 72 are débitage, ten are cores and nine are tools. The tools are all unifacially retouched blanks. Artifacts were made exclusively from Mudayy formation chert, which outcrops as large nodules, plaquettes and tabular slabs.

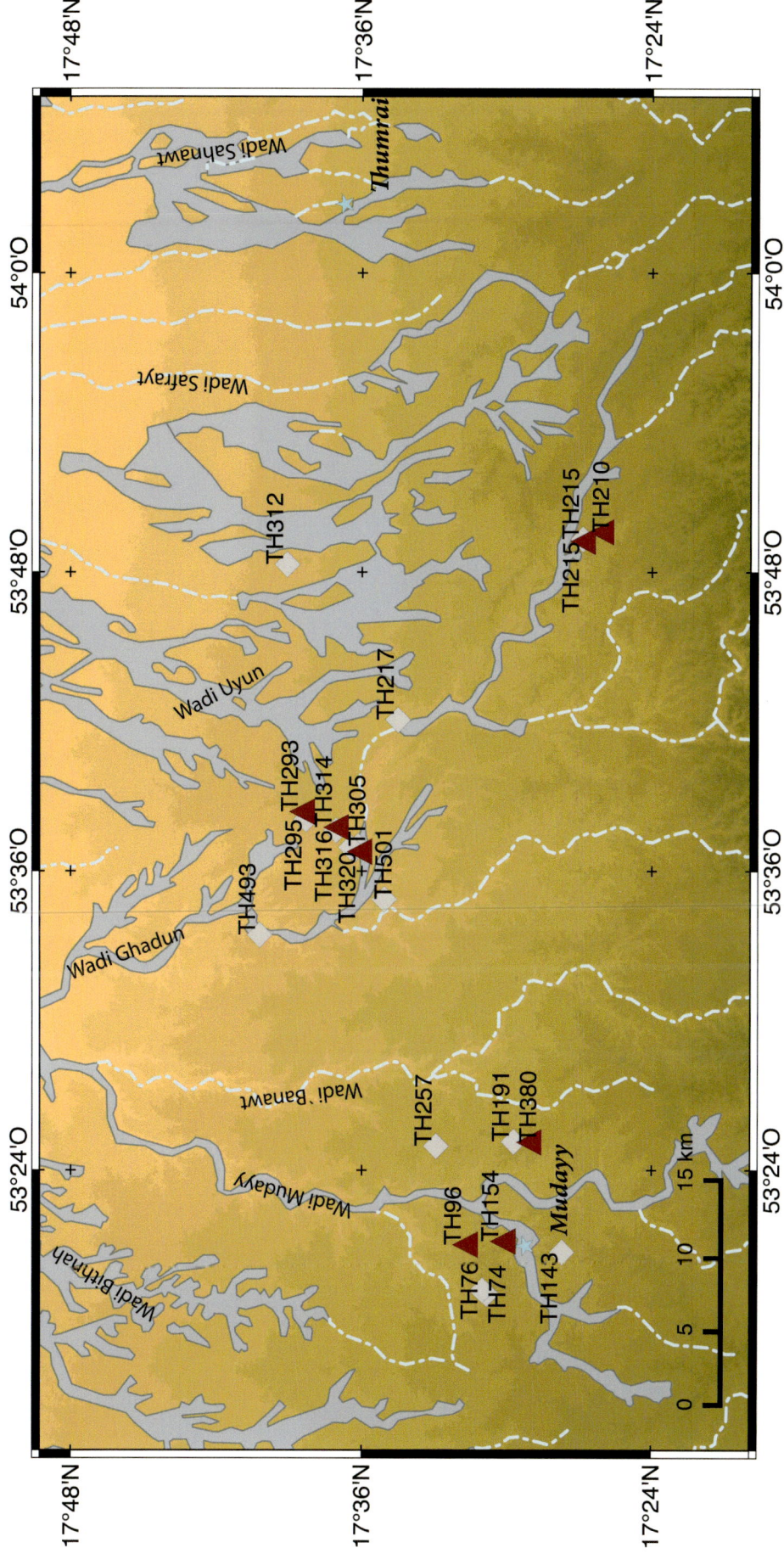

Figure 2.7. Map showing the location of Lower Palaeolithic sites (gray squares) and isolated handaxes (red triangles) on the central-western Nejd Plateau (image by the authors).

Figure 2.8. Volumetric cores from TH.501a: (1) core showing blade scar reduced in semi-tournant manner and (2) core showing flake negatives produced on nodule reduced in unidirectional-parallel manner (photographs by Y.H. Hilbert).

5 cm

Figure 2.9. Flat cores from TH.501a: (1-4) discoid cores, (2) flat unidirectional-lateral core, (3) flat core with bilateral distal negatives on the dorsal surface (photographs by Y.H. Hilbert).

The artifacts from TH.501a show intense chemical dissolution, where the majority of the original surface has been obliterated. The edges and ridges are moderately to severely rounded, sometimes making it difficult to determine dorsal scar patterns. Patination is quite thick, producing dark brownish-black surfaces. Due to the advanced stages of chemical dissolution, the original patinated surface area tends to be low and restricted to the undissolved edges of the pieces.

Cores and débitage from TH.501a show some variability in terms of their reduction strategies. Cores are either volumetric (n=6) or flat (n=11); the manner in which the striking platforms and core working surfaces were arranged vary considerably. The volumetric cores were reduced by single platform unidirectional-parallel and unidirectional-convergent strategies. These were made on nodules of much different size, reflected in the size range of the blanks that were produced. The majority of the unidirectional-parallel single platform cores have flake negatives that are typically transverse (wider than they are long). One example, shown in Figure 2.8: 1, exhibits blanks struck from an unprepared platform, giving the core a prismatic appearance.

The flat cores from TH.501a were divided into discoids and other unprepared cores. These were reduced using either centripetal, convergent or bidirectional strategies (Figure 2.9). The majority of flat cores were high-backed discoids with flakes struck from the ventral surface, exhibiting mostly cortex and just a few preparatory flake removals on the dorsal face. In a few cases, both dorsal and ventral faces were reduced by an alternating centripetal reduction strategy. In this respect, most of the discoidal cores from TH.501a do not fit the classic discoid category, which dictates that both ventral and dorsal surfaces are exploited without hierarchical distinction (i.e., alternating dorsal and ventral reduction). Flat cores have little variance in size, averaging 10 cm in maximum length, 9 cm in maximum width and 10 cm in thickness reflecting the high-backed morphology of the dorsal surfaces. While no hammer stones were found at the site, a small percentage of the cores display impact fractures on rounded cortical ends (Figure 2.10). It is possible that these cores (n=3) were also used as percussion tools.

There were two choppers within the TH.501a toolkit (Figure 2.11). Both were made on chert nodules and retain cortical butts. The choppers exhibit acute working edges that were formed by just two or three removals. The chopper depicted in figure 2.11: 1 has a pointed worked edge and percussion scars at the intersection of the working edge and butt, while the other specimen exhibits a straight working edge.

The 27 handaxes from TH.501a demonstrate a high amount of variability in terms of shape, size and symmetry. Handaxe shapes are cordiform (Figure 2.12: 5), ovate (Figure 2.13) lanceolate (Figure 2.12: 2), triangular (Figure 2.12: 1), amygdaloid and trapezoid. They are generally asymmetrical and most working edge cross sections (n=20) are sinuous. Seven specimens display straight, biconvex working edges. This is significant for discerning tool functionality: straight cutting edges are effective for pulling and cutting mechanics, while sinuous edges are more useful for sawing and chopping movements.

The handaxes from TH.501a were made on nodules with thick, often rhomboidal cross sections and unworked butts. One handaxe was reused as a single platform core with a unidirectional parallel scar pattern (Figure 2.14). The scars from core reduction display slightly less patination, chemical dissolution and rounding, suggesting that the piece was recycled during a subsequent stage of workshop activity.

TH.501a handaxes are fairly homogeneous in size, averaging 11 cm in maximum length, 8 cm in maximum width and 5 cm in medial thickness. The largest specimen measures 14 cm in maximum length, 10 cm in maximum width and 5 cm in medial thickness, while the smallest measures 8 cm in maximum length, 6 cm in maximum width and 3 cm in medial thickness. All of the handaxes were made from nodules, with the exception of one small specimen manufactured from a blank (Figure 2.15).

Figure 2.10. Impact marks on the distal end of a discoid core (#4 in figure 2.9). Such impact marks are typical and indicate that the piece was also used as a percussor (photograph by Y.H. Hilbert).

5 cm

Figure 2.11. Choppers made on chert nodules from TH.501a (photographs by Y.H. Hilbert).

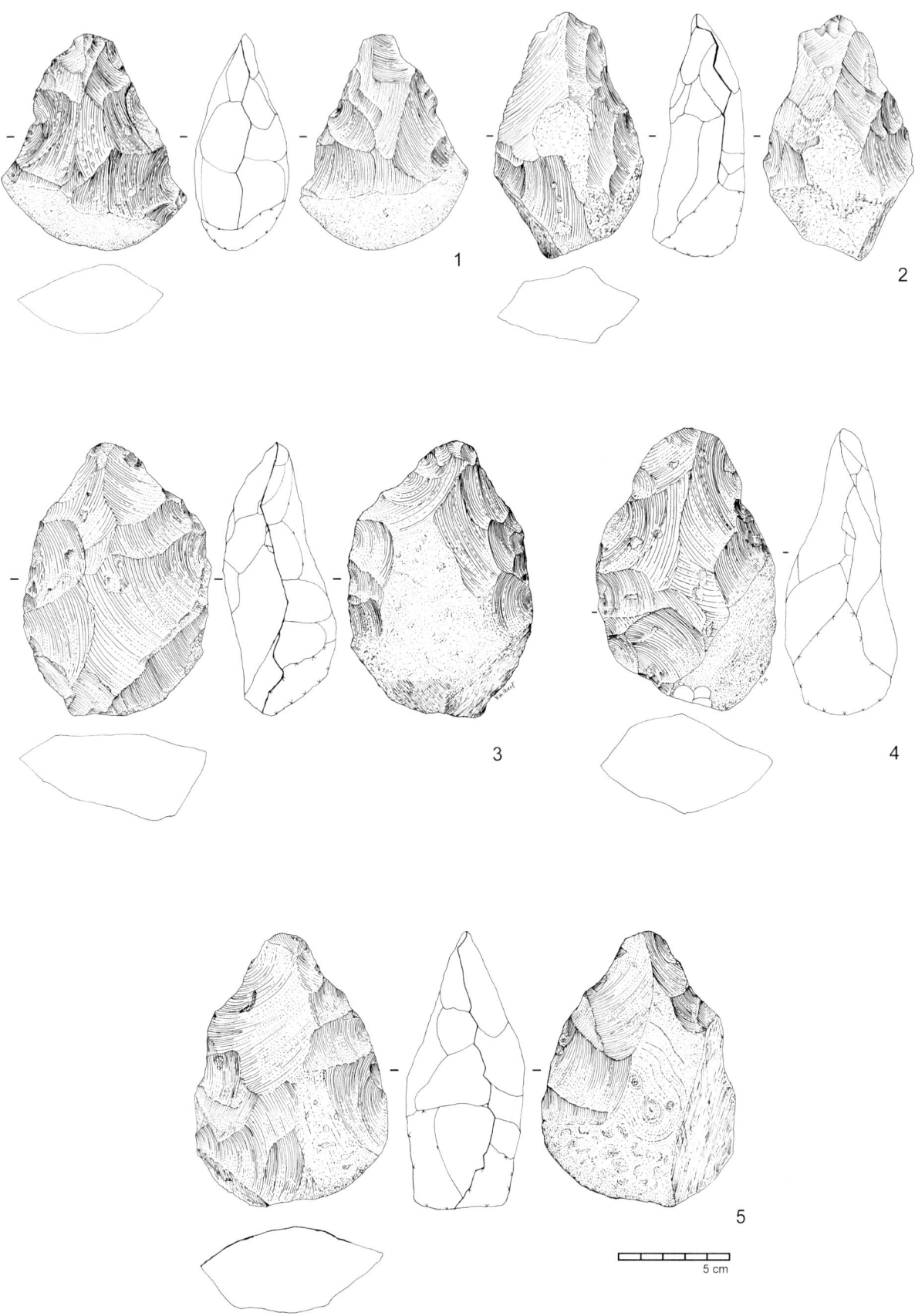

Figure 2.12. Handaxes from TH.501a: (1) triangular handaxe with cortical butt and asymmetric edges, (2) lanceolate-shaped handaxe with cortical butt, (3-5) cordiform handaxes (illustrations by Y.H. Hilbert).

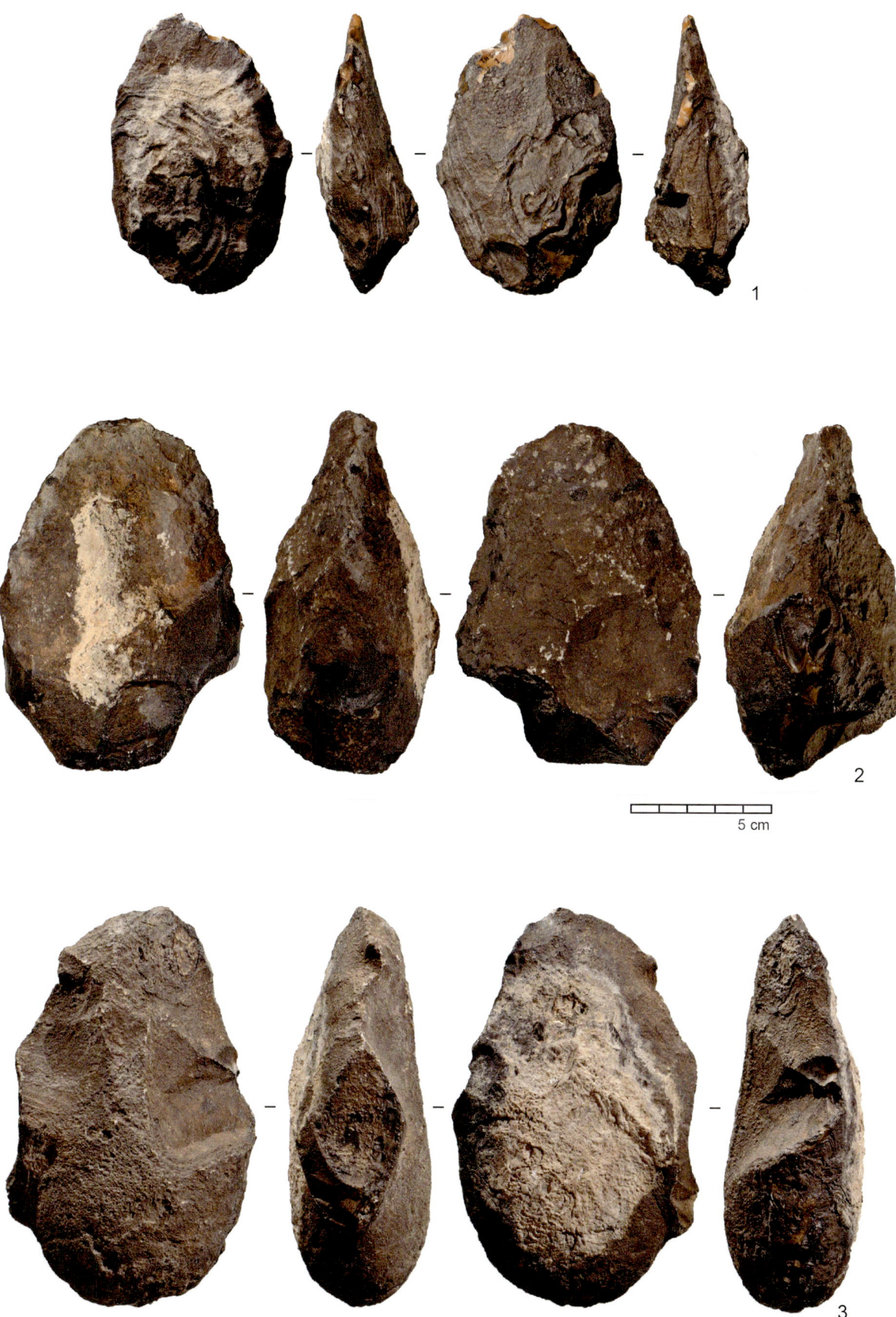

5 cm

Figure 2.13. Ovate handaxes from TH.501a: (1) handaxe made on flake, (2-3) handaxe made on nodules (photographs by Y.H. Hilbert).

5 cm

Figure 2.13. Handaxe from TH.501a subsequently used as a unidirectional core. The patination of the artifacts is homogenous, suggesting that the two different uses of the piece were roughly contemporary (photographs by Y.H. Hilbert).

TH.501b

The TH.501b surface scatter, located some 150 m north of TH.501a, is a workshop site utilizing the same extensive local chert outcrop. In comparison to TH.501a, the artifacts from TH.501b have less rounded ridges. While chemical dissolution of the original silicate surface also shows advanced stages of degradation, they seldom exceed 75% of the knapped surfaces. In contrast, the artifact's surfaces at TH.501a exhibit nearly 100% dissolution.

The majority of débitage from TH.501b are blades (n=42), followed by cortical pieces (n=16), flakes (n=12) and two débordant elements. Among the blades, scar patterns are predominantly unidirectional (n=35) and typically exhibit just one or two scars. Lateral edges on the blades are mostly parallel (n=25) and expanding (n=11), with rare instances of convergent forms. The majority of striking platforms are unfaceted (n=30), while seven blades had faceted platforms with three or more preparatory removals. Distal terminations tend to be overpassed or feathering with cortex. Most of the blades have at least one cortical-lateral edge (n=30), indicating that the blanks were removed from the edge of the core's working surface. The blades tend to exhibit twisted longitudinal profiles, evidence of their removal from the side of the core. The remaining débitage – flakes and cortical pieces – show similar attributes to the blades in terms of dorsal scar patterns, striking platforms and distal terminations.

Of the ten cores, nine are single platform unidirectional and one bidirectional with opposed platforms. The cores' working surfaces are typically located on the broad face, with only one specimen showing blades struck from the narrow working surface. As was the case with the debitage, the majority of cores have unmodified striking platforms, while three have faceted platforms. Most cores demonstrate just two or three negatives on the working surface. The cores and débitage show a concise range of attributes that suggest the elongated blanks were the products of a specific core reduction strategy aimed at producing blades.

The toolkit from TH.501b includes two convex sidescrapers, one inversely retouched convex side scraper, a notch, a denticulate and four retouched blades. The tools were made on blades, flakes and cortical flakes; there is no evidence for deliberate blank type selection. Convergent, expanding and biconvex shaped blanks were selected over blanks with parallel edges. Given the more advanced stages of weathering in comparison to nearby Middle Palaeolithic assemblage associated with the same chert outcrop, as well as the absence of any prepared core technologies, TH.501b is thought to fall between the Acheulean complex Lower Palaeolithic and Nubian complex Middle Palaeolithic chronological phases.

TH.76

The TH.76 findspot occurs on the high plateau between Wadi Aybut and Wadi Mudayy, roughly five kilometers northwest of Mudayy village on the central-west Nejd (Figure 2.7). It is a multi-occupation workshop spread across three low (<1 m) step-scarps, with high quality chert slabs outcropping along each rise. Different lithic scatters were identified at the site, exhibiting a wide range of weathering patterns and technologies from Lower, Middle and Late Palaeolithic to Neolithic periods.

As part of an inter-site investigation into spatial patterning in lithic taphonomy and technology at palimpsest workshop sites, the artifacts collected from TH.76 were piece-plotted and geo-referenced using a total station. From this assemblage, we recorded technological attributes and taphonomic data observed in the degree of surface weathering, ridge rounding, edge damage, patination and chemical dissolution.

Cluster analysis of these taphonomic patterns indicates that the Lower Palaeolithic material can be divided into two groups (Figure 2.16). Artifacts from cluster 1 show moderately advanced stages of surface deterioration with up to 75% surface dissolution, patination ranging between brown and black and moderate edge rounding. Artifacts from cluster 2 display more advanced state of weathering, with surface deterioration nearly 100% on most specimens, patination is similar to cluster 1 and edge rounding is severe. Spatially and technologically, there is little variance between clusters.

The lithic assemblage attributed to cluster 1 is composed primarily of cores and débitage (n=23); tools are rare and consist of four handaxes. The core assemblage is highly variable, including both flat and volumetric core types. Unidirectional-parallel flakes and blades were struck from volumetric cores. The cores tend to be rectangular with plain striking platforms. The flat cores are more varied in shape and architecture, demonstrating an array of bidirectional-lateral, bidirectional, unidirectional-parallel, lateral-distal and unidirectional-lateral-dorsal scar patterns. Striking platforms are generally unmodified; cortical platforms were used without preparation when suitable angles for reduction were available.

Four handaxes occur within the TH.76 Lower Palaeolithic cluster 1 assemblage. These are more lightly patinated than the handaxes from cluster 2 and display different technical characteristic. Two were made on large flakes (Figure 2.17), rather than nodules or chunks as in cluster 2. They are also smaller than the cluster 2 handaxes and symmetrical with straight edges. The other two specimens are distal fragments and also appear to be symmetrical with straight edges and well-formed tips.

The Lower Palaeolithic cluster 2 sample is composed of handaxes (n=20), cores (n=6) and débitage (n=18) including flakes, blades and cortical flakes. Among the cores, there is one classic discoid, a flat core and four single platform blade cores. The single platform cores exhibit unidirectional-parallel scars with a broad working surface. One has been reduced from both frontal and lateral edges (Figure 2.18). The discoid shows centripetal scar patterns on just the dorsal surface and is considerably smaller that the single platform cores.

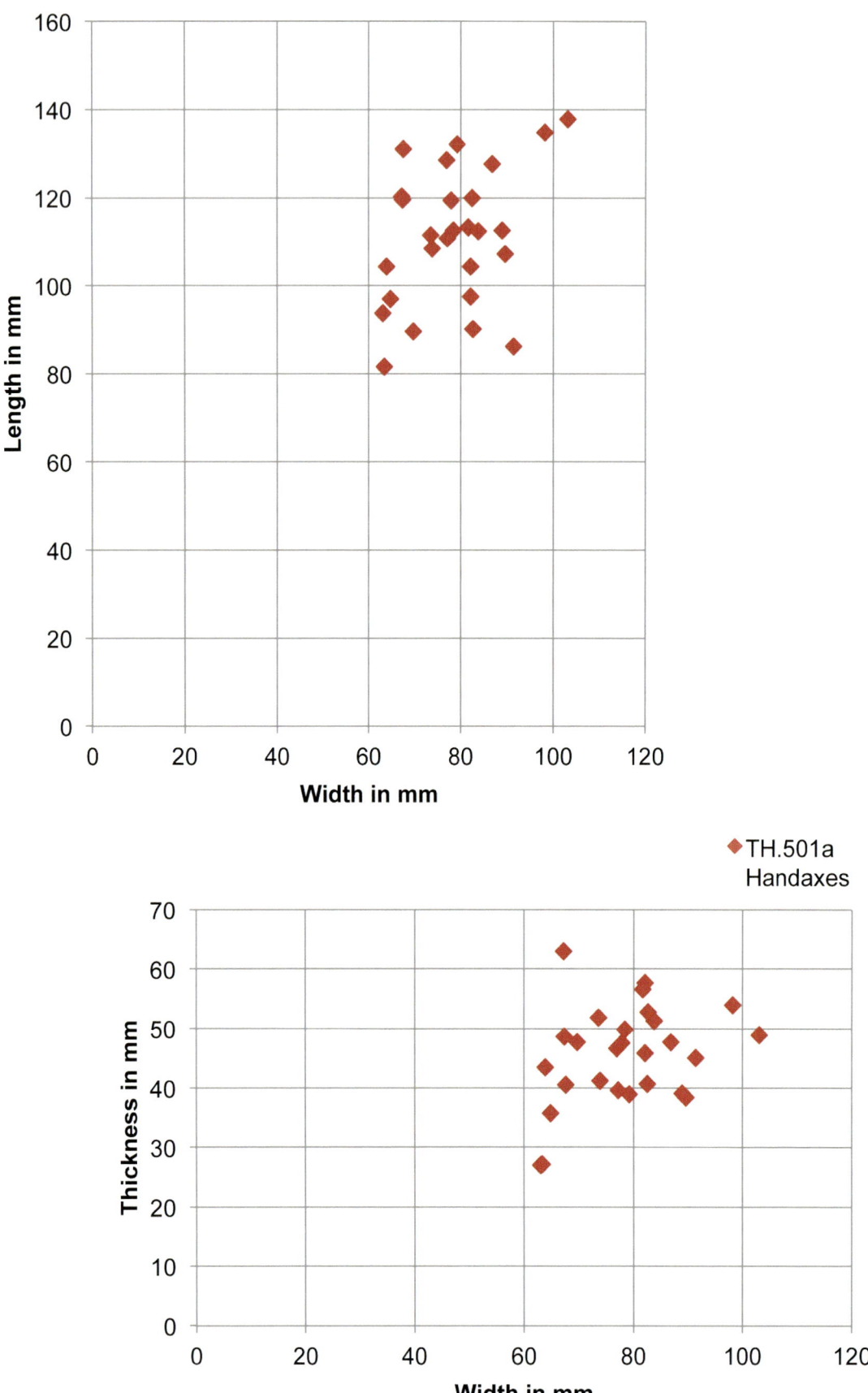

Figure 2.15. TH.501a handaxe metrics (figure plots by Y.H. Hilbert).

Aybut ath Thalith (TH.76) Lower Paleolithic cluster 1

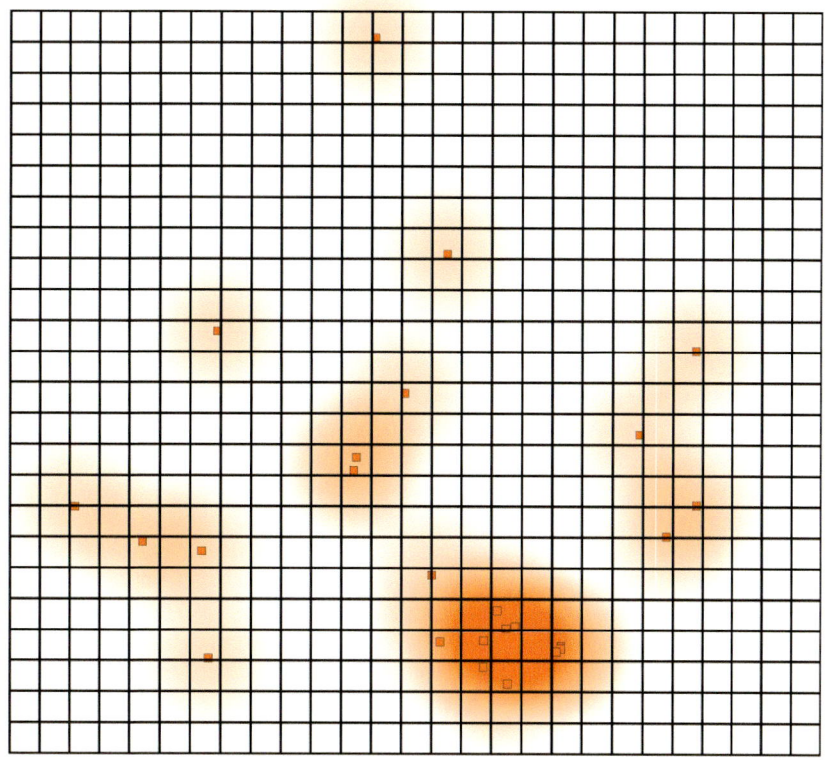

Aybut ath Thalith (TH.76) Lower Paleolithic cluster 2

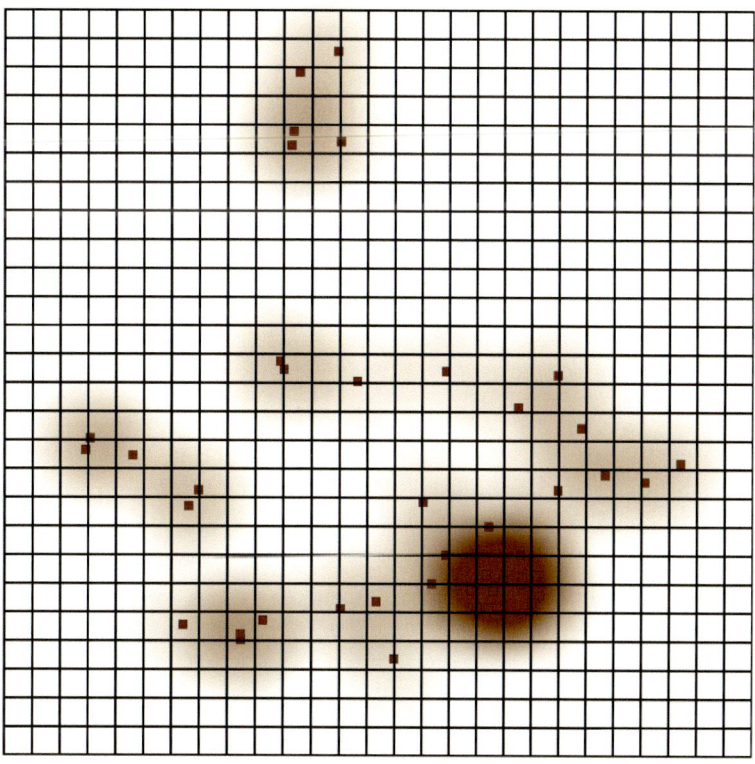

Figure 2.16. Heat map showing the distribution of differentially weathered Lower Palaeolithic artifacts from TH.76 (figure plots by Y.H. Hilbert).

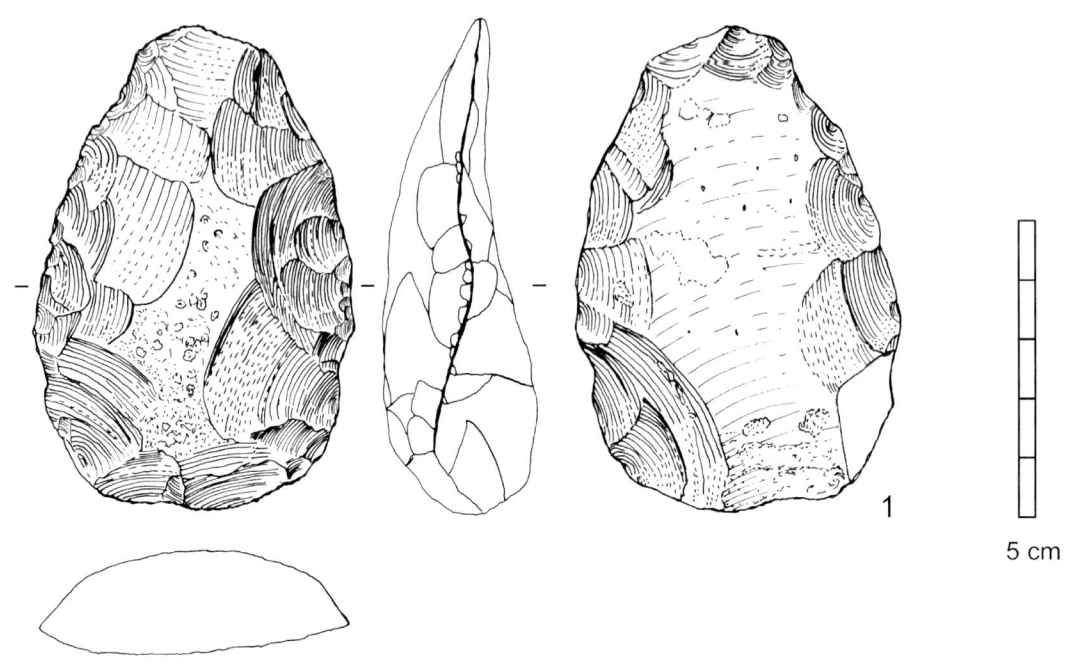

5 cm

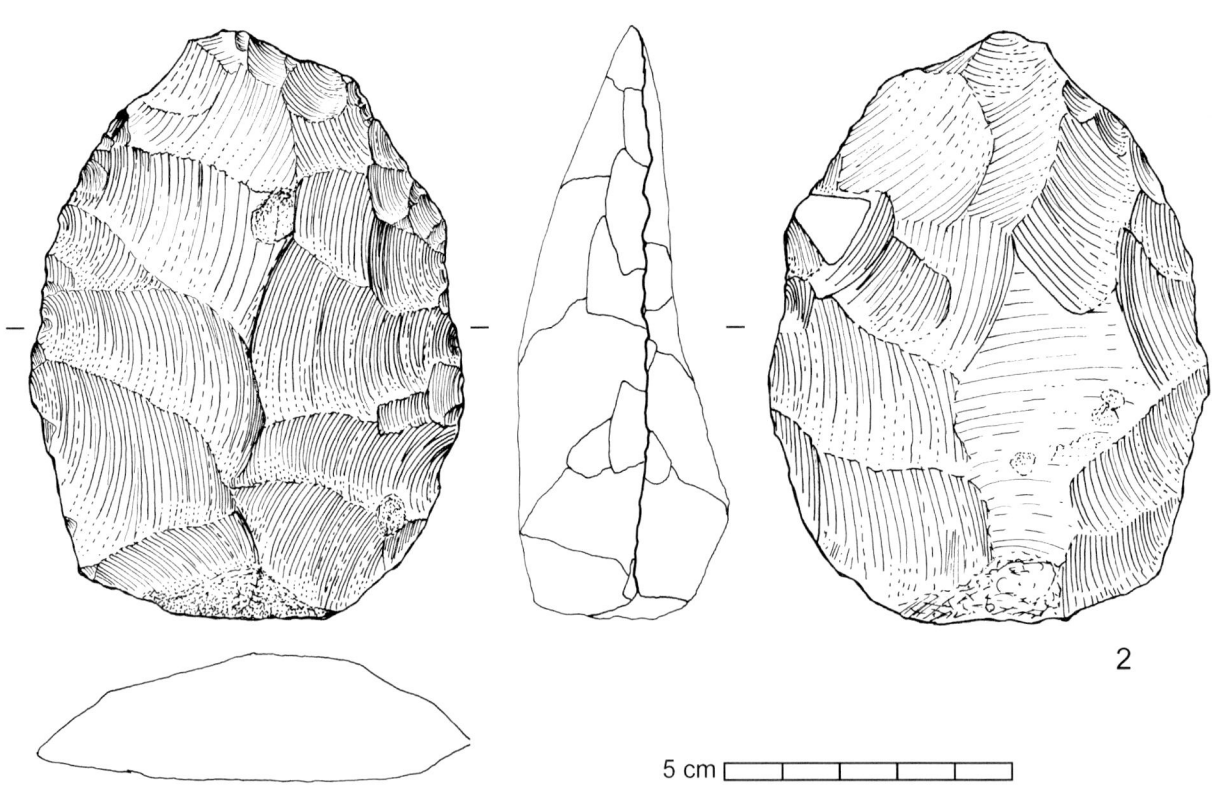

5 cm

Figure 2.17. Handaxes made on cortical blanks from TH.76 (illustrations by Y.H. Hilbert).

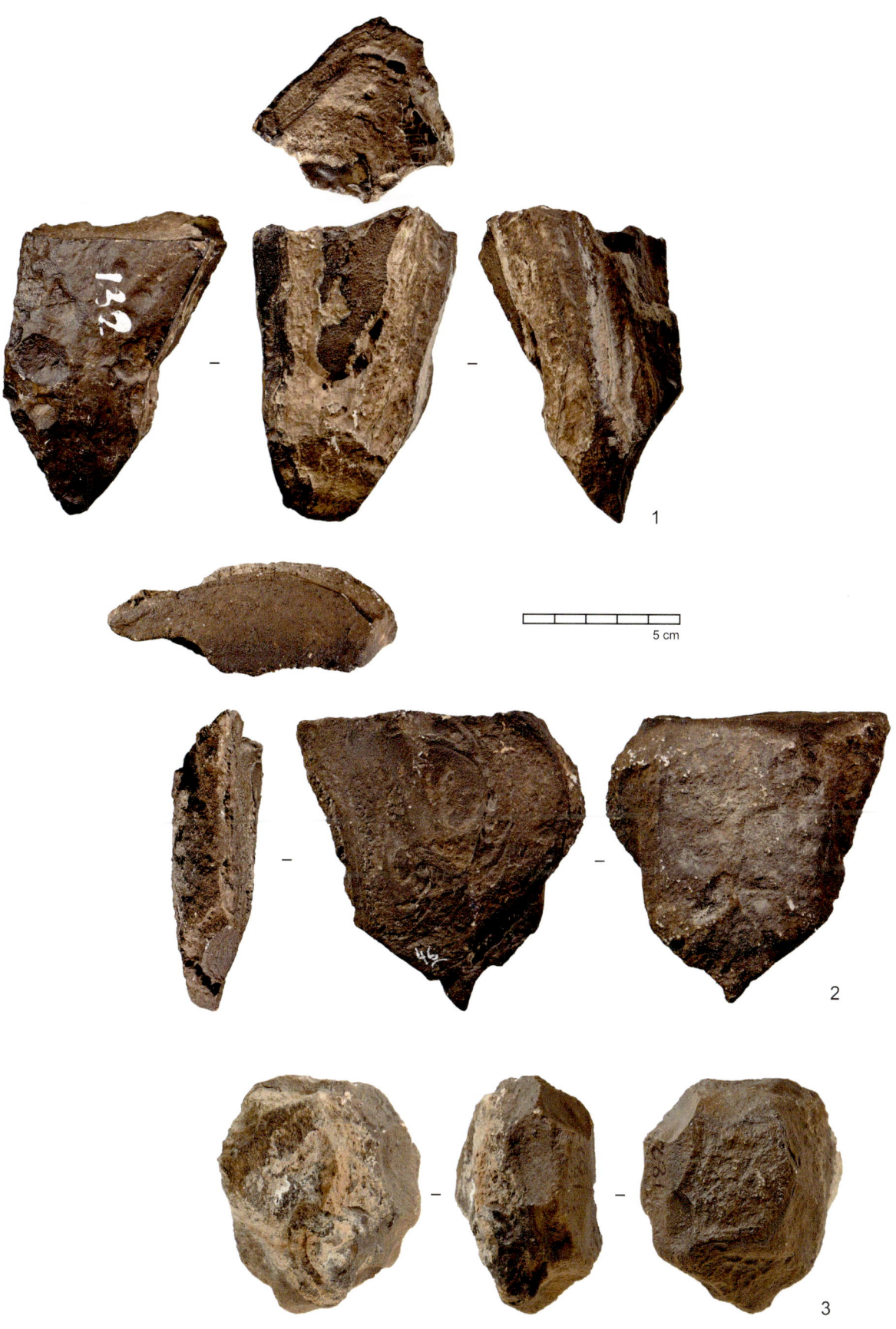

Figure 2.18. Cores from TH.76: (1) unidirectional single platform core reduced in semi-tournant manner, (2) unidirectional parallel single platform flat core, (3) discoid core (photographs by Y.H. Hilbert).

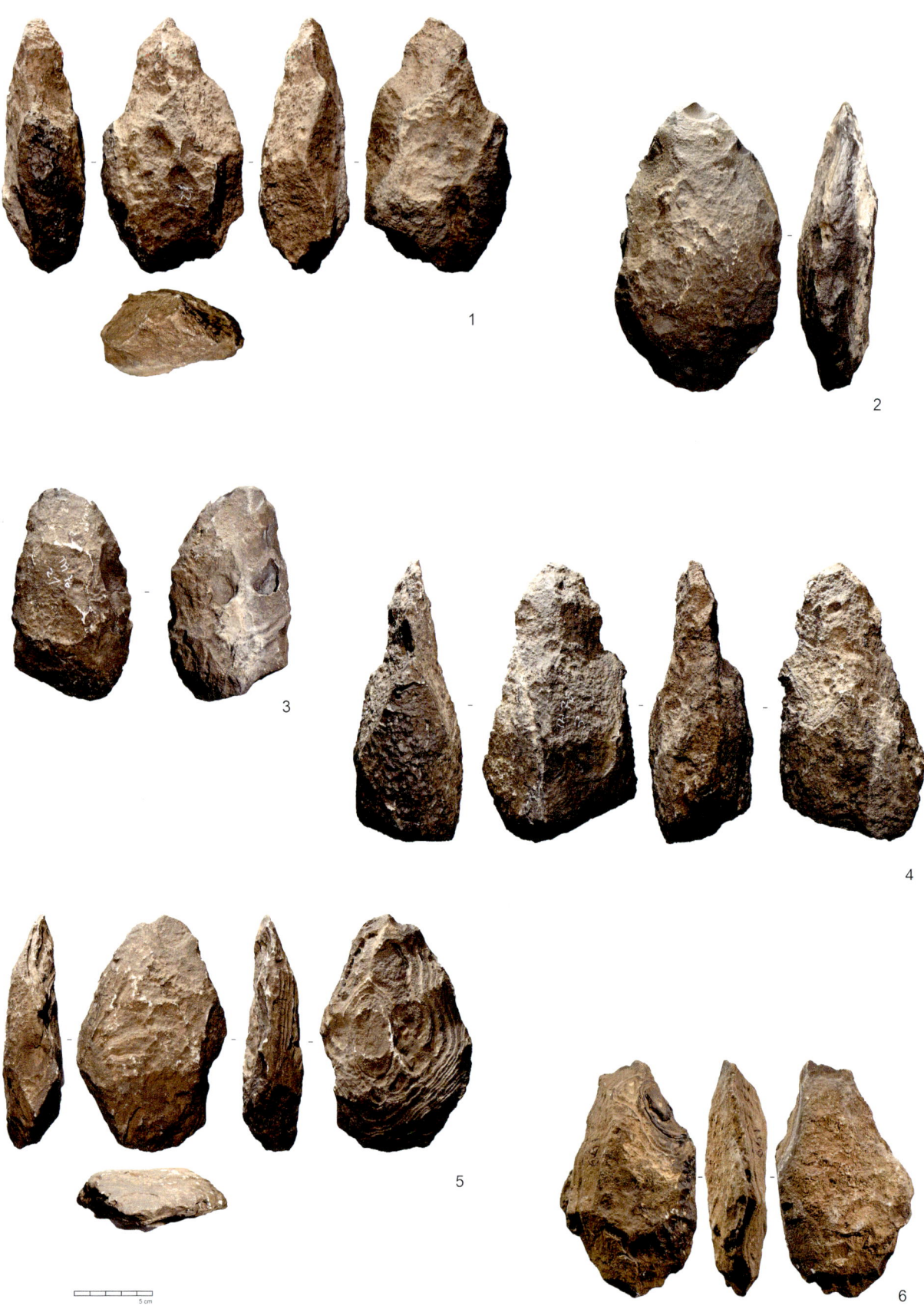

Figure 2.19. Handaxes from TH.76: (1) thick sub-triangular, (2) amygdaloid on flat nodule, (3) small asymmetrical ovate, (4) large lanceolate with cortical butt, (5,6) symmetrical ovate handaxes (photographs by Y.H. Hilbert).

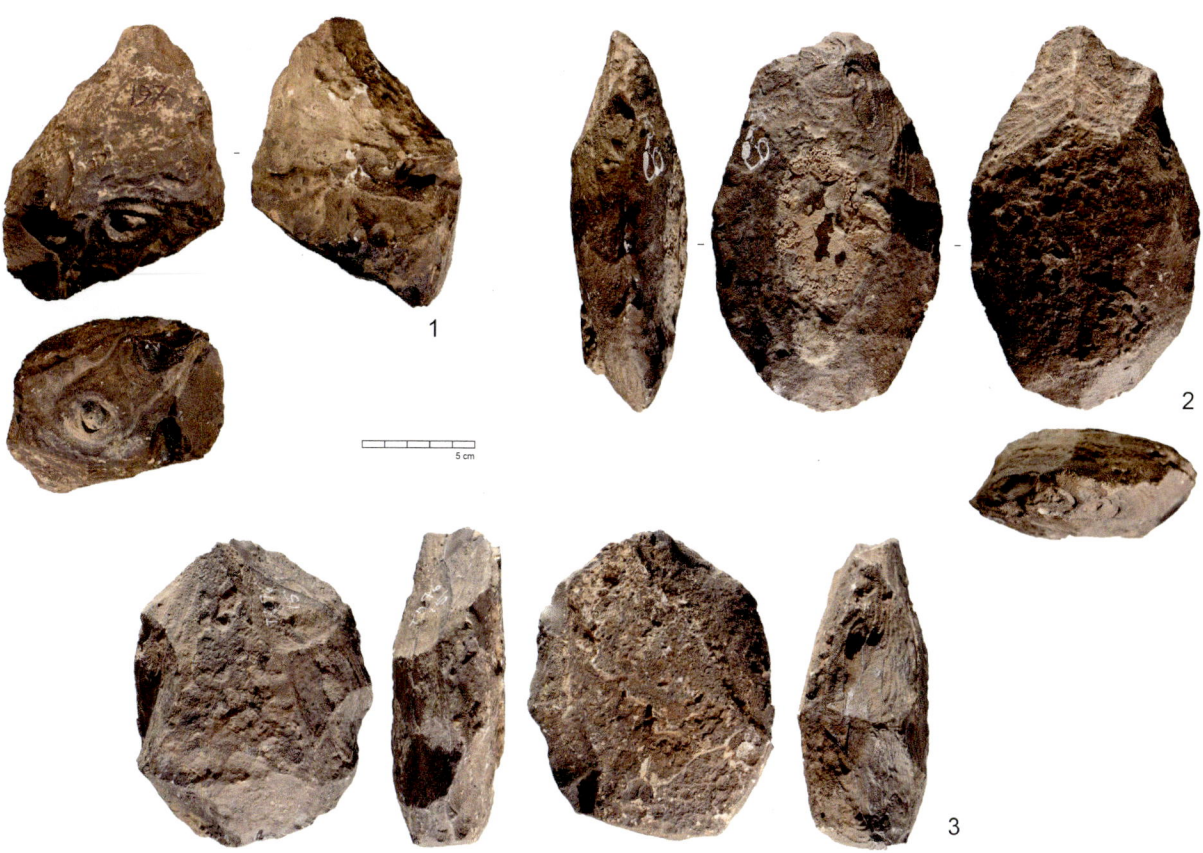

Figure 2.20. Handaxes from TH.76: (1) handaxe subsequently used as core, the butt was removed by unidirectional-parallel removals, (2) symmetrical amygdaloid handaxe with tip removed by a series of removals oriented transverse to the technological axis of the artifact, (3) handaxe with tip removed by blows to the edge (photographs by Y.H. Hilbert).

The handaxes from TH.76 cluster 2 are taphonomically homogenous, appearing to have reached a "weathering equilibrium". The original worked surfaces are completely deteriorated and the formation process of a new cortex is advanced. Cortical and worked areas of the tools exhibit the same dark color and edges are severely rounded (Figure 2.19). Ovate shaped handaxes are most prevalent (n=10), followed by amygdaloid (n=4), lanceolate (n=3), cordiform (n=2) and triangular (n=1) variations. Edges and longitudinal cross-sections are generally asymmetric. The majority of medial cross-sections are thick and rhomboidal, with only five specimens demonstrating thin biconvex cross-sections. We also note the recycling of these tools as cores during subsequent occupation phases, as well as removals from the tip by a diagonally placed blow on the distal lateral edge of some specimens (Figure 2.20).

TH.143a

Assemblage TH.143a was found in Jebel Sanoora, an area of steep terraced hills one kilometer southeast of the Mudayy fracture springs. We discovered the remains of a modern Arabian wildcat (*Felis silvestris gordoni*) during our initial visit, so began referring to the hilly region as Jebel Sanoora. Jebel Sanoora has multiple limestone terraces; each rise has a seam of chert eroding from the base, suggesting that the erosional terraces are formed by the hard armor of the horizontal chert beds.

Figure 2.21. Panorama overlooking the Jebel Sanoora terraces (photograph by the authors).

The terraces average 20 m deep and extend for several hundred meters along the tributaries of Wadi Aybut (Figure 2.21). Given its strategic position, access to fresh water and abundance of high quality chert, it is not surprising that the archaeology of this region was found to be one of the richest and most diverse in Dhofar.

Over the course of multiple seasons we made several systematic collections from Jebel Sanoora, targeting artifacts from different Palaeolithic periods. This section will focus on the results from TH.143a, representing the Lower Palaeolithic component of the site. The TH.143a assemblage was collected from the first terrace, some 20 m above a steeply incised tributary of Wadi Aybut. The same sampling strategy used at TH.76 was replicated here. Lithic artifacts were recovered within a transect that extended from the raw material outcrop at the back of the terrace to the edge overlooking the *wadi*. Individual artifacts were piece-plotted and geo-referenced using a total station. In the laboratory, we recorded technological attributes and taphonomic data observed in the degree of surface weathering, ridge rounding, edge damage, patination and chemical dissolution. There were 58 artifacts included in the Lower Palaeolithic component of the transect. These were primarily found at the edge of the terrace, while more recent Middle and Late Palaeolithic assemblages were found closer to the actively eroding chert seam toward the back. All artifacts were made from the same relatively homogenous local outcrop of Mudayy chert slabs. The Lower Palaeolithic artifacts are extremely weathered, showing advanced signs of chemical dissolution and thermal fracturing, evidenced by the large and deep potlid scars on one or both surfaces. Edges are highly rounded from aeolian abrasion and there is severe edge damage from post-depositional movement. The patinas tend to be grayish-brown in color and none of the pieces possess their original silicate surfaces.

The majority of Lower Palaeolithic artifacts are débitage (n=46), primarily blades and débordant blades. There were 11 cores and no retouched tools or bifacial pieces. The débitage is almost exclusively elongated blanks with large plain striking platform, unidirectional-parallel scar patterns and thick trapezoidal cross-sections (Figure 2.22). Most of the blades exhibit cortex on the lateral edge, indicating they were struck from the edge of the core's working surface. From the débitage, we conclude that Lower Palaeolithic toolmakers at TH.143a produced elongated blanks using a hard hammer, recurrent, unidirectional technology. This is evident from the cores as well; of which six were classified as single platform cores with unidirectional scar patterns (Figure 2.23).

Three cores have double working surfaces oriented on the broad faces of chert nodules; these surfaces were reduced independently from one another. Metric analysis shows that blades and débordant blades are longer than the cores themselves (Figure 2.24). This might suggest that the cores were intensively reduced on-site, meaning the assemblage represents primary workshop activity. The fact that blank technological attributes remain consistent throughout the entire reduction sequence indicates there were no changes in strategy, maintenance, or rejuvenation as the core was exploited.

From the relative position of the TH.143a scatter furthest from the actively eroding chert seam, as well as the taphonomic weathering patterns relative to Middle and Late Palaeolithic artifacts on the terrace, we infer that the TH.143a artifacts pre-date all other assemblage types at the site. Consequently, TH.143a is classified as late Lower Palaeolithic.

Figure 2.22. Unidirectional-parallel cores from TH.143 (photographs by Y.H. Hilbert).

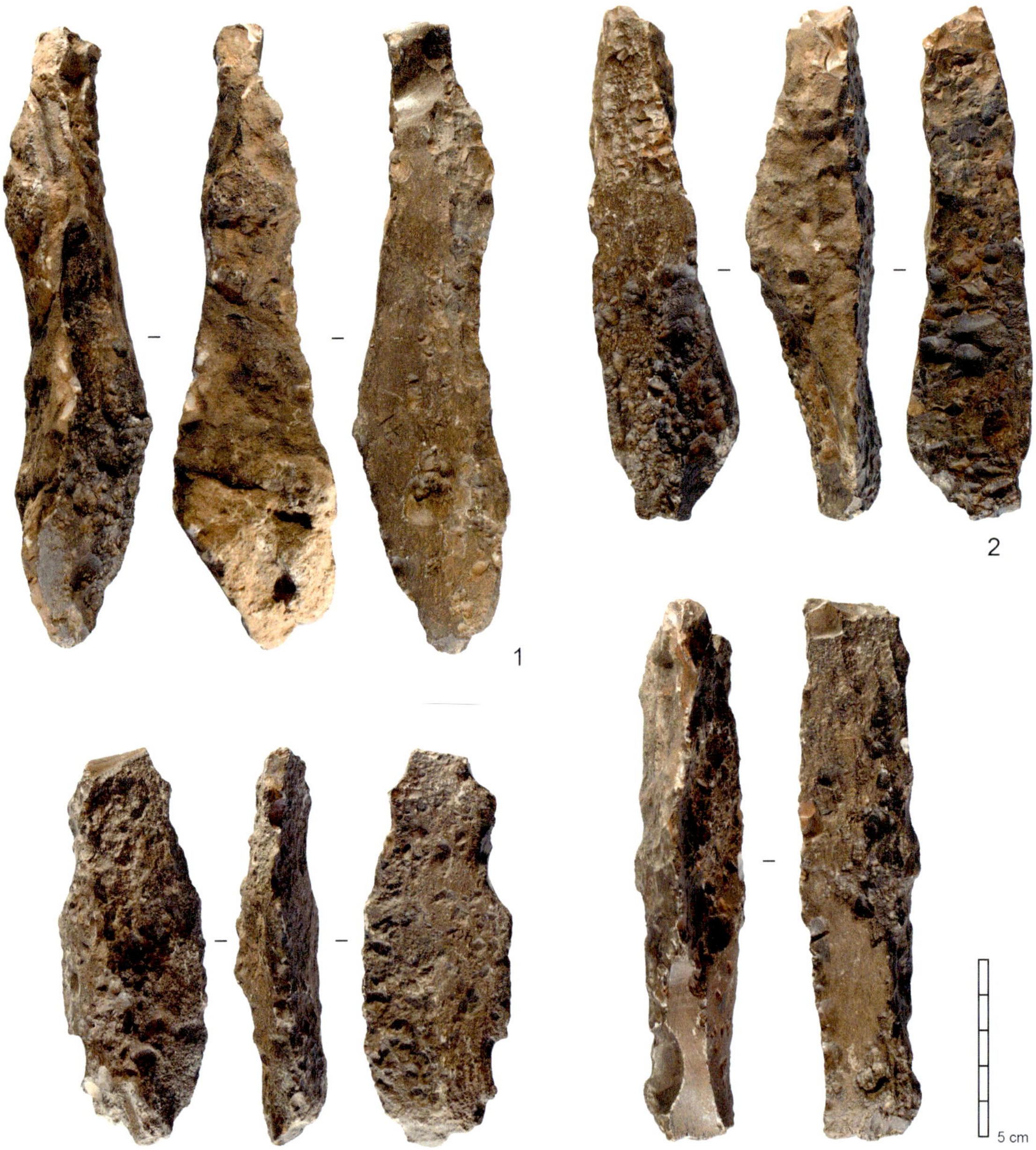

Figure 2.23. Unidirectional-parallel blades from TH.143 (photographs by Y.H. Hilbert).

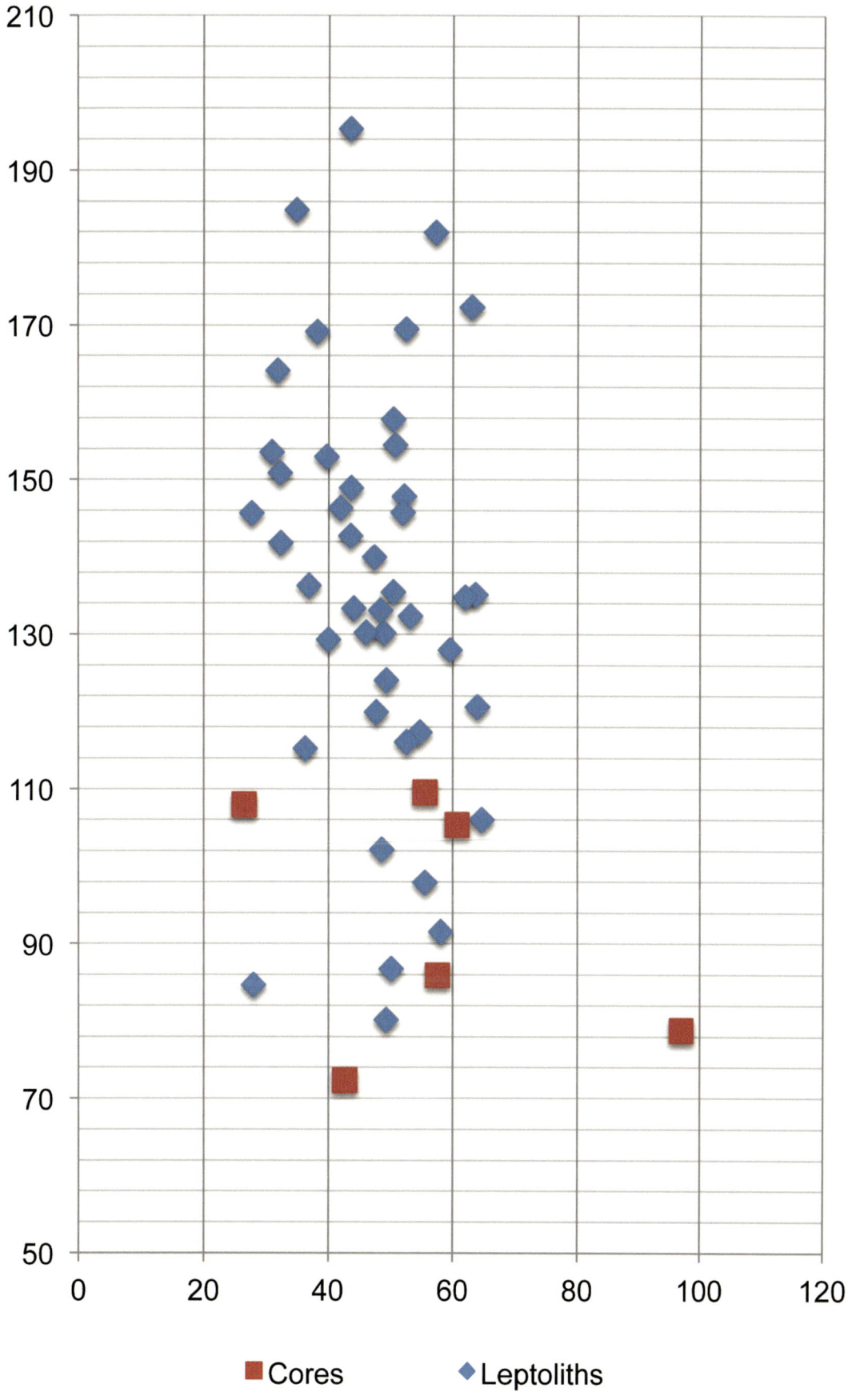

Figure 2.24. TH.143 blade and core metrics (figure plot by Y.H. Hilbert).

Figure 2.25. Panorama overlooking Wadi Khasheem with TA.23 site located inside the red dotted line (photograph by the authors).

Figure 2.26. Surface of the Wadi Khasheem terrace (photograph by the authors).

TA.23

During the 2010 coastal survey, our team mapped Lower Palaeolithic findspot TA.23 along Wadi Khasheem, some ten kilometers west of Khor Rori. A diffuse scatter of artifacts was collected on the second and third terraces, across a wide extent measuring approximately 1.5 km long and 300 m wide along the left bank of the *wadi* (Figures 2.25 and 2.26).

The terrace is an ancient alluvial fan that extends three kilometers southward from the Dhofar escarpment. In this location, Wadi Khasheem has incised the fan deposit, exposing an eight meter section of large rounded cobbles cemented in silt. The TA.23 artifacts were found scattered over a large area; no discrete clusters could be identified. Raw material used for stone tool production does not appear to be of local origin. One source of similar raw material, a light gray quartzite, was observed about 20 km to the east, in the vicinity of Mirbat. Although it is coarse-grained, experimentation with the quartzite shows that it fractures well and could have been suitable for tool manufacture. The TA.23 specimens are extremely rounded, exhibit a yellow-orange color and have heavily damaged edges (Figure 2.27). The assemblage is composed mostly of débitage and cores, with a small handful of tools made on flakes as well as one diminutive handaxe.

Flakes are medium to large in size, with thick cross-sections and unprepared striking platforms. The deep striking platforms and prominent bulbs of percussion suggest a forceful and high-velocity impact from a heavy stone percussor. In addition to simple unidirectional flake and blade blanks, the débitage included medium and large-sized flakes with dihedral and faceted striking platforms and radial and crossed dorsal scar patterns (Figure 2.28).

Among the cores, there were both volumetric and flat types. The few volumetric cores are spheroids and polyhedrons typically with unidirectional-parallel scar patterns. Most other cores are irregular multi-platform and high-backed radial cores found in small, medium and large sizes. The ventral surfaces are usually covered in cortex and were left unexploited.

Tools were made on both large and small flakes and have irregular retouch with little morphological standardization. The handaxe is approximately six centimeters in length and fully worked on both faces, with a well-articulated tip and asymmetric edges (Figure 2.29). It is impossible to date the TA.23 assemblage with any precision, other than to suggest an earlier Lower Palaeolithic age based on the condition of the artifacts, tool types and core technology.

Summary of Lower Palaeolithic Findings

The results of the DAP suggest there were multiple waves of occupations in southern Oman throughout the Early and Middle Pleistocene, supporting the conclusions of prior surveys carried out in the region (Cremaschi and Negrino 2002; Whalen *et al.* 2002; Zarins 2001). Lower Palaeolithic surface scatters are found in every ecological zone of Dhofar, except the mountain highlands and seaward slopes. We cannot rule out low archaeological visibility in this zone as one reason for the absence of sites.

While the Lower Palaeolithic findspots in Dhofar indicate the presence of hominids in South Arabia, it is unlikely that the Acheulean sites from Dhofar reflect a preserved Acheulean landscape such as that identified by Jennings *et al.* (2015) at Saffaqah in central Saudi Arabia. The plateau in Dhofar experienced considerable erosion and downcutting throughout the Quaternary. The escarpment, which is composed of shallow marine sediments, underwent tectonic uplift until the Late Miocene (Lepvrier *et al.* 2002; Platel and Roger 1989).

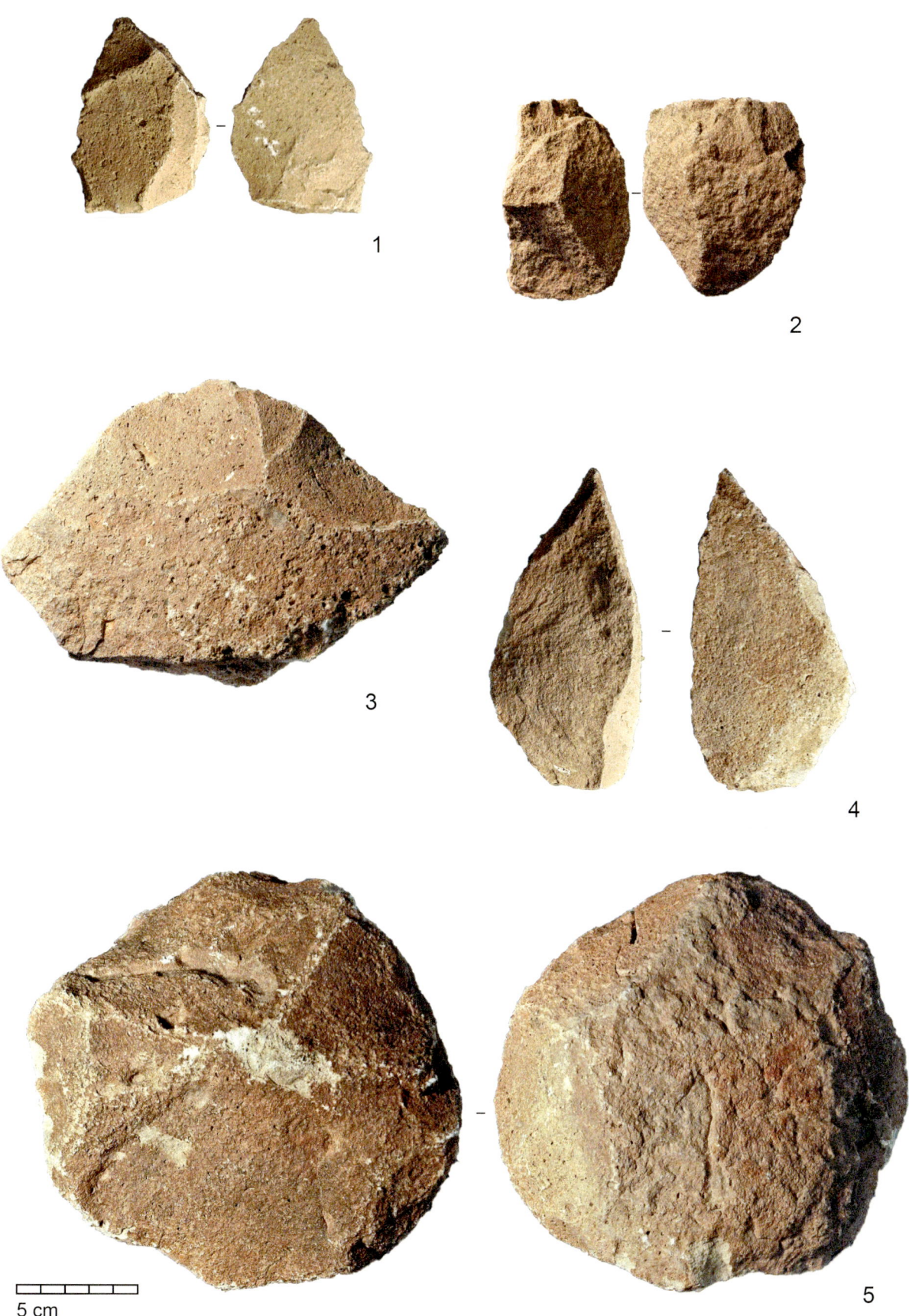

5 cm

Figure 2.27. Lower Palaeolithic artifacts from TA.23: (1-4) flakes, (2) single platform core, (3) retouched cortical flake, (5) massive discoid core (photographs by Y.H. Hilbert).

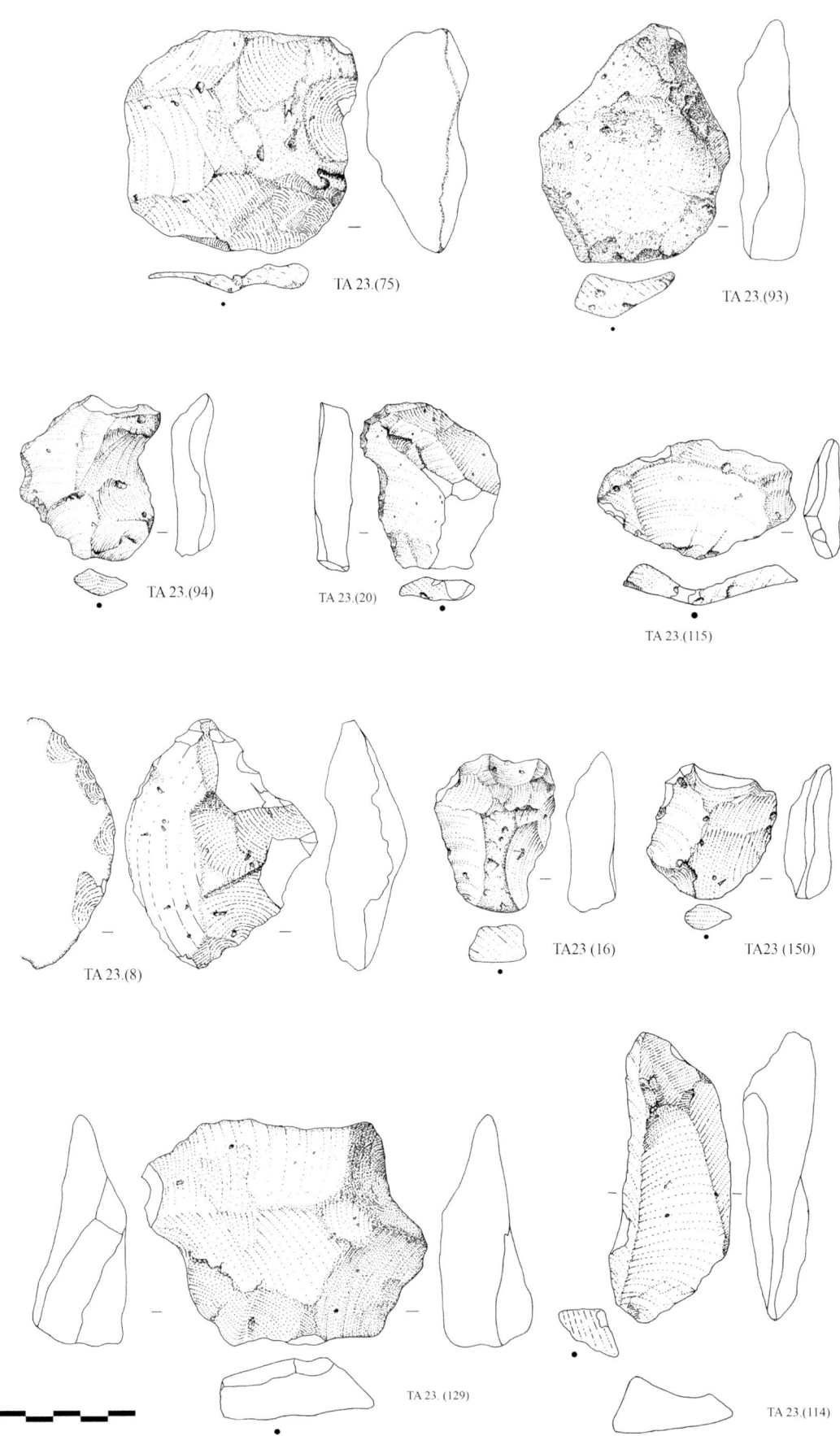

TA 23.(75)

TA 23.(93)

TA 23.(94)

TA 23.(20)

TA 23.(115)

TA 23.(8)

TA23 (16)

TA23 (150)

TA 23. (129)

TA 23.(114)

Figure 2.28. Débitage from TA.23 (illustrations by A. Beshkani).

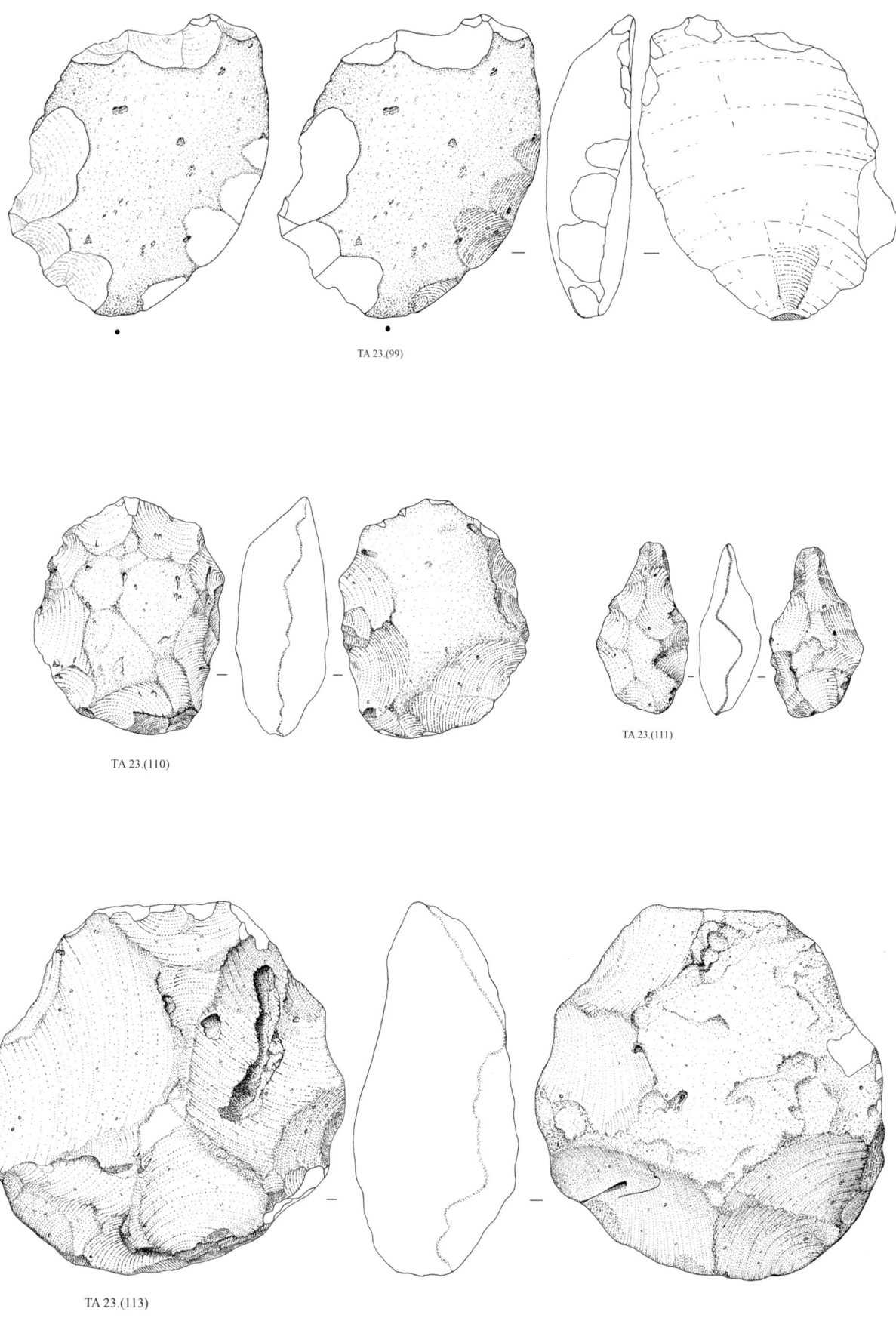

TA 23.(99)

TA 23.(110)

TA 23.(111)

TA 23.(113)

Figure 2.29. Tools and cores from TA.23 (illustrations by A. Beshkani).

This means that the first toolmakers in Dhofar, arriving sometime in the Early Pleistocene lived on a vastly different landscape than that of today. It is possible that the major extant *wadis* of the Nejd were not yet formed, given that the earlier Lower Palaeolithic scatters were found on the uppermost terraces and high desert plateau.

We recognize two general types of Lower Palaeolithic assemblages in Dhofar. The seemingly older group is characterized by the prevalence of handaxes, choppers, radial cores, discoids and volumetric cores. The later group of assemblages is consistently less weathered and is characterized by large blades produced using a volumetric, unidirectional-parallel blank production system. Assemblages from this later phase are sometimes accompanied by bifacial foliates and handaxes. We have not yet scratched the surface from this time period; more study is required to articulate the full range of techno-typological variability to build a chronological framework for the Lower Palaeolithic of Dhofar.

Chapter 3

The Middle Palaeolithic in Dhofar

The Middle Palaeolithic period is bracketed between approximately 300,000 and 40,000 years BP. During this technological phase, we see the continued development of prepared core technologies, which started to appear in the archaeological record toward the end of the Lower Palaeolithic. This was also a period of regional diversification, when distinct local lithic traditions developed across different parts of the globe. Some innovative toolmakers began to construct composite tools with interchangeable stone elements hafted onto a shaft of wood, bone, horn, antler, or ivory, in some cases attached using a chemically fabricated resin adhesive.

Researchers working in Europe, Asia and North Africa use the term Middle Palaeolithic for this phase, while archaeologists in sub-Saharan Africa traditionally use the designation Middle Stone Age. In both Middle Palaeolithic and Middle Stone Age assemblages, blade and prepared core reduction strategies become increasingly prevalent. One of the hallmarks of this period is the development of the Levallois method, a specific prepared core reduction strategy that creates a predetermined endproduct.

The Levallois method first appeared in the East African Middle Pleistocene and, over the course of the late Middle Pleistocene and early Late Pleistocene, developed into a variety of regional techniques. Levallois cores display a specific suite of morphological characteristics that are clearly recognizable and often chronologically diagnostic. In every variant of the Levallois method, the initial steps are to prepare a convex working surface and to facet the striking platform perpendicular to the working surface. In the case of preferential Levallois cores, one or two preferential blanks were struck from the prepared platform, leaving a signature dorsal scar pattern (Figure 3.1). The dorsal surface could be prepared using a variety of different organizational systems, which in some cases are time-transgressive (e.g. centripetal preparation) and in others are regionally and temporally discrete (e.g. Nubian preparation).

There are three types of Levallois preferential end products, whose shapes are controlled by the shape of the prepared core and the organizational system used to form the working surface: Levallois points, flakes and blades. Points were created by either unidirectional-convergent or Nubian Levallois techniques, while Levallois flakes were struck from ovate working surfaces with centripetal preparation. Levallois blades were produced by a recurrent reduction strategy that developed out of the classic preferential Levallois method in the later Middle Palaeolithic. Blades were struck from opposed platforms in alternating bidirectional removals to maintain convexity while producing multiple endproducts.

One reason for this apparent regional diversification during the Middle Palaeolithic and Middle Stone Age is the development of different hunting technologies and subsistence strategies. Hominids in the Middle Palaeolithic and Middle Stone Age actively preyed upon large, medium and small animals. Hafted tools and chemical adhesives led to more efficient weapons that could be hurled longer distances at higher velocities. At the Middle Palaeolithic site of Umm el Tlel in Syria, Levallois flakes and points still have traces of bitumen used for adhesive (Boëda *et al.* 2008). In Europe, toolmakers made a resinous pitch out of birch bark to fasten lithic tools (e.g., Grünberg 2002; Mazza *et al.* 2006) and at the Middle Palaeolithic Nubian Complex site of Sodmein Cave in the Egyptian Red Sea Hills, early modern humans created a concoction of charcoal, ochre and resin to haft their tools (Rots *et al.* 2011).

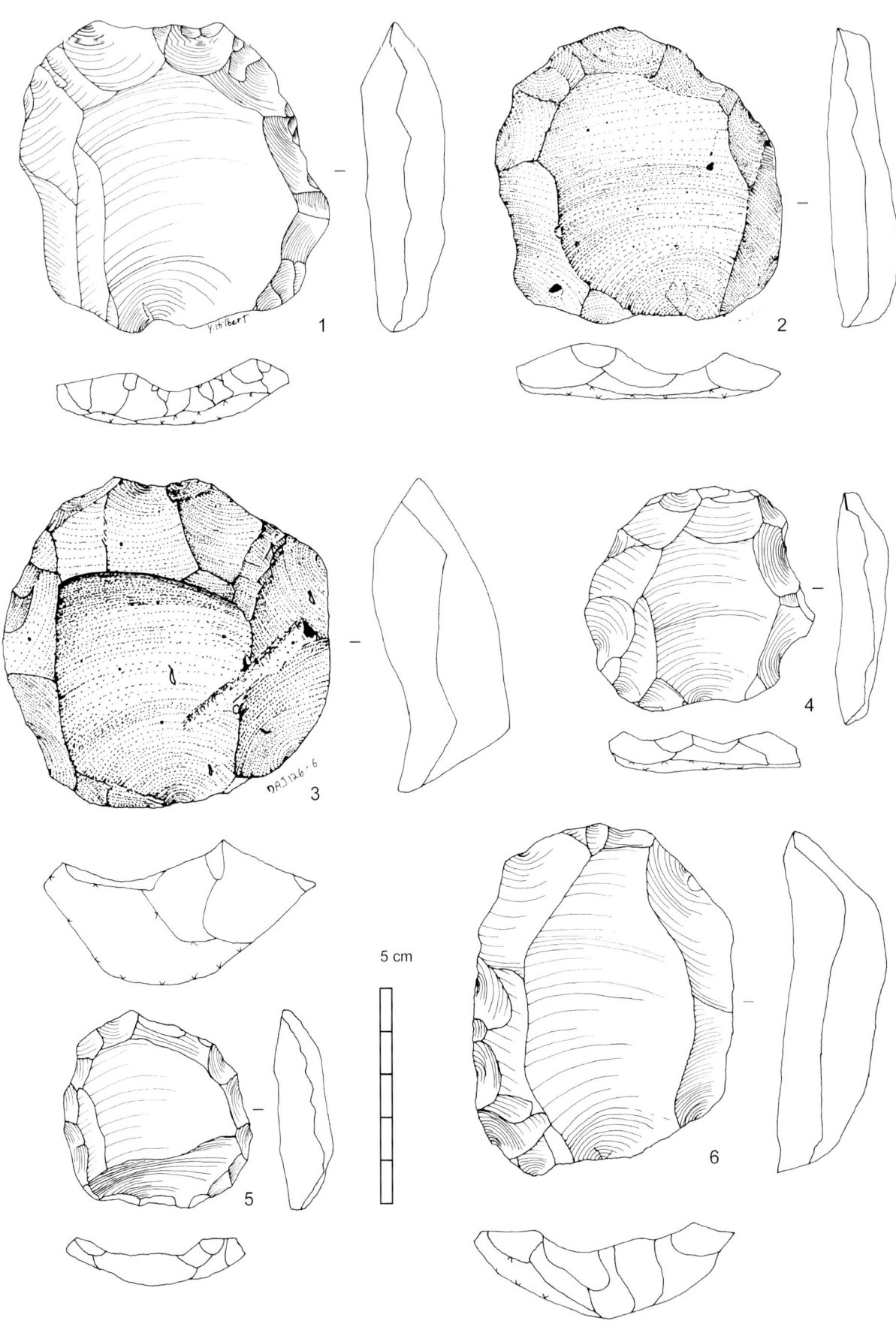

5 cm

Figure 3.1. Preferential Levallois flake cores from northern Saudi Arabia (after Hilbert et al. 2015a).

Hominid groups also used organic materials such as bone, wood, shell and antler for manufacturing tools and other cultural remains. The first documented bone points and carved decorative objects artifacts are found in the Middle Palaeolithic of Europe (Villa and D'errico 2001) and African Middle Stone Age (Bouzouggar *et al.* 2007; Henshilwood *et al.* 2009; McBrearty and Brooks 2000).

The oldest skeletal remains with anatomically modern human features have been found in Morocco and the Levant between approximately 350,000 and 200,000 years ago (Hershkovitz *et al.* 2018; Hublin *et al.* 2017; Shimelmitz *et al.* 2011, 2016). In sub-Saharan Africa, the earliest anatomically modern human specimens date between 200,000 and 150,000, discovered in the Omo River Valley in Ethiopia (McDougall *et al.* 2005), Singa in southern Sudan (McDermott *et al.* 1996) and Mumba Cave in Kenya (Bräuer and Mehlman 1988).

There is a longstanding debate as to the timing, route, quantity and direction of early human expansions into and out of Africa. The genetic, palaeoanthropological and archaeological records paint somewhat different pictures of how this process unfolded. One point of agreement is the geographic importance of the Arabian Peninsula in early human dispersal, largely due to the glacial-interglacial climatic cycles that drove demographic movement and cultural change.

South Arabia is one of just two conduits for human groups exiting or entering Africa. It is also the region most directly affected by Indian Ocean monsoon rainfall, serving as a refugium for plant and animal species. In this light, the Middle Palaeolithic archaeological record of Dhofar and all of southern Arabia, hold important clues as to the origins and spread of *Homo sapiens*.

The Afro-Arabian Nubian Complex

Artifacts from the Middle Palaeolithic period are among the most frequent on the expansive prehistoric landscapes of Arabia and most thoroughly documented in recent years. Like in Africa and Eurasia, Arabian archaeological research has uncovered a picture of regional diversity developing over the course of the Middle Palaeolithic. Across southern Arabia, from the Ramlat As Sabatayn desert in central Yemen to the foothills of Jebel Akhdar in northern Oman, thousands of regionally distinct Middle Palaeolithic sites have been discovered, in one of the richest zones of habitation on the Peninsula (Amirkhanov 2006; Beshkani *et al.* 2017b; Crassard 2008a; Inizan and Ortlieb 1987; Rose *et al.* 2011; Rose and Hilbert 2014; Usik *et al.* 2013; Zarins 2001).

The vast majority of Middle Palaeolithic assemblage types in southern Arabia belong to the Nubian Technocomplex (or Complex). Nubian Complex sites demonstrate a distinct constellation of technological features first reported from northern Sudan in the late 1960s (Guichard and Guichard 1965; Marks 1968), distinguished by a characteristic and highly standardized method of preferential Levallois reduction, "mass-produced from an elaborate archetype" (Guichard and Guichard 1965). Nubian core technology (Figure 3.2) is a regional variant of the preferential Levallois method for producing points, recognized by triangular/sub-triangular shaped cores, faceted striking platforms and specific preparation of the median distal ridge on the working surface, from which Levallois blanks were struck. There are three sub-types of Nubian Levallois core preparation, referred to as Nubian Type 1, Type 2 and Type 1/2. The primary working surface of a Type 1 core is formed by two distal-divergent removals that create a steeply angled median distal ridge for the removal of an elongated blade or point. Although the elongated endproduct is the same, Type 2 cores use bilateral shaping to construct the primary working surface. In some cases, the working surface of the Nubian core exhibits a combination of distal and lateral shaping, termed Type 1/2.

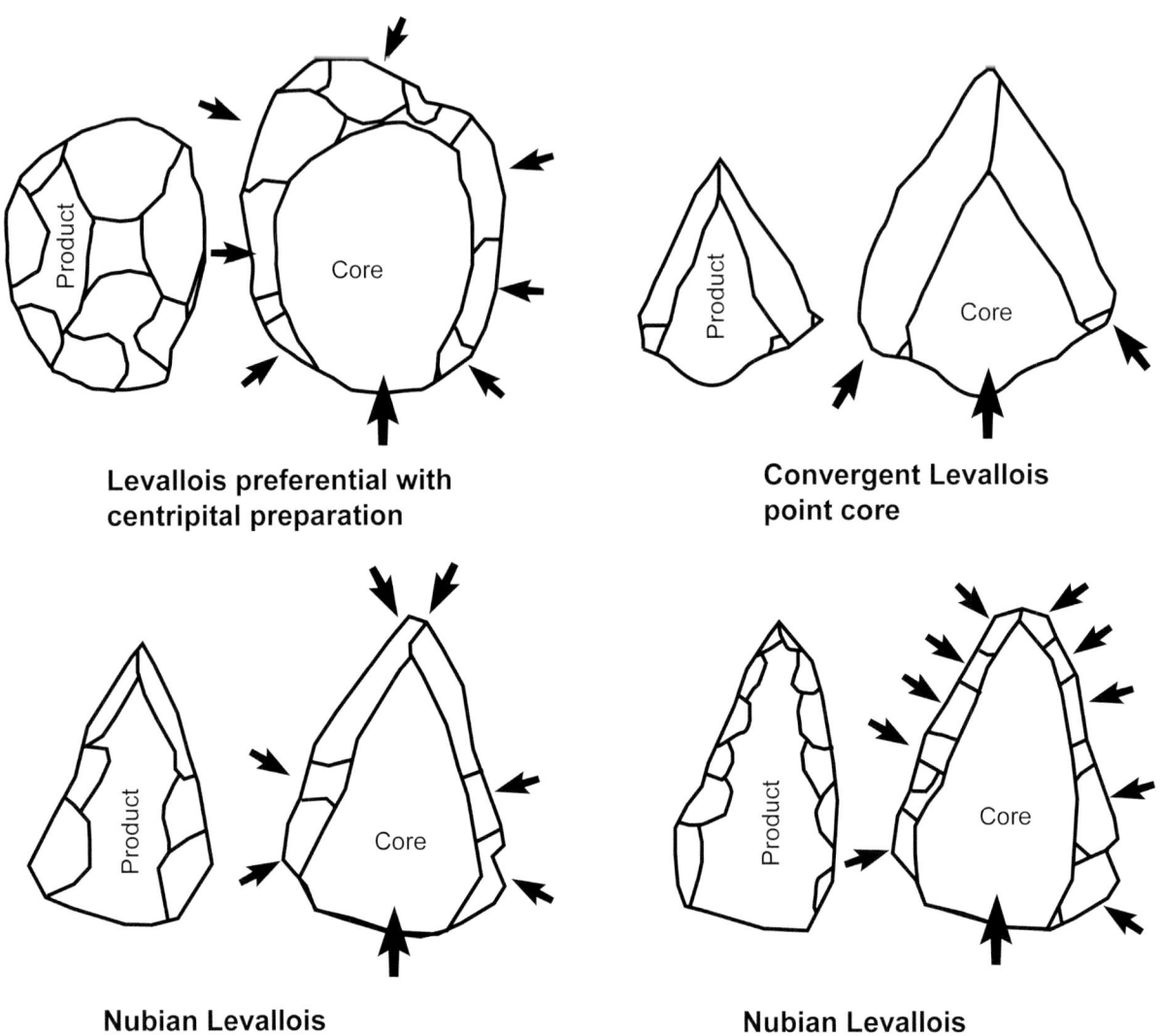

Levallois preferential with centripital preparation

Convergent Levallois point core

Nubian Levallois

Nubian Levallois

Figure 3.2. Schema of preferential centripetal Levallois, unidirectional convergent Levallois and Nubian Levallois methods (after Crassard and Hilbert 2013).

Assemblages belonging to the Nubian Complex have been found throughout the Nile Valley catchment system and high plateau (Olszewski *et al.* 2010; Van Peer 1992; Van Peer *et al.* 2003, 2010; Van Peer and Vermeersch 2007), around palaeolakes of the eastern Sahara (Kindermann *et al.* 2017; Smith *et al.* 2007; Wendorf and Schild 1980) and in the Egyptian Red Sea hills (Mercier *et al.* 1999; Van Peer *et al.* 1996). In sub-Saharan Africa, Nubian Complex findspots were discovered in Ethiopia (Clark 1988; Kurashina 1987), Somalia (Clark 1954) and Eritrea (Beyin 2013) (Figure 3.3).

In Africa, early Nubian Complex industries fall between 130,000 and 115,000 BP, while dates for the late Nubian Complex cluster between 85 and 70 ka BP (Mercier *et al.* 1999; Schmidt *et al.* 2015; Van Peer *et al.* 2010; Vermeersch *et al.* 1998). A single set of OSL dates from the site of Aybut Al-Auwal on the western Nejd Plateau in Dhofar places the Nubian Complex in southern Arabia before 106,000 years ago (Rose *et al.* 2011). Nubian Complex toolmakers were anatomically modern humans. At Taramsa 1 in Egypt, an anatomically modern human child was discovered dating to around 70,000 BP (Van Peer *et al.* 2010).

The prevalence of Nubian Complex assemblages in southern Arabia provides evidence for demographic connections across the Red Sea during MIS 5; however, the directionality of these population movements remains an open question (Crassard and Hilbert 2013; Goder-Goldberger *et al.* 2016; Hilbert *et al.* 2017; Rose *et al.* 2011; Rose and Marks 2014; Usik *et al.* 2013).

A regionally distinct *facies* of the late Nubian Complex has been mapped on the western Nejd, concentrated around fracture springs near the village of Mudayy. This industry, called the Mudayyan, includes Nubian core technology and the production of Nubian Levallois points, but differs in several aspects. Mudayyan artifacts consistently exhibit less chemical and mechanical weathering than do the classic Nubian assemblages found in the same immediate areas. In some cases, heavily patinated earlier Nubian cores have been reworked using Mudayyan core reduction strategies. Consequently, it is likely that the Mudayyan is temporally later than the Dhofar Nubian, but sufficiently close in time to demonstrate technological continuity. Typical Mudayyan Levallois cores are smaller than those of the Dhofar Nubian and show a decrease in the thickness of the median distal ridge. These small Nubian Levallois cores grade into flat bidirectional cores with facetted platforms that produce blades and elongated points. In addition to Levallois points, the Mudayyan toolkit includes end scrapers, burins and perforators.

DAP Middle Palaeolithic Sites

A total of 262 Middle Palaeolithic surface sites were mapped by the DAP between 2010 and 2013 (Figure 3.4). These vary in size, density and function depending on distance to raw material, distance to fresh water, landscape gradient and local geomorphology. Middle Palaeolithic sites are most often found atop the high plateau and upper terraces overlooking the major drainage systems of the western Nejd: Wadis Ghadun, Banawt, Amawt, Mudayy, Aybut, Stum, Aydam and Tanfarawt. The vast majority of Middle Palaeolithic sites are found on our near chert outcrops, while rare occurrences are found in secondary position within *wadi* gravels, or as isolated Levallois points and cores far from raw material sources.

Middle Palaeolithic Sample Assemblages

TH.418

TH.418 is an expansive, multi-occupation lithic workshop site with exceptionally well-preserved artifacts. The site is located on the high plateau (20-30 m) above an anastomosing tributary of Wadi Aybut, just over one kilometer west of the extant fracture spring in Mudayy village (Figure 3.5). The scatter occurs on and around a low hill (ca. 2 m) at the center of the site, which has a high quality chert seam actively eroding from the scarp. The low hill is capped by a harder beige bioclastic limestone that overlies a soft whitish dolomitic chalk. The surrounding plateau landscape, including nearby site TH.419, is composed of these step-scarp erosional features (Figure 3.6). In 2012, we systematically collected artifacts from three separate locations at the site. Collection Area 1 was a 5 x 5 m grid near the edge of the plateau, Collection Area 2 was a 5 x 5 grid roughly halfway between the edge of the plateau and hill with the chert seam and Collection Area 3 was a 3 x 3 grid close to the base of the hill. These results showed us that there was technological and taphonomic variability between the collection areas, appearing to correlate with distance to the actively eroding chert seam. Consequently, we returned during the 2013 campaign and piece plotted all diagnostic artifacts along a 30 x 5 m transect radiating outward from the chert outcrop.

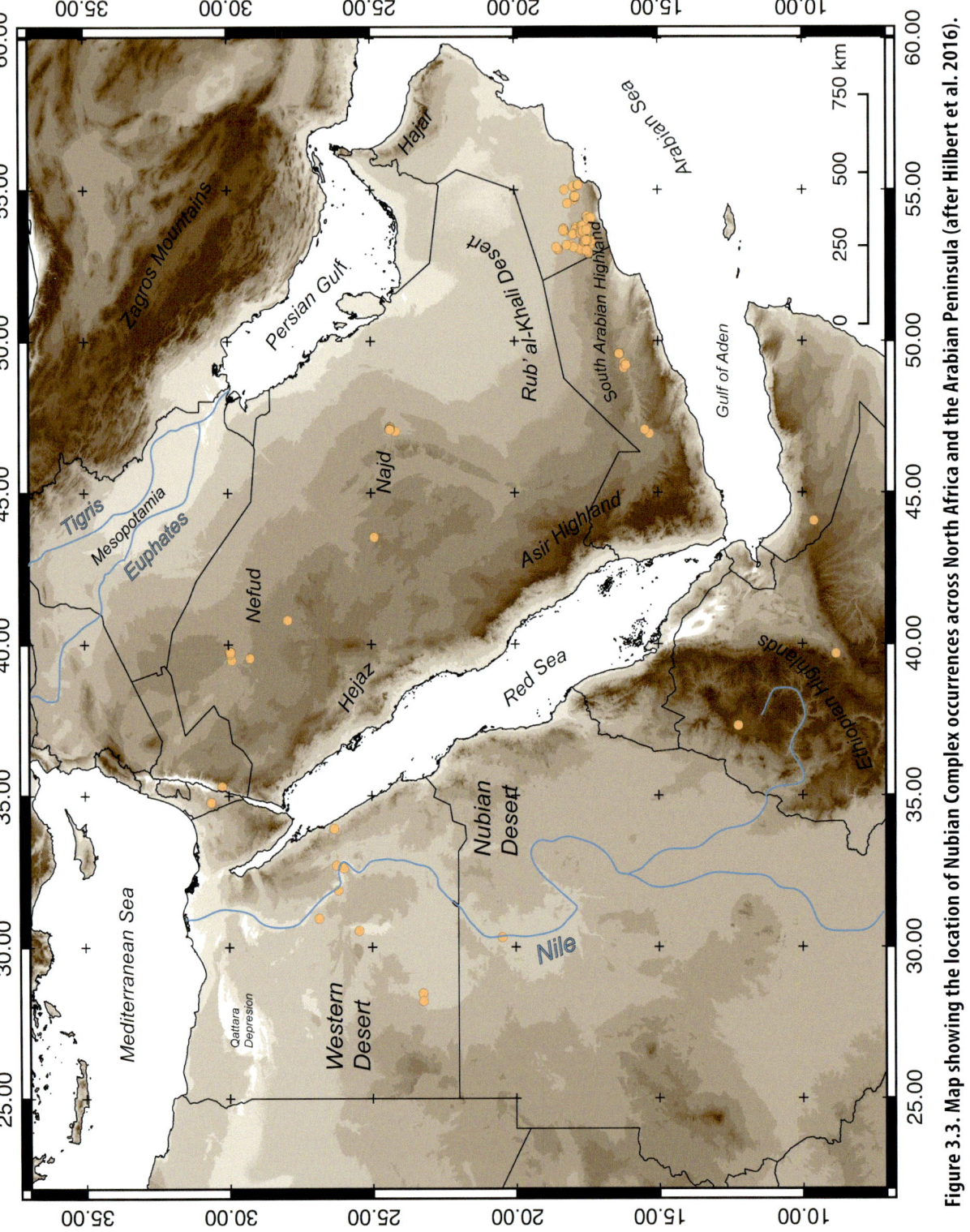

Figure 3.3. Map showing the location of Nubian Complex occurrences across North Africa and the Arabian Peninsula (after Hilbert et al. 2016).

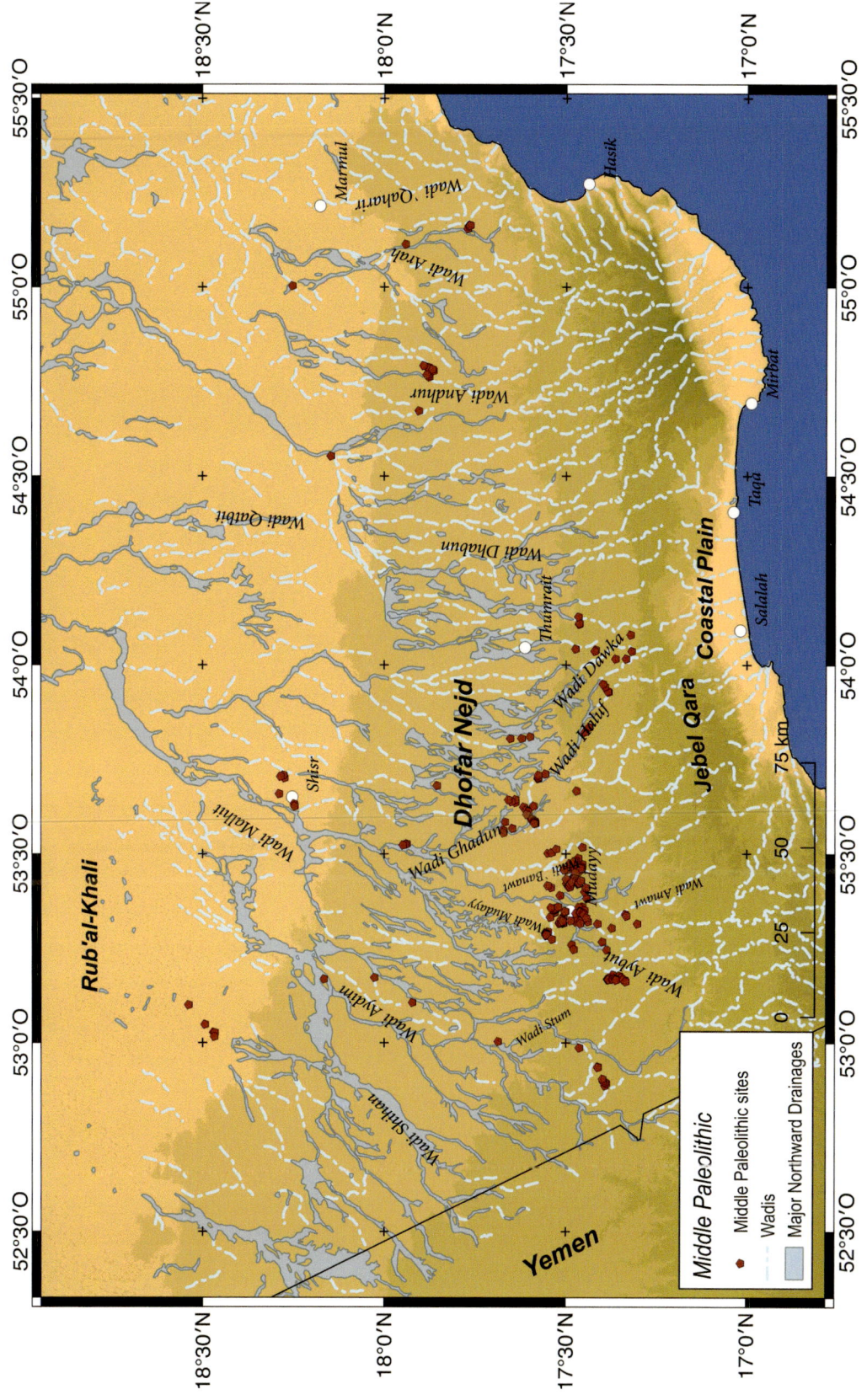

Figure 3.4. Map showing the location of Middle Palaeolithic findspots recorded by the Dhofar Archaeological Project between 2010 and 2013.

Figure 3.5. TH.418 upper terrace (photograph by the authors).

The surface of the transect study area is relatively flat and dips gently (1.4°) away from the low hill scarp. In general, Late Palaeolithic artifacts were found clustering closer to the chert outcrop, while Middle Palaeolithic Mudayyan artifacts were found further away. There is some spatial overlap with Late Palaeolithic material scattered further away from the outcrop, superimposed over the Middle Palaeolithic artifacts, as would be expected from a chronologically later occupation. Conversely, there are few Mudayyan specimens mixed with the Late Palaeolithic artifact cluster (Figure 3.7). The spatial distribution at TH.418 upholds the trend of younger artifacts being closer to the actively eroding chert seam, while taphonomic patterns exhibit less surface weathering on artifacts closer to the seam. Older Nubian elements were clearly distinguished by their black patina and moderate chemical dissolution, in comparison to the lighter brown and beige patina of the Mudayyan and Late Palaeolithic artifacts.

The following is a description of the Mudayyan assemblage from Collection Area 2 (Table 3.1). Among the 600 total artifacts, there are an unusually large number of cores in relation to débitage. Tools predominantly include Levallois points and flakes, as well as rare end scrapers, perforators, burins and notches. Débitage is composed mostly of flakes and cortical pieces. Half of the cores are single platform, unidirectional blade cores reduced from the narrow working surface of thin nodules. Of the remaining core types, 42% are Levallois cores, including both classic Nubian and bidirectional preferential Levallois variants. Also present is a hybrid technology that utilizes the narrow working surface of the raw material to produce elongated blanks from opposed faceted striking platforms.

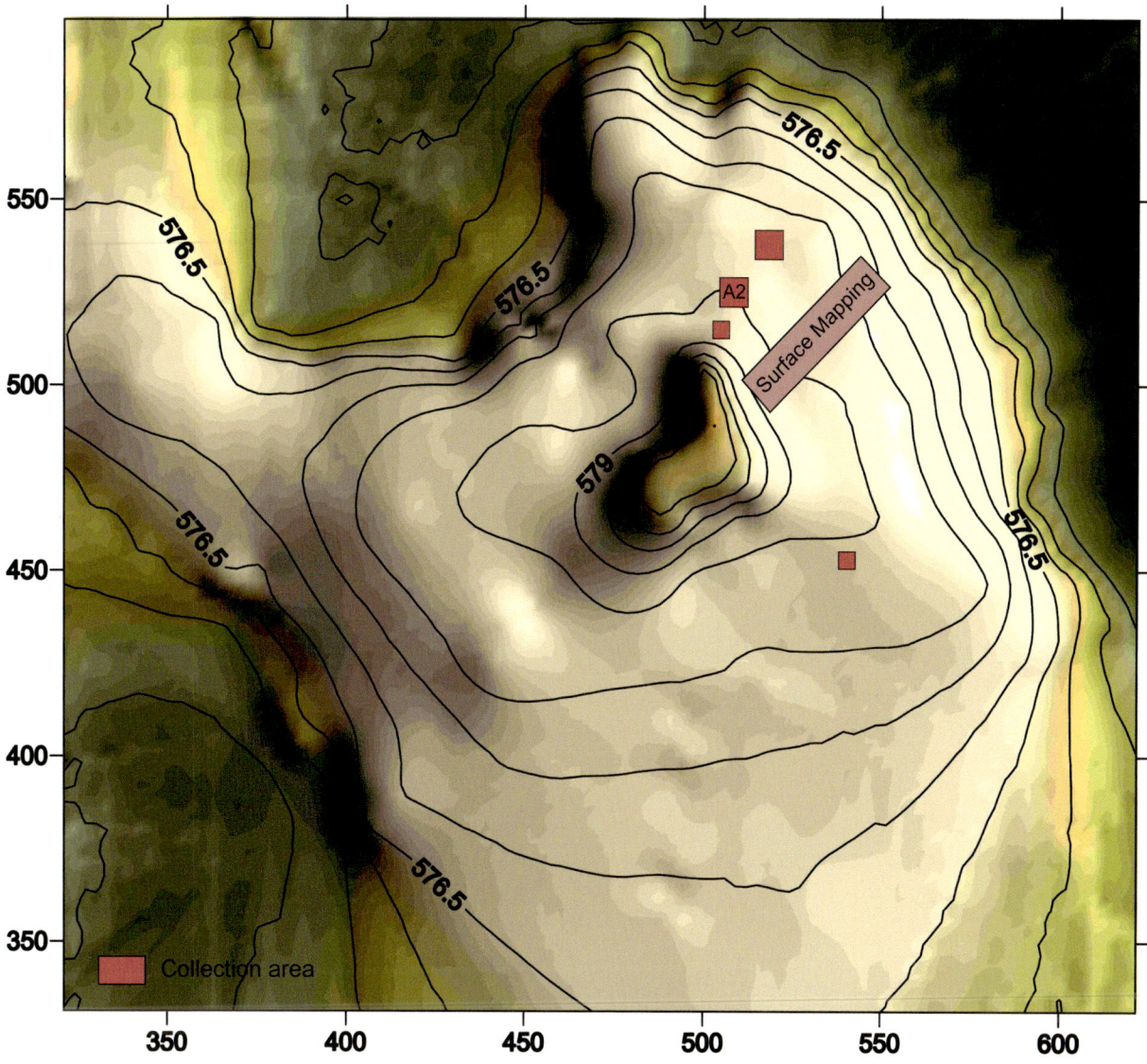

Figure 3.6. Topographic map of TH.418 (figure plot by Y.H. Hilbert).

In terms of metrics, the assemblage is relatively small, with Levallois points ranging between 4 and 7 cm (Figures 3.8 and 3.9). This may be due to the cores being thoroughly reduced and recycled during repeated visits to the quarry, a change in reduction strategy that deliberately produced smaller points and/or relatively small size of the chert nodules. Most of the bidirectional and unidirectional (non-Nubian) Levallois cores are flat and exhausted with a final overpassed flake obscuring the distal platform, suggesting these may have begun the reduction sequence as classic Nubian cores.

The primary reduction strategies observed at TH.418 are 1) classic Nubian Levallois, 2) recurrent bidirectional cores with opposed, faceted platforms, and 3) blades struck from the narrow working surface of single platform cores (Figures 3.10 and 3.11). There are taphonomic and technological differences between the Late Palaeolithic blade cores with semi-tournant working surfaces from Collection Area 3 and the Mudayyan blade cores in Collection Area 2 with frontal, narrow surfaces.

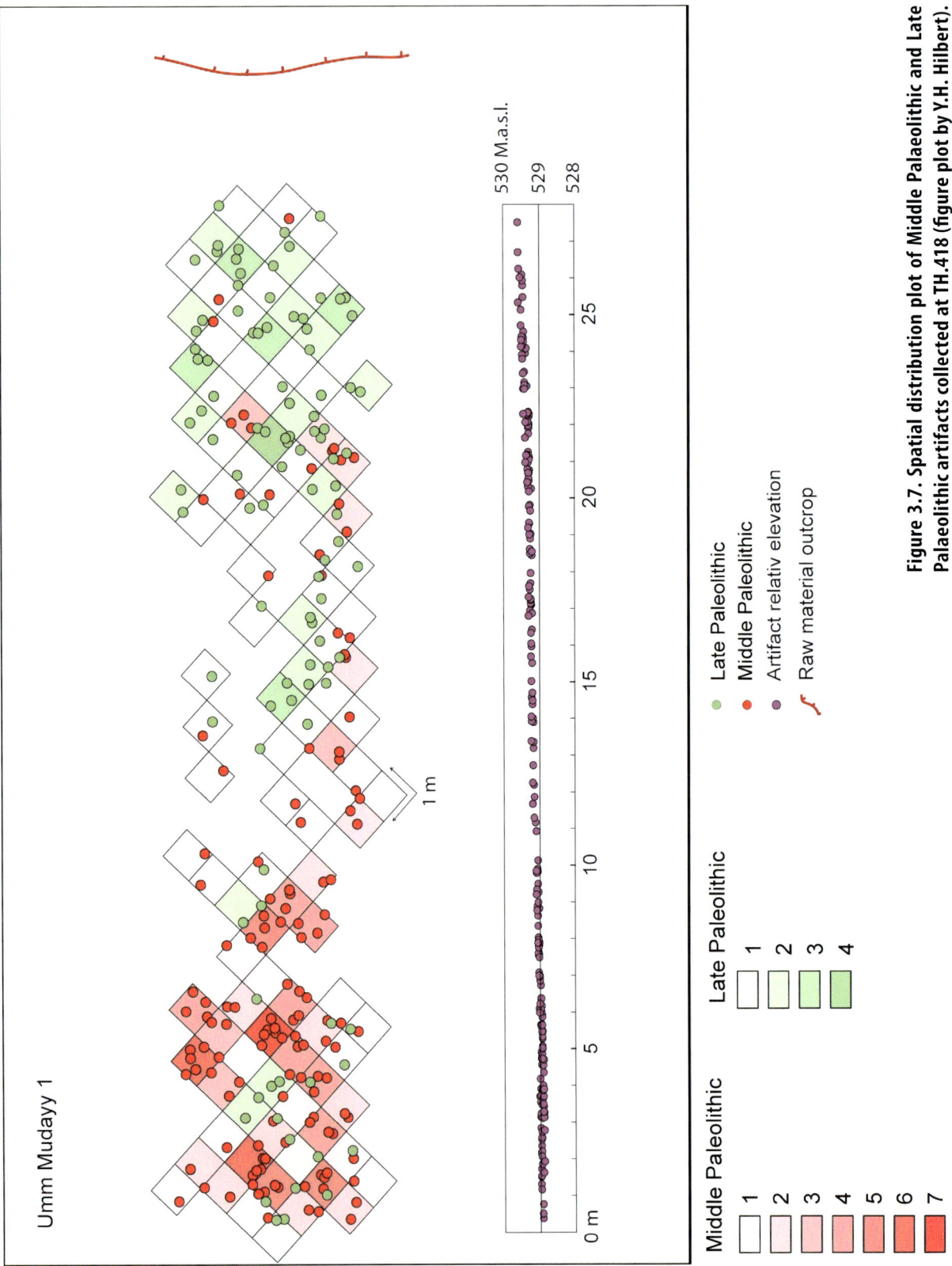

Figure 3.7. Spatial distribution plot of Middle Palaeolithic and Late Palaeolithic artifacts collected at TH.418 (figure plot by Y.H. Hilbert).

Table 3.1. Artifact counts from TH.418.

Umm Mudayy 1	N	Percentage
Debitage	**402**	**67%**
Flakes	*107*	*27%*
Cortical Flakes	*164*	*41%*
Débordant Flakes	*15*	*4%*
Blades	*22*	*5%*
Cortical blades	*44*	*11%*
Débordant blades	*30*	*7%*
Crested blades	*5*	*1%*
Core tablets	*1*	*0%*
Core trimming elements	*8*	*2%*
Nubian diagnostic debitage	*6*	*2%*
Cores	**166**	**28%**
Single platform	*16*	*9%*
Single platform, narrow working surface	*36*	*22%*
Bidirectional	*16*	*10%*
Bidirectional, narrow working surface	*2*	*1%*
Bidirectional, adjacent working surfaces	*3*	*2%*
Bidirectional Levallois	*10*	*6%*
Nubian Levallois	*26*	*16%*
Nubian Levallois, fragment	*8*	*5%*
Pre-core, with cresting	*1*	*0%*
Pre-core Nubian	*10*	*6%*
Levallois, indeterminate/exhausted	*15*	*9%*
Indeterminate	*2*	*1%*
Fragments	*21*	*13%*
Tools	**32**	**5%**
Levallois points	14	44%
Levallois flakes	3	10%
Notches	1	3%
Double Notches	2	7%
Perforators	2	6%
Burins, single	2	6%
Burins, on retouched edge	1	3%
Endscrapers, convex	1	3%
Endscrapers, atypical	2	6%
Endscrapers, fragment	1	3%
Naturally-backed knife	1	3%
Retouched pieces	2	6%
Total	**600**	**100%**

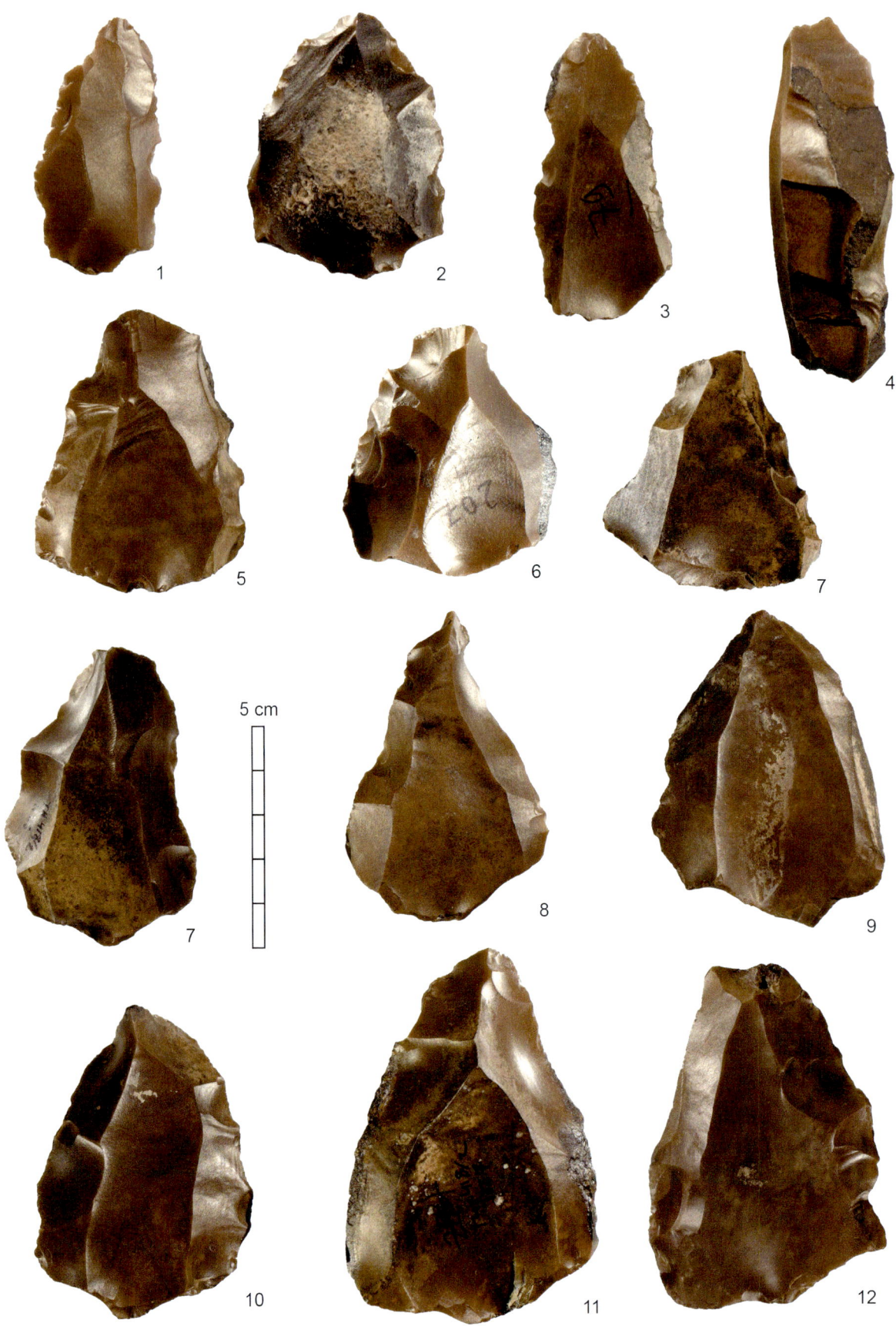

Figure 3.8. Nubian Middle Palaeolithic artifacts from TH.418: (1-3) Nubian Levallois points, (4) débordant blade, (5-12) Nubian Levallois cores (photographs by A. Beshkani).

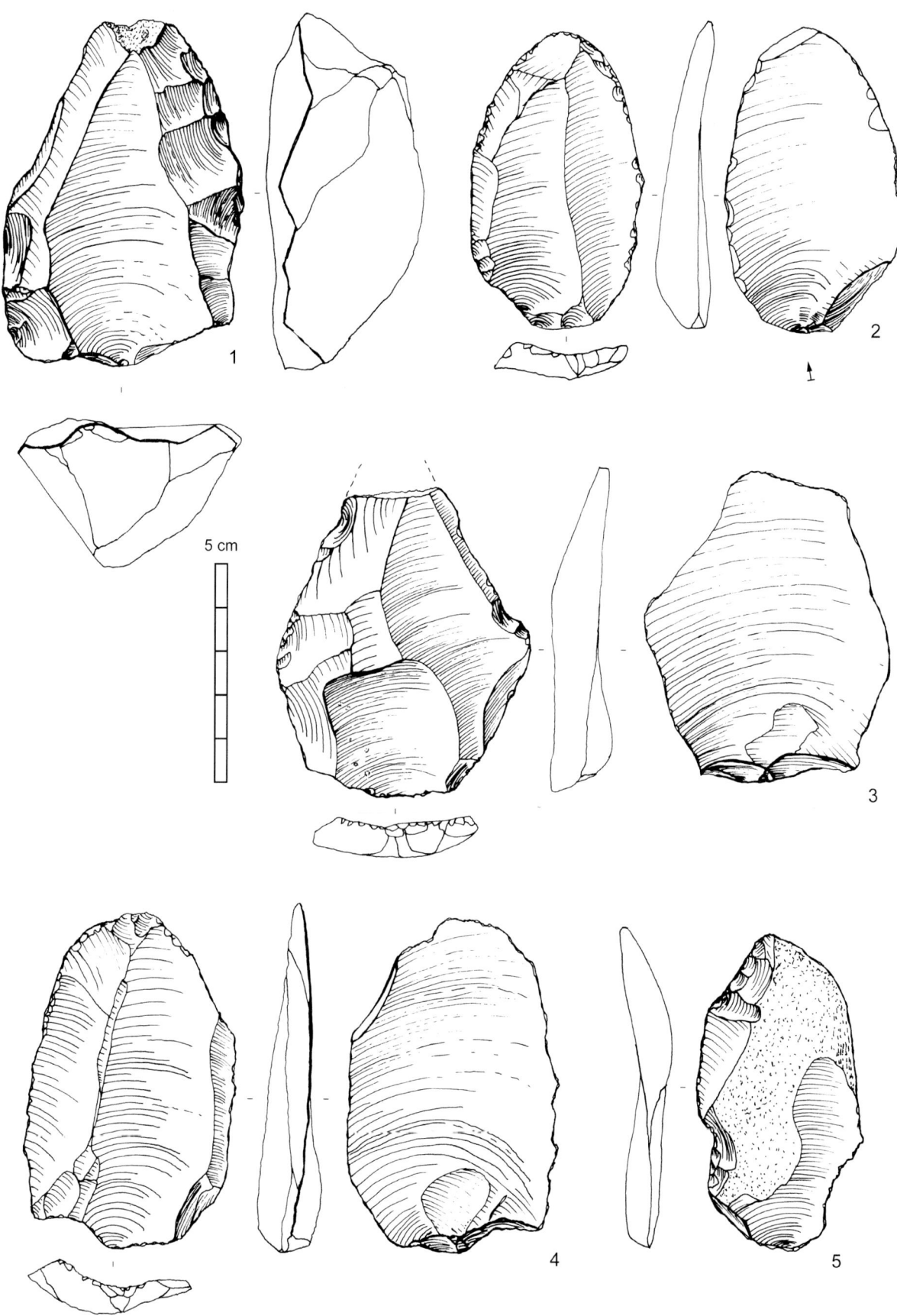

5 cm

Figure 3.9. Nubian Middle Palaeolithic artifacts from TH.418: (1-4) Nubian Levallois cores, (2) Levallois flake with discontinuous lateral retouch, (3) Nubian Levallois point, (5) notch (illustrations by Y.H. Hilbert).

5 cm

Figure 3.10. Bidirectional Middle Palaeolithic cores from TH.418 (photographs by A. Beshkani).

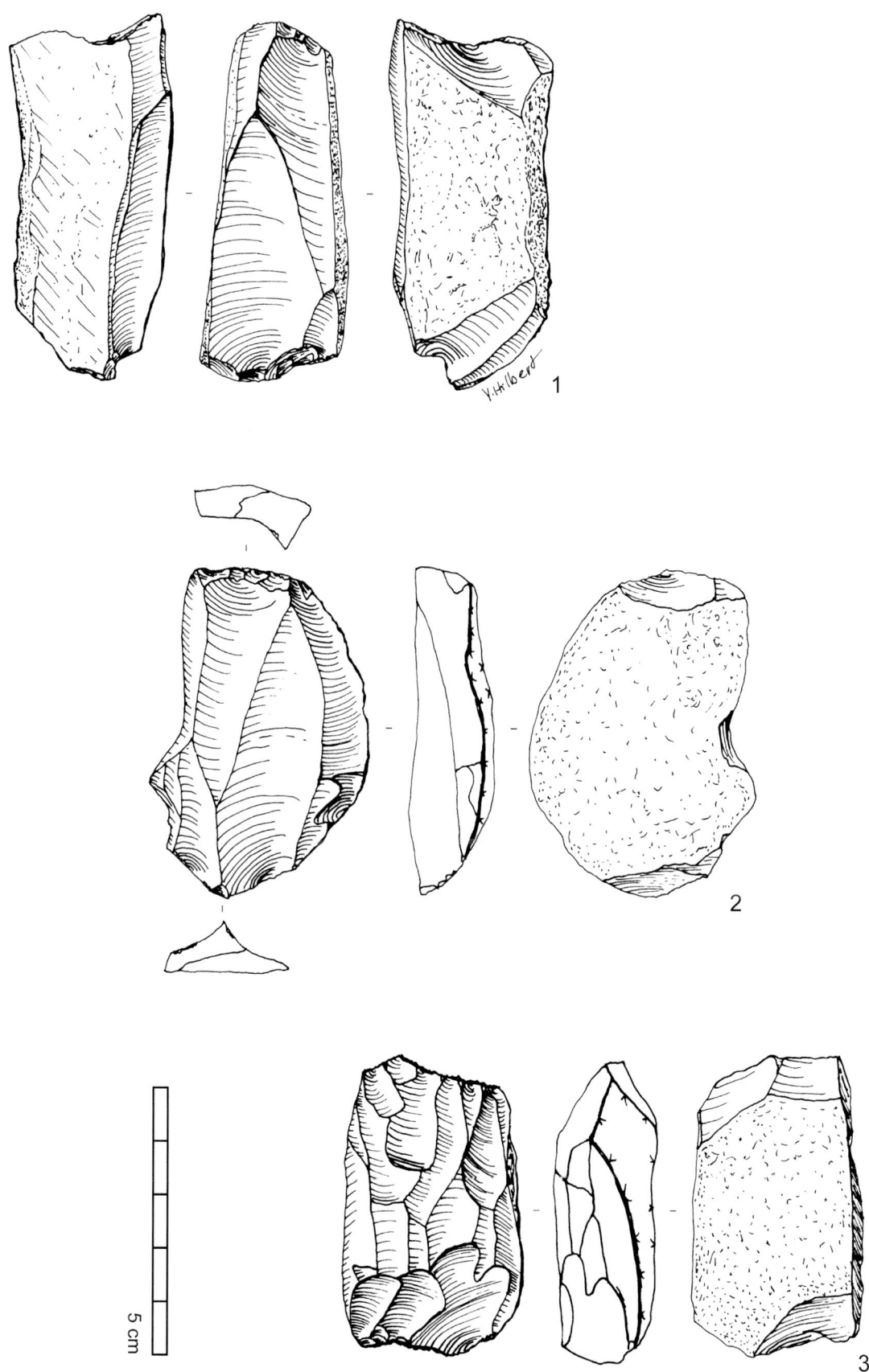

Figure 3.11. Bidirectional Middle Palaeolithic cores from TH.418: (1) bidirectional Levallois core on narrow surface of plaquettes, (2) bidirectional Levallois core, (3) exhausted bidirectional blade core (illustrations by Y.H. Hilbert).

5 cm

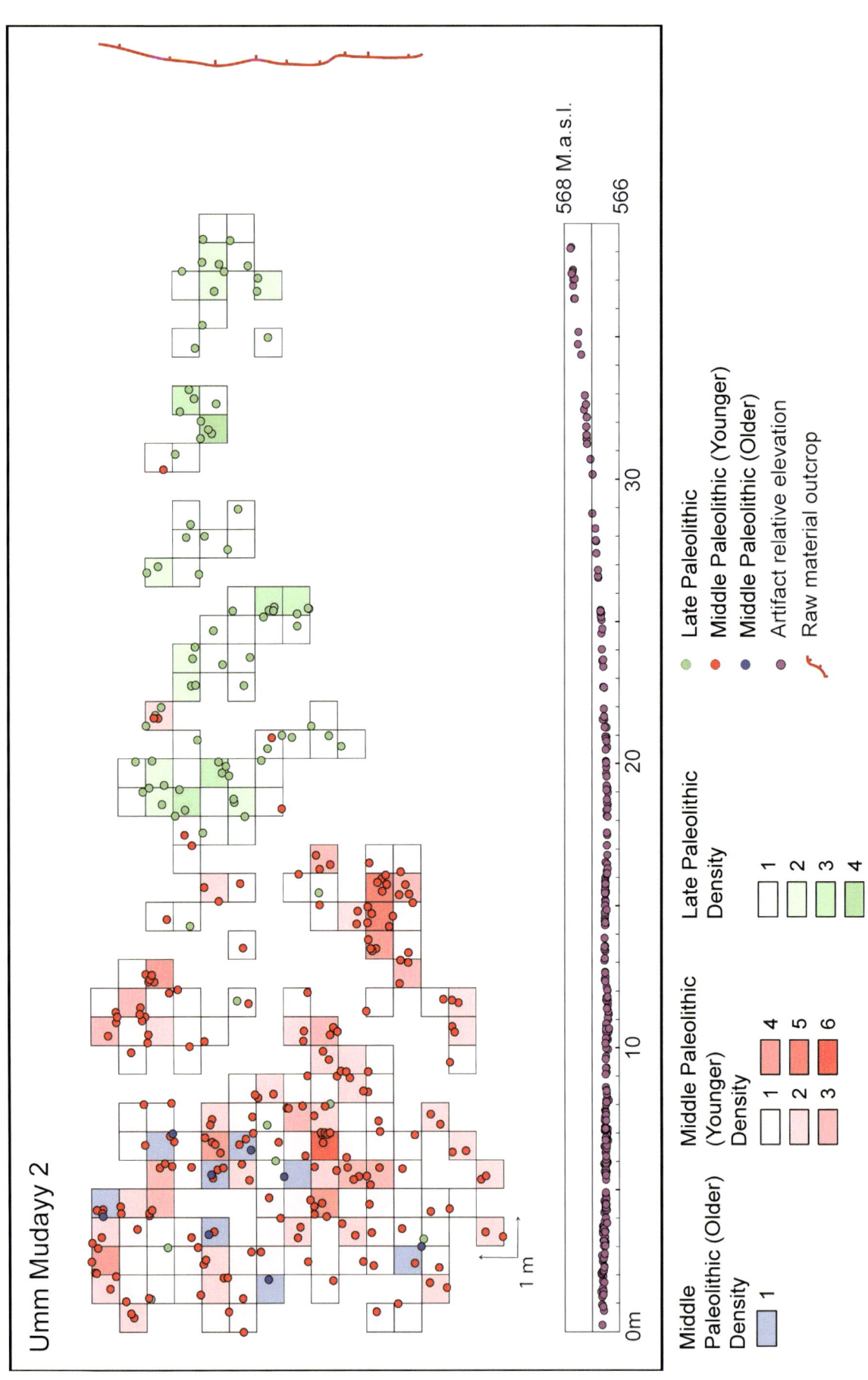

Figure 3.12. Spatial distribution plot of Middle and Late Palaeolithic artifacts from TH.419 (figure plot by Y.H. Hilbert).

TH.419

Findspot TH.419 is located on the same landscape as TH.418, approximately 300 m to the east. The artifacts found there are associated with a similar chert outcrop eroding from a low scarp in the same manner as TH.418. The TH.419 collection methodology was the same as at TH.418. We plotted all diagnostic artifacts within a 30 x 15 m transect, collecting a total of 300 specimens (Figure 3.12). Middle and Late Palaeolithic artifacts were found on a nearly horizontal surface that rises slightly toward the low scarp. The Late Palaeolithic specimens have a widespread but sparse distribution across the surface, found in highest concentrations at the base of the low hill scarp. Lightly weathered Middle Palaeolithic Mudayyan artifacts cluster somewhat further away from the outcrop, while a few heavily weathered, larger Nubian cores were found furthest from the scarp.

Most the Mudayyan artifacts within the collection area are in relatively good condition, although with moderate edge damage. There is low to moderate chemical dissolution and the pieces tend to exhibit a mustard-brown patina. There is a high frequency of recycling, nearly a quarter of the artifacts are manufactured on older Nubian cores and flakes. The TH.419 assemblage includes a large amount of tools and cores in relation to débitage (Table 3.2). Among the débitage, flakes and blades are the most common blank types, many exhibiting diagnostic scar patterns and striking platforms indicative of Nubian Levallois preparation and curation (e.g., blades with crested dorsal scars, technical blanks struck from the median distal ridge of a Nubian core, etc). Cortical pieces are also numerous, indicating that initial stages of core reduction took place at the site.

The Mudayyan assemblage includes 170 cores. The majority are classified as small (<7 cm in length) classic Nubian Levallois cores. Slightly less frequent are bidirectional Levallois cores, recurrent bidirectional cores and single platform blade cores exploiting the narrow working surface of local nodules. Tools include retouched Levallois blanks and a large number of end scrapers and burins. Of the ten retouched Levallois flakes and points, six were retouched into endscrapers and perforators. Scraper retouch is semi-steep and continuous, most often convex. In every instance, perforators are double-shouldered.

The reduction strategies identified at TH.419 include Nubian Levallois (Figure 3.13) and bidirectional Levallois cores with flat, secondary opposed platform (Figures 3.14 and 3.15). From the large sample size, it appears that preferential bidirectional Levallois cores fall within a single technological continuum grading into recurrent bidirectional cores. In both cases, the opposed platforms are faceted. The determining factor is whether the opposed platform is primary or secondary. Blade cores infrequently display some form of rudimentary crest preparation, as well as the rare removal of core tablets to rejuvenate the striking platform. The blade cores range from frontal to semi-tournant and are both single and opposed platform.

TH.123

The extensive TH.123 surface scatter was found on the high plateau approximately three kilometers northwest of Mudayy village. Like the other lithic workshops site presented above, TH.123 is a multi-occupation site with spatially confined areas of reduction that correlate with distance to the active chert outcrop. A dense scatter of Late Palaeolithic blade blanks was observed directly on top of the local outcrop (Figure 3.16). During the initial site visit in 2011, we systematically collected a 10 x 10 m grid consisting almost exclusively of a Middle Palaeolithic Nubian assemblage (Rose *et al.* 2011), approximately 20 m from the chert seam (Figures 3.17 and 3.18)

Table 3.2. Artifact counts from TH.419.

Umm Mudayy 2	N	Percentage
Debitage	**128**	**37%**
Flakes	*46*	*36%*
Cortical Flakes	*22*	*17%*
Débordant Flakes	*5*	*4%*
Blades	*22*	*17%*
Cortical Blades	*6*	*5%*
Débordant Blades	*10*	*8%*
Crested blades	*9*	*7%*
Core tablets	*1*	*1%*
Nubian diagnostic blades	*7*	*5%*
Cores	**170**	**49%**
Single platform	*18*	*11%*
Single platform, narrow working surface	*16*	*9%*
Narrow working surface, with cresting	*5*	*3%*
Bidirectional	*20*	*12%*
Bidirectional, narrow working surface	*4*	*2%*
Bidirectional, adjacent working surfaces	*1*	*1%*
Nubian Levallois	*52*	*31%*
Nubian Levallois, fragment	*2*	*1%*
Levallois, unidirectional	*17*	*10%*
Levallois, bidirectional	*23*	*13%*
Pre-core, with cresting	*1*	*1%*
Pre-core, Micro-Nubian	*7*	*4%*
Indeterminate	*4*	*2%*
Tools	**48**	**14%**
Levallois points	*6*	*13%*
Levallois flakes	*1*	*2%*
Levallois points, retouched	*8*	*17%*
Levallois flakes, retouched	*2*	*4%*
Notches	*1*	*2%*
Double Notches	*1*	*2%*
Sidescrapers, straight	*3*	*6%*
Perforators	*4*	*8%*
Perforators, double	*1*	*2%*
Burins, single	*1*	*2%*
Burins, dihedral	*2*	*4%*
Burin on retouched edge	*2*	*4%*
Endscrapers, convex	*8*	*17%*
Endscrapers, nosed	*2*	*4%*
Endscrapers, thumbnail	*1*	*2%*
Endscrapers, straight	*3*	*6%*
Endscrapers, atypical	*1*	*2%*
Hammerstone	*1*	*2%*
Total	**474**	**100%**

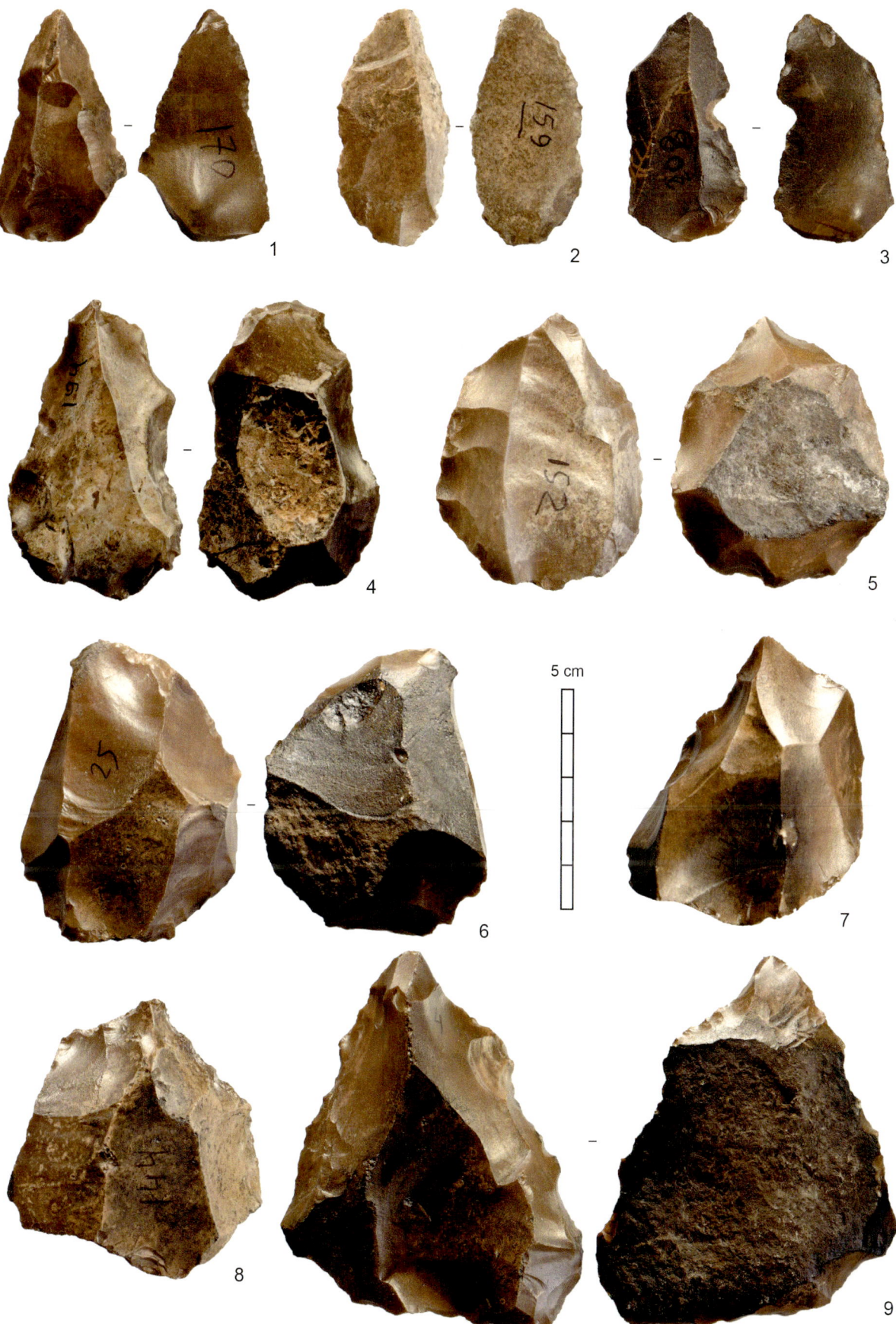

Figure 3.13. Nubian Levallois cores and products from TH.419: (1-3) Nubian Levallois points, (4-9) Nubian Levallois cores (photographs by A. Beshkani).

Figure 3.14. Bidirectional cores from TH.419: (1-2) bidirectional blade cores, (3) bidirectional Levallois core, (4) bidirectional Levallois core made on darker patinated flake (photographs by A. Beshkani).

Figure 3.15. Bidirectional Levallois cores from TH.419 (photographs by A. Beshkani).

Figure 3.16. Late Palaeolithic blade scatter at TH.123 (photograph by the authors).

During the 2011 fieldwork campaign, a total of 1141 Middle Palaeolithic Nubian artifacts were collected from the 10 x 10 m grid (Table 3.3). The high frequency of débitage and chips suggests that little post-depositional displacement has affected this part of the site. The majority of the cores are Nubian Levallois, of which most show moderate to advanced surface weathering, resulting in chemical dissolution over more than half the original knapped surface (Figure 3.19). We note that the seemingly older, more weathered Nubian cores are larger and more voluminous than the smaller Nubian cores, which still display most of the original knapped surface (Figure 3.20).

We returned to the site in 2013 to analyze the spatial distribution of Late and Middle Palaeolithic artifacts. A sample of diagnostic artifacts were mapped inside a transect measuring 32 x 5 m, within which the terrain is relatively flat, sloping about 2 degrees downward from the modern outcrop (Figure 3.21). We plotted a total of 120 artifacts, including 68 heavily weathered Middle Palaeolithic Nubian artifacts, 14 more lightly weathered Middle Palaeolithic Mudayyan artifacts and 38 Late Palaeolithic cores, tools and débitage with little to no patina, chemical dissolution, rounding, or edge damage. Although of lower resolution given the smaller sample size, the relative distribution of artifacts and taphonomic weathering patterns at TH.123 follows the same patterns observed at other multi-occupation workshop sites in Dhofar.

Figure 3.17. TH.123 surface collection area prior to sampling in 2011 (photograph by the authors).

Figure 3.18. TH.123 surface collection during sampling in 2011 (photograph by the authors).

5 cm

Figure 3.19 More heavily weathered Nubian cores from TH.123 (photographs by A. Beshkani).

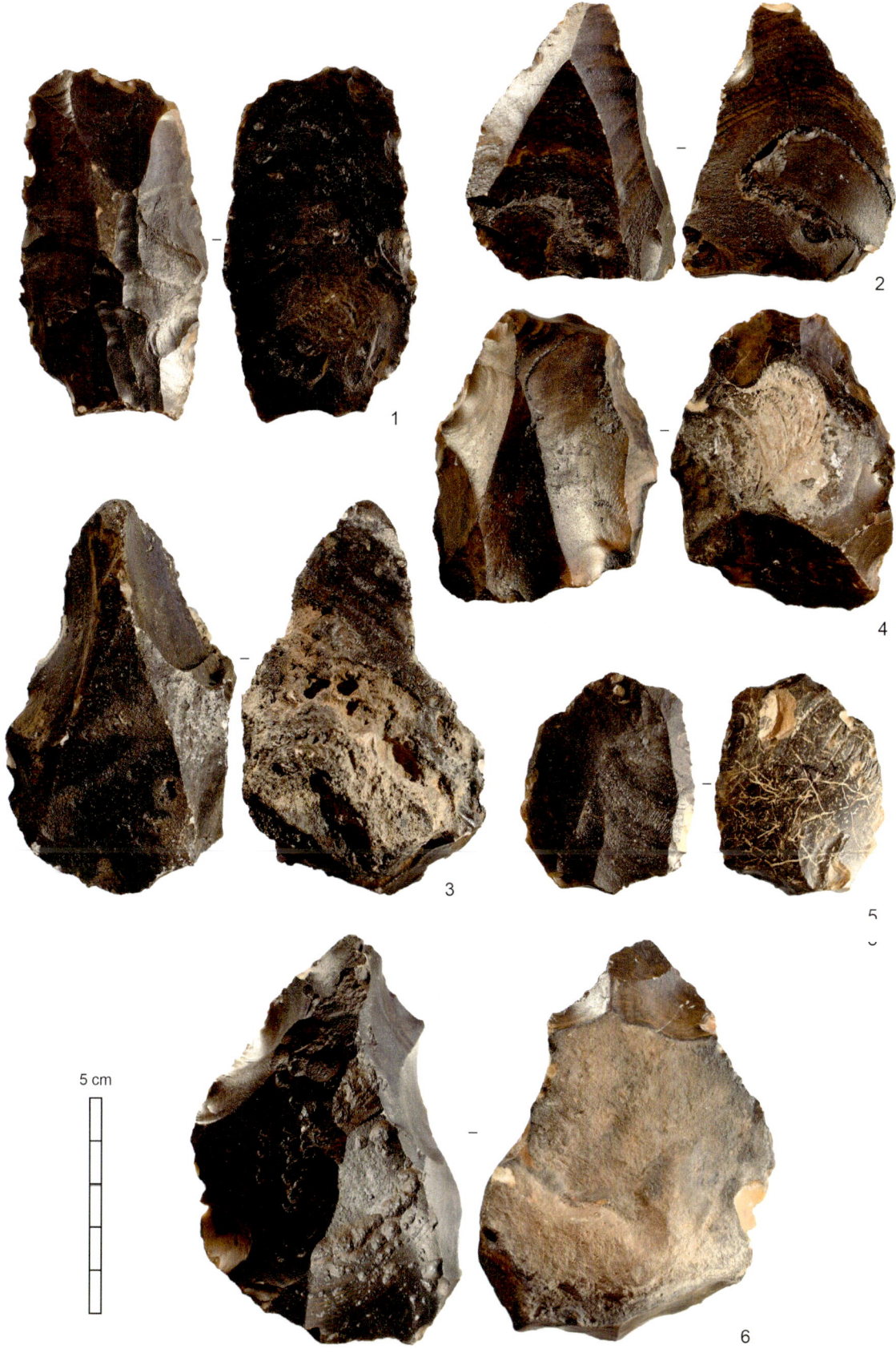

5 cm

Figure 3.20. Less heavily weathered Nubian artifacts from TH.123: (1) Levallois blade, (2) Levallois point, (5) Levallois flake fragment with rootlet patina on the ventral side, (3,6) Nubian Levallois cores, (4) Levallois core (photographs by A. Beshkani).

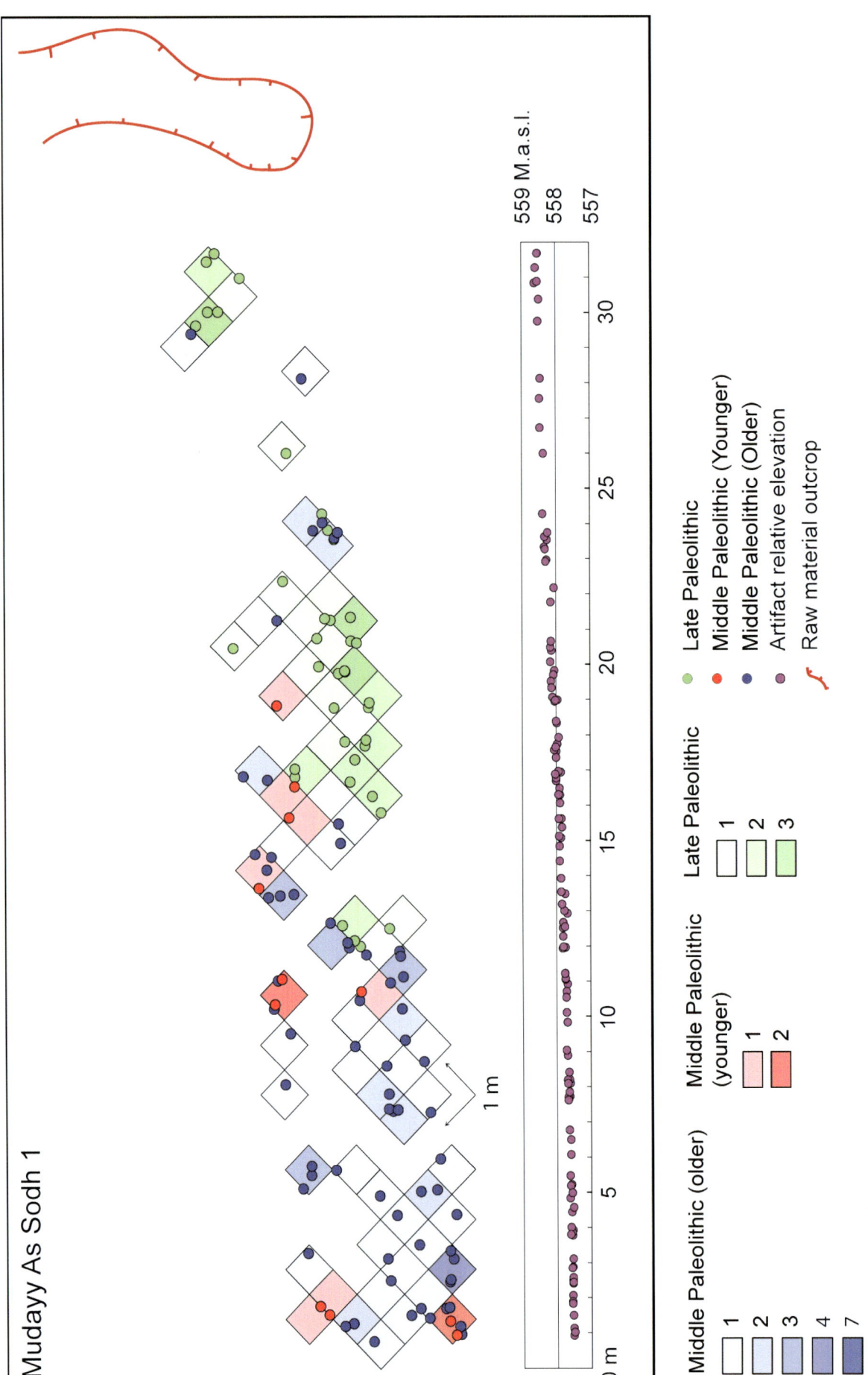

Figure 3.21. Spatial distribution plot of Middle and Late Palaeolithic artifacts from TH.123 (figure plot by Y.H. Hilbert).

Table 3.3. Artifact counts from TH.123.

Mudayy as Sodh 1	N	Percentage
Debitage	**997**	**87%**
Levallois blade	*5*	*0%*
Levallois point	*18*	*2%*
Levallois flake	*14*	*1%*
Primary flakes	*182*	*18%*
Primary blades	*19*	*2%*
Flakes	*496*	*50%*
Blades	*107*	*11%*
Chips	*156*	*16%*
Cores	**112**	**10%**
Two platforms	*2*	*2%*
Crossed	*2*	*2%*
Orthogonal flat core	*2*	*2%*
Single platform (broad)	*10*	*9%*
Nubian Levallois	*61*	*54%*
Nubian Levallois, early stage	*11*	*10%*
Levallois preferential core	*2*	*2%*
Bidirectional	*2*	*2%*
Pre-core	*9*	*8%*
Core fragment	*11*	*10%*
Tools	**32**	**3%**
Side Scraper	*7*	*22%*
End Scraper	*7*	*22%*
Denticulate	*7*	*22%*
Notch	*4*	*12%*
Retouched piece	*7*	*22%*
Total	**1141**	**100%**

TH.143

The Middle Palaeolithic assemblages from TH.143 were collected from the same terrace as the Lower Palaeolithic material described in the previous chapter. During the 2011 campaign, we made three separate collections targeting Late and Middle Palaeolithic artifact clusters (Figure 3.22), the results of which are already available in publication (Rose *et al.* 2011). We returned to the site in 2013 to plot a sample of diagnostic artifacts within a 28 x 4 m transect, mapping 218 diagnostic artifacts inside the collection area.

The assemblage includes 69 Lower Palaeolithic artifacts, 106 Middle Palaeolithic artifacts with advanced stages of weathering, 10 Middle Palaeolithic artifact with less weathering and 33 Late Palaeolithic artifacts with minimal evidence of surface degradation (Figure 3.23). Among the Middle Palaeolithic artifacts (Table 3.4), the majority are Nubian Levallois cores (Figures 3.24 and 3.25). They vary little in size, averaging 10 cm in length.

Table 3.4. Artifact counts from TH.143 Middle Palaeolithic component.

Jebel Sanoora 1 (MP)	N	Percentage
Debitage	**43**	**37%**
Flake	*8*	*18%*
Blade	*5*	*12%*
Levallois preferential flake	*2*	*5%*
Levallois point	*2*	*5%*
Levallois flake	*3*	*7%*
Levallois débordant	*13*	*30%*
Cortical débordant	*10*	*23%*
Cores	**67**	**58%**
Single platform core flake	*3*	*5%*
Single platform core blade	*6*	*9%*
Bidirectional opposed core	*3*	*4%*
Levallois preferential core	*6*	*9%*
Nubian Levallois core	*44*	*66%*
Levallois core early stage	*5*	*7%*
Tools	**6**	**5%**
Side Scraper	*4*	*67%*
End scraper with lateral retouch	*1*	*16%*
Denticulate	*1*	*17%*
Total	**116**	**100%**

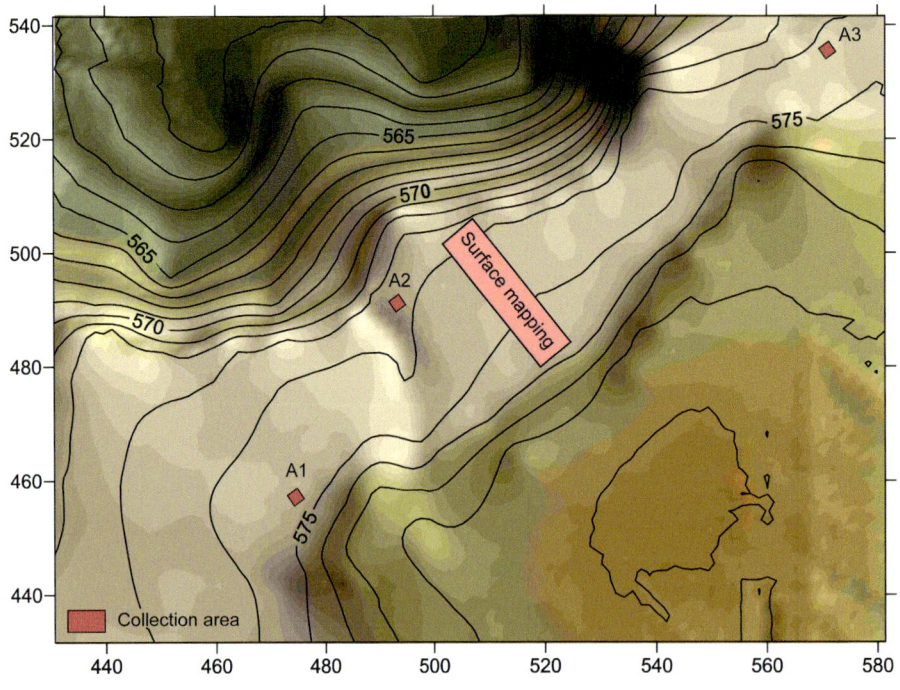

Figure 3.22. Topographic map of TH.143 showing locations of systematic collection areas and location of transect where the artifacts were piece-plotted (figure plot by Y.H. Hilbert).

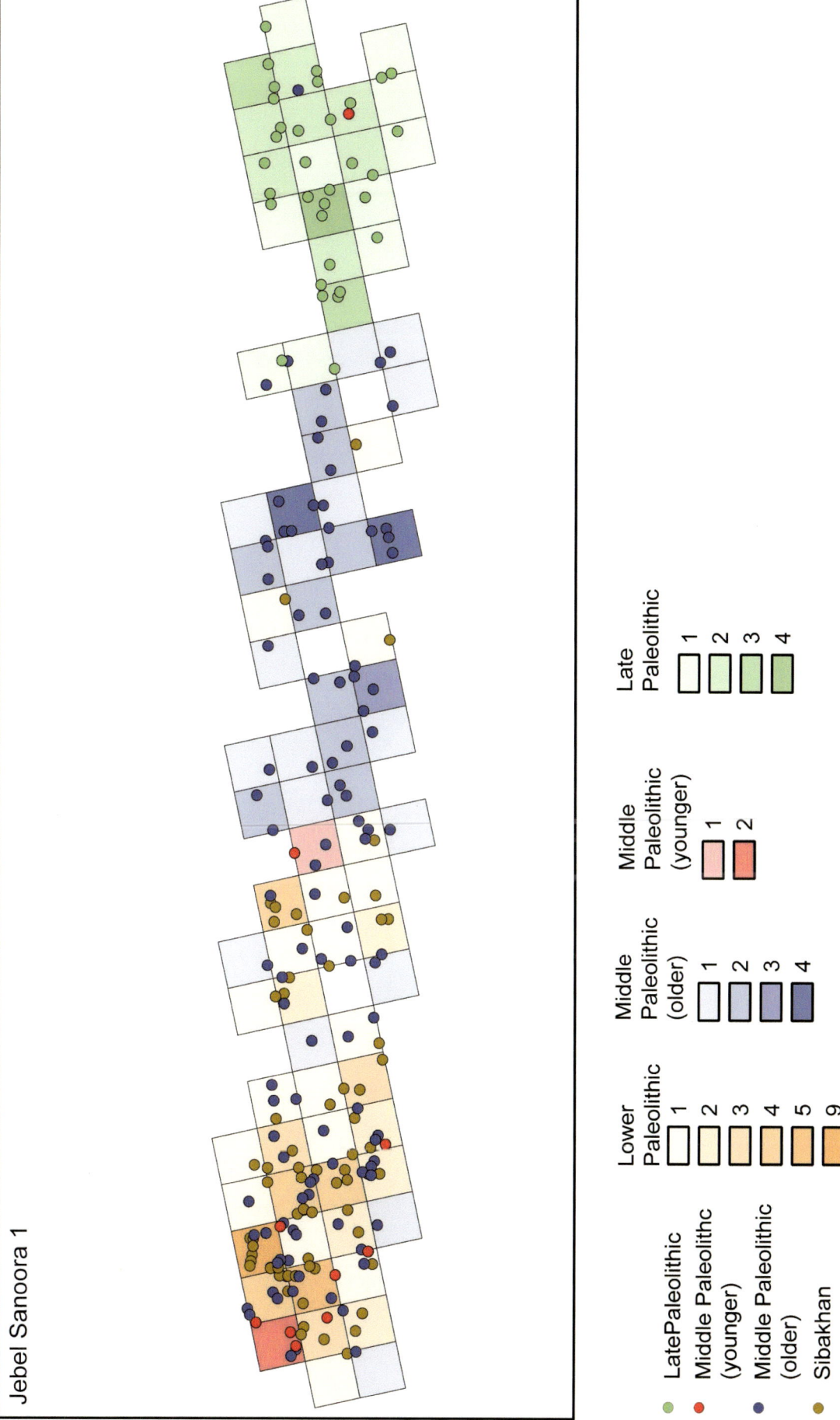

Figure 3.23. Spatial distribution plot of Middle Palaeolithic and Late Palaeolithic artifacts from TH.143 (figure plot by Y.H. Hilbert).

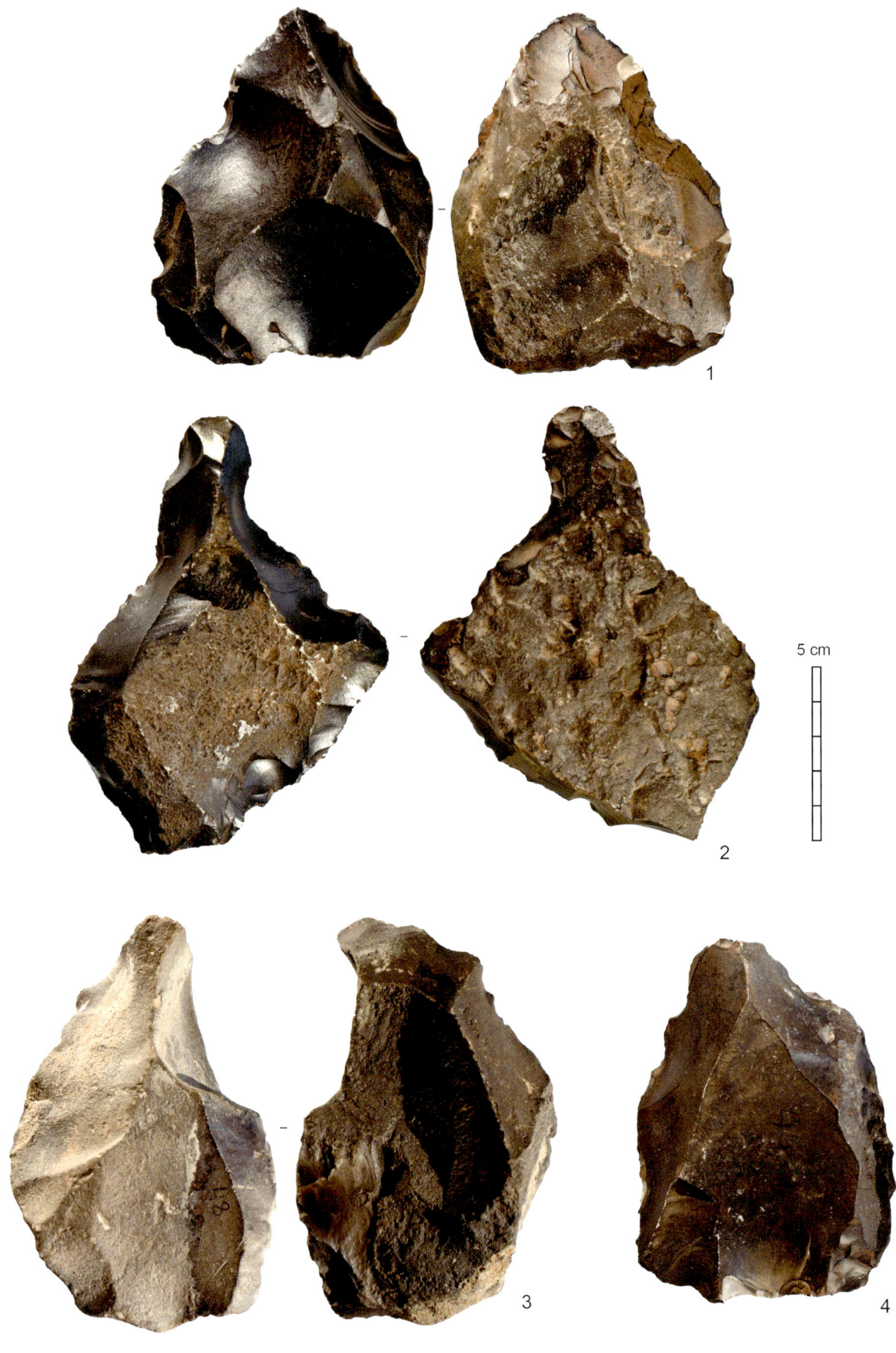

5 cm

Figure 3.24. Nubian Levallois cores from TH.143 (photographs by A. Beshkani).

5 cm

Figure 3.25. Nubian Levallois cores from TH.143 (photographs by A. Beshkani).

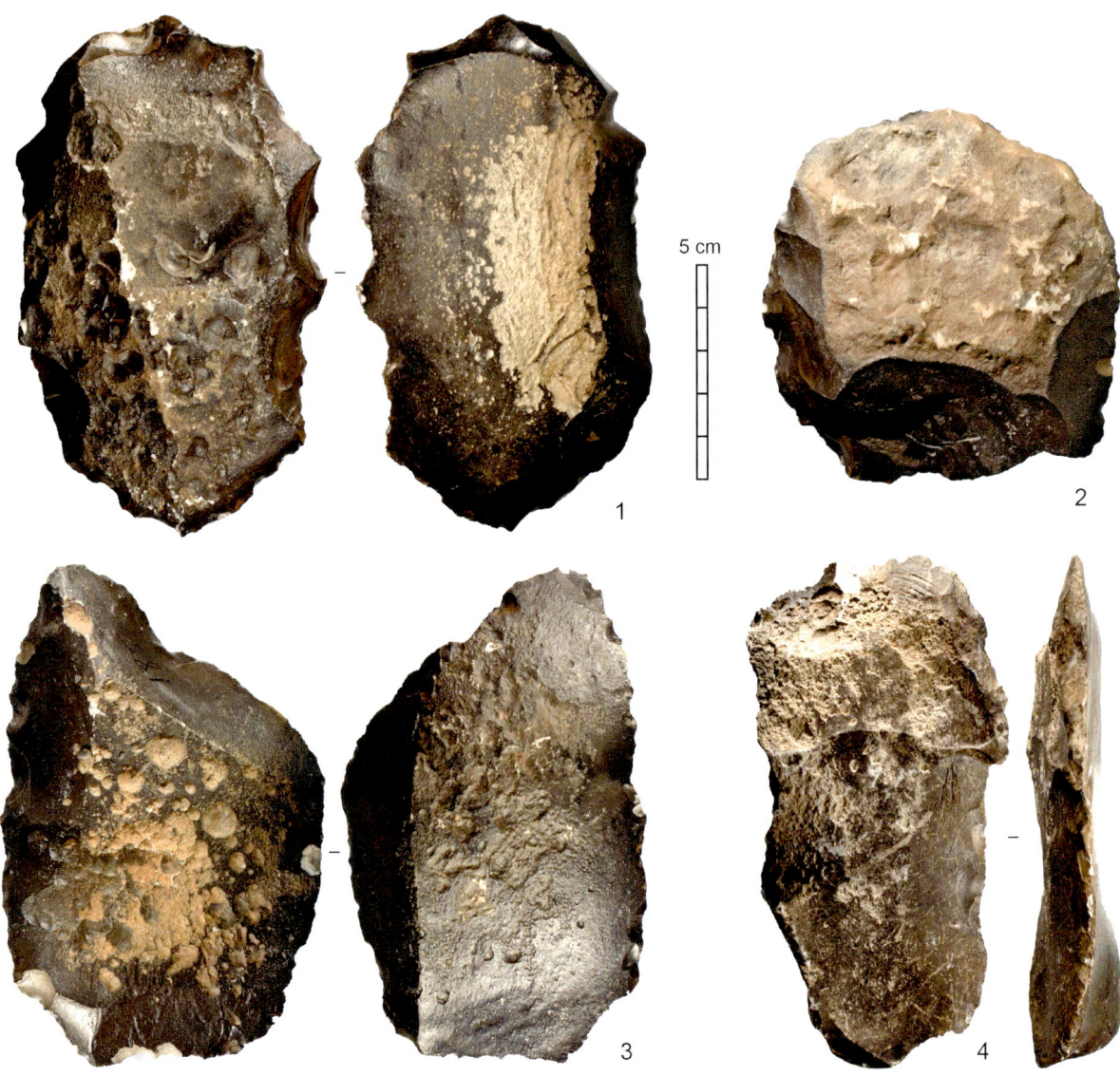

5 cm

Figure 3.26. Middle Palaeolithic tools from TH.143: (1) denticulate, (2-4) sidescrapers (photographs by A. Beshkani).

Some of the Levallois cores were recycled from more heavily weathered blade blanks and blade cores. Single platform blade cores, bidirectional cores and preferential bidirectional Levallois cores are also present. The few recognizable tools consist primarily of thick side scrapers (Figure 3.26).

TH.76

The TH.76 multi-component workshop site yielded a wide array of artifacts belonging to Lower, Middle and Late Palaeolithic phases (Figure 3.27). Unlike the other workshop sites with a single outcropping chert seam, the stepped surface of TH.76 had multiple exposed seams. Rather than collect a narrow transect, this configuration required a large square collection zone measuring 51 x 55 m. A total of 222 diagnostic artifacts were mapped inside the grid; the surface of which is characterized as an undulating horizontal gradient dipping slightly to the southwest.

A total of 110 Middle Palaeolithic artifacts are included in the TH.76 surface assemblage (Table 3.5), of which the majority are Nubian Levallois cores and débitage (Figure 3.28). Nubian Levallois points show different proportions and morphological characteristics, some being broad and short, while others are elongated and narrow. Nubian cores occur as large and heavily weathered specimens (Figure 3.29), or smaller (< 10 cm) with minor chemical dissolution, minimal edge damage, only slight amounts of rounding and a dark glossy patina (Figure 3.30). We identified six conjoins in the Middle Palaeolithic assemblage, the majority of these refittings being the reattachment of Levallois points to Nubian cores (Figures 3.31 and 3.32).

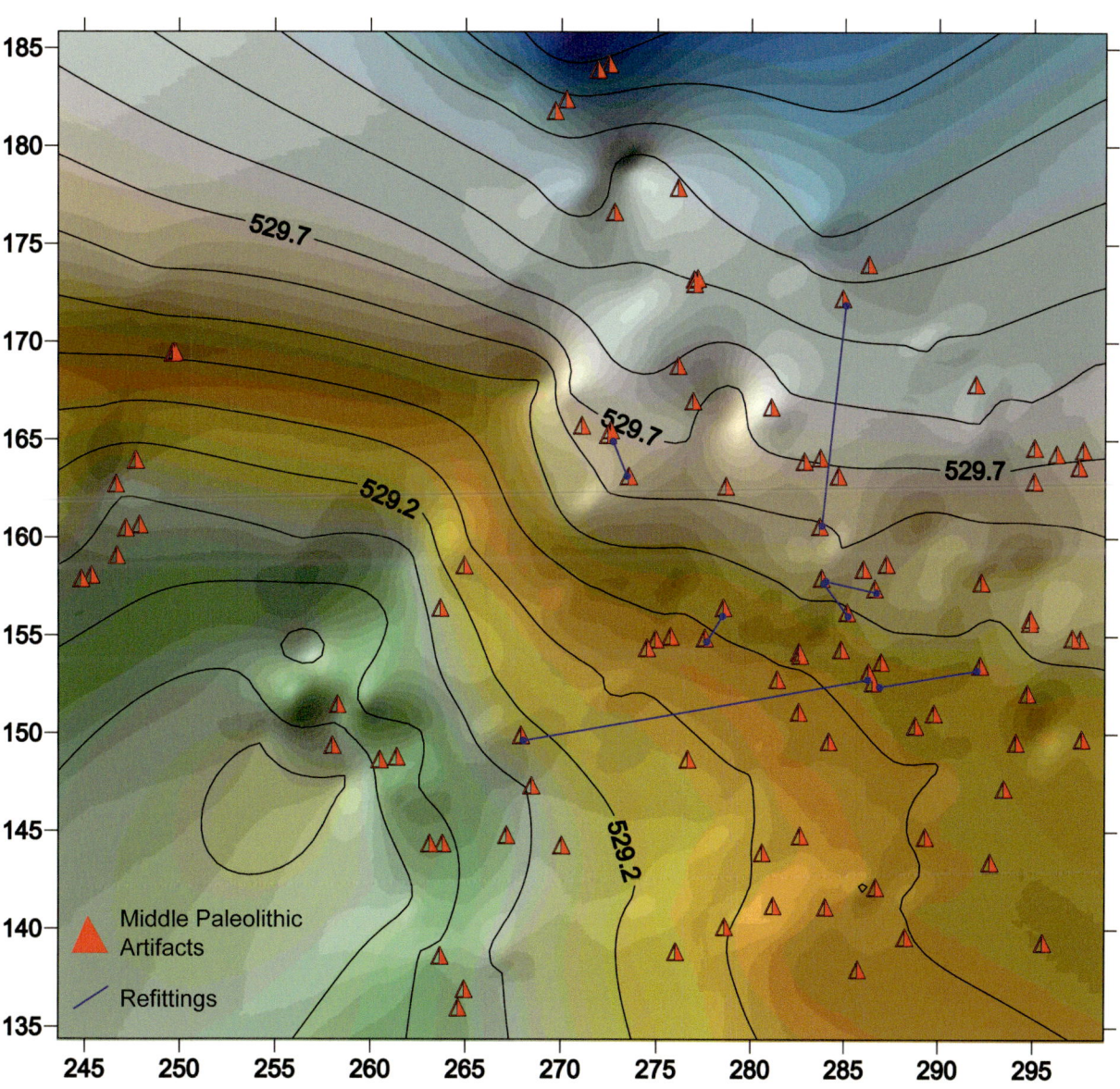

Figure 3.27. Spatial distribution plot of Middle Palaeolithic artifacts from TH.76 showing refittings (figure plot by Y.H. Hilbert).

Table 3.5. Artifact counts from TH.76 Middle Palaeolithic component.

Aybut at Thalith (MP)	N	Percentage
Debitage	**54**	**49%**
Flake	7	13%
Blade	13	24%
Levallois point	8	15%
Levallois flake	9	17%
Levallois débordant	11	20%
Cortical débordant	6	11%
Cores	**42**	**38%**
Single platform core, flake	5	12%
Single platform core, blade	3	7%
Bidirectional opposed core	2	5%
Levallois preferential core	1	2%
Nubian Levallois core	14	33%
Precore Levallois	12	29%
Core preform	5	12%
Tools	**14**	**13%**
Retouched piece	2	14%
Side scraper	5	36%
Notch	4	29%
Endscraper with lateral re-touch	1	7%
End scraper	2	14%
Total	**110**	**100%**

TH.268a

The TH.268a lithic scatter was identified on top of a star-shaped inselberg, which we refer to as Jebel an Najm (Figure 3.33). Jebel An-Najm rises about 15 m above a gently undulating plain of heavily weathered black chert and limestone. It is one of several inselbergs associated with archaeological remains in a particularly rich prehistoric landscape on the high plateau between Wadis Amawt and Banawt. Chert nodules are actively eroding from the sides of the inselberg (Figures 3.34 and 3.35). Preliminary analyses of the Middle Palaeolithic assemblage have already appeared in publications (Rose and Marks 2014; Usik *et al.* 2013); additional information on the lithic technology, artifact illustrations and site data are provided here.

The TH.268a collection area was placed at the center of Jebel An-Najm inselberg. A moderate-high density of artifacts was recovered within a 4 x 4 m grid. The artifacts were all made on the same local chert nodules and display a similar range of surface weathering. The raw material is Gahit chert, indicated by the fossil inclusions, thin cortex and very fine-grained silicate matrix.

Figure 3.28. Nubian Levallois points from TH.76 (photographs by A. Beshkani).

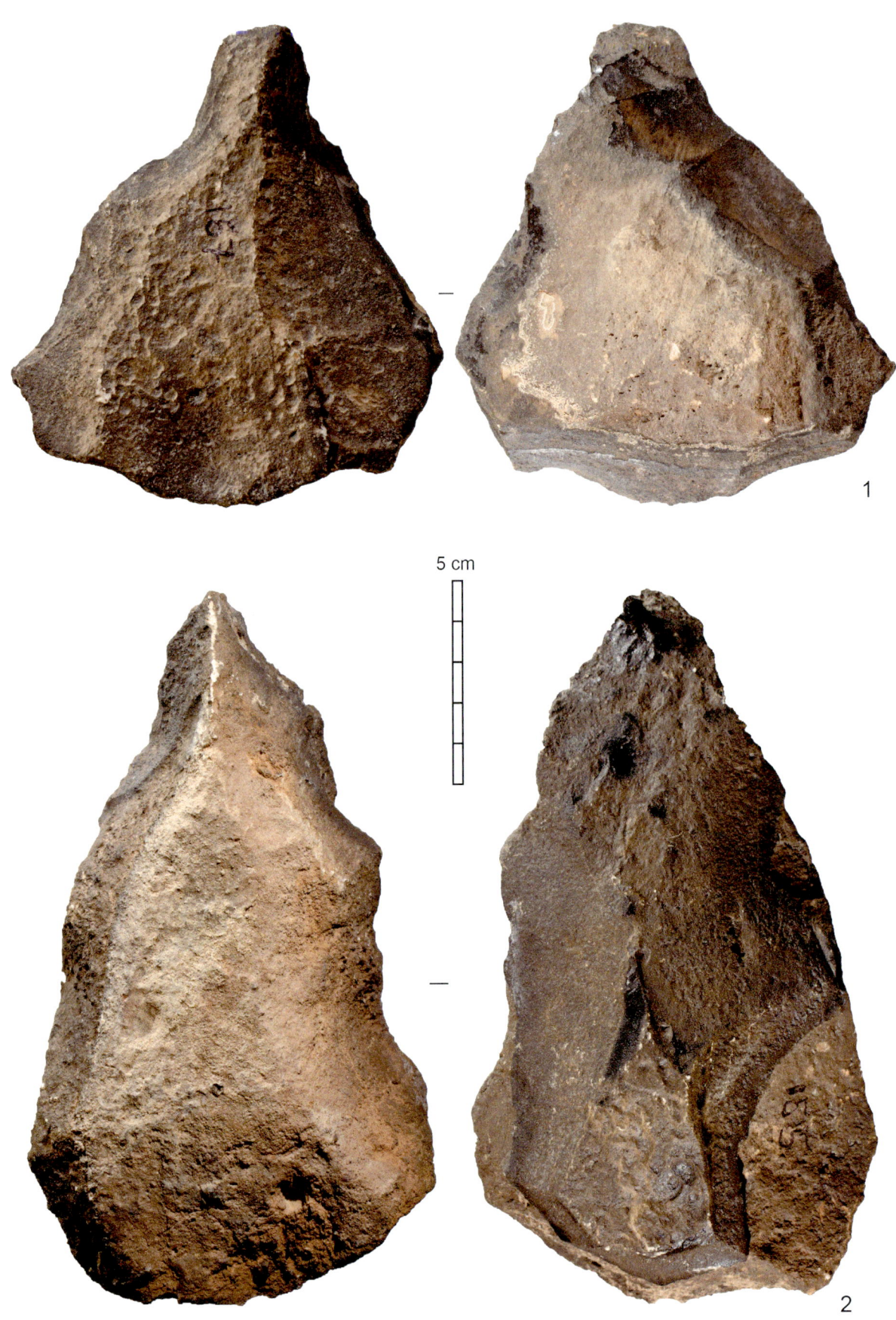

5 cm

1

2

Figure 3.29. More heavily weathered Nubian cores from TH.76 (photographs by A. Beshkani).

Figure 3.30. Less heavily weathered Middle Palaeolithic artifacts from TH.76: (1-3) bidirectional Levallois cores, (2) Nubian Levallois core; 4) Recurrent bidirectional blade core (photographs by A. Beshkani).

The artifacts typically show no signs of rounding from aeolian abrasion, no chemical dissolution, minimal mechanical edge damage, light brown patina and a glossy surface (Figure 3.35). The assemblage is composed of 220 cores, 444 pieces of débitage and 20 retouched tools (Table 3.6).

Core are numerous and exhibit different reduction strategies typical of the Mudayyan industry. Both Levallois and non-Levallois technological systems are present, evidence of the former being more prevalent. Nubian Levallois are the most numerous core types identified at the site (Figures 3.36 and 3.37). These were most often-prepared using bidirectional or bilateral dorsal preparation. Their size is relatively small, not exceeding 10 cm, despite the fact that local Gahit chert nodules are up to five times larger than any of the cores found at the site. This suggests that the diminution of Nubian technology was a deliberate choice, rather than a constraint placed upon the toolmakers by the raw material.

There are other Levallois variants and non-Levallois reduction strategies within the TH.268a assemblage (Figure 3.38). Non-Nubian Levallois cores are infrequent and represent either failed attempts in Levallois preparation, early stages of core preparation, or exhausted Levallois cores in which the distal platform has been removed by an overpassed flake.

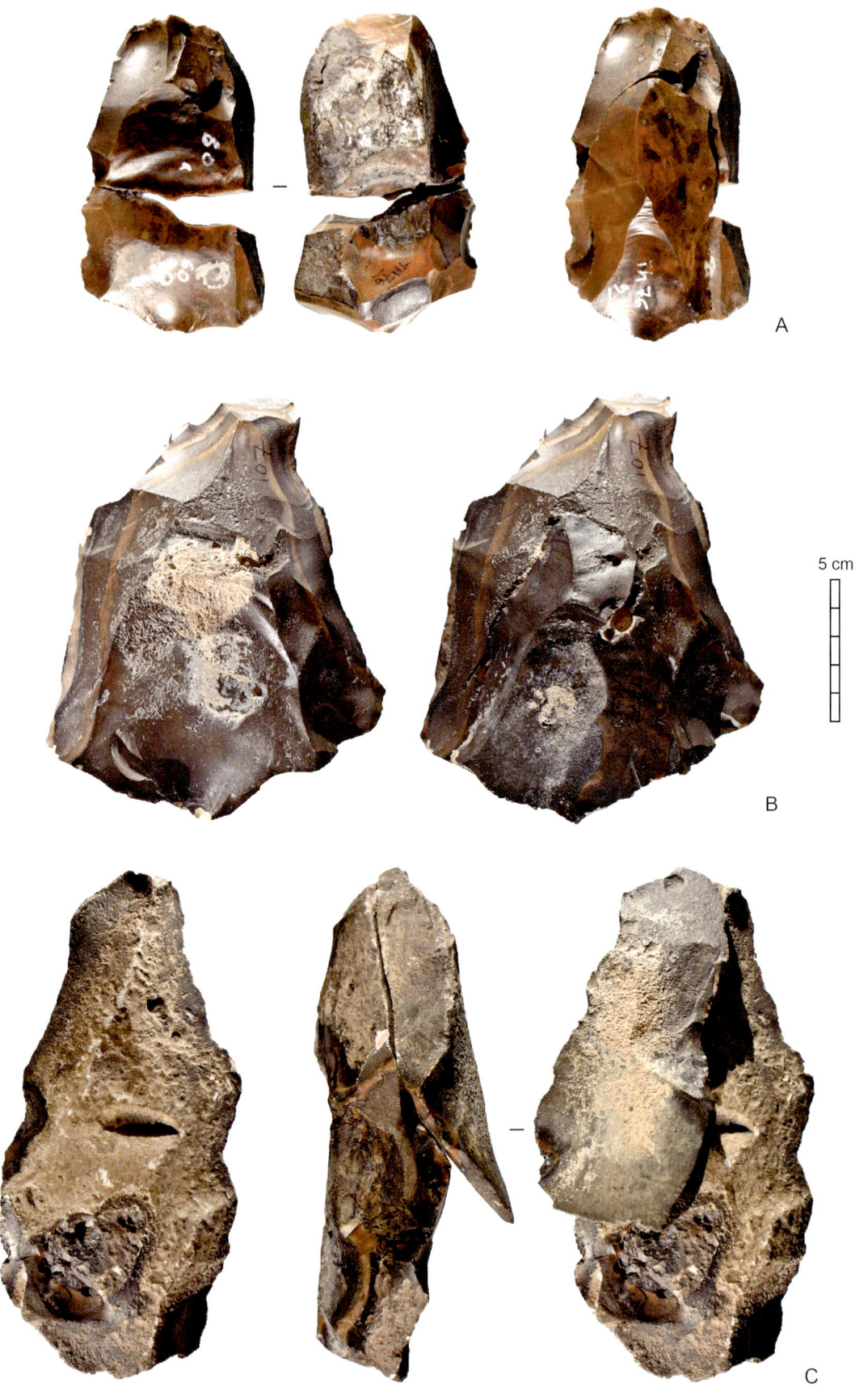

5 cm

Figure 3.31. Refittings from TH.76: (A) fragmented Nubian Levallois core and point, (B) Nubian Levallois core and point, (C) distal preparation removal conjoined to Nubian Levallois core (photographs by A. Beshkani).

Figure 3.32. Refittings from TH.76. Nubian core and point with distal preparation débordant blade (photographs by A. Beshkani).

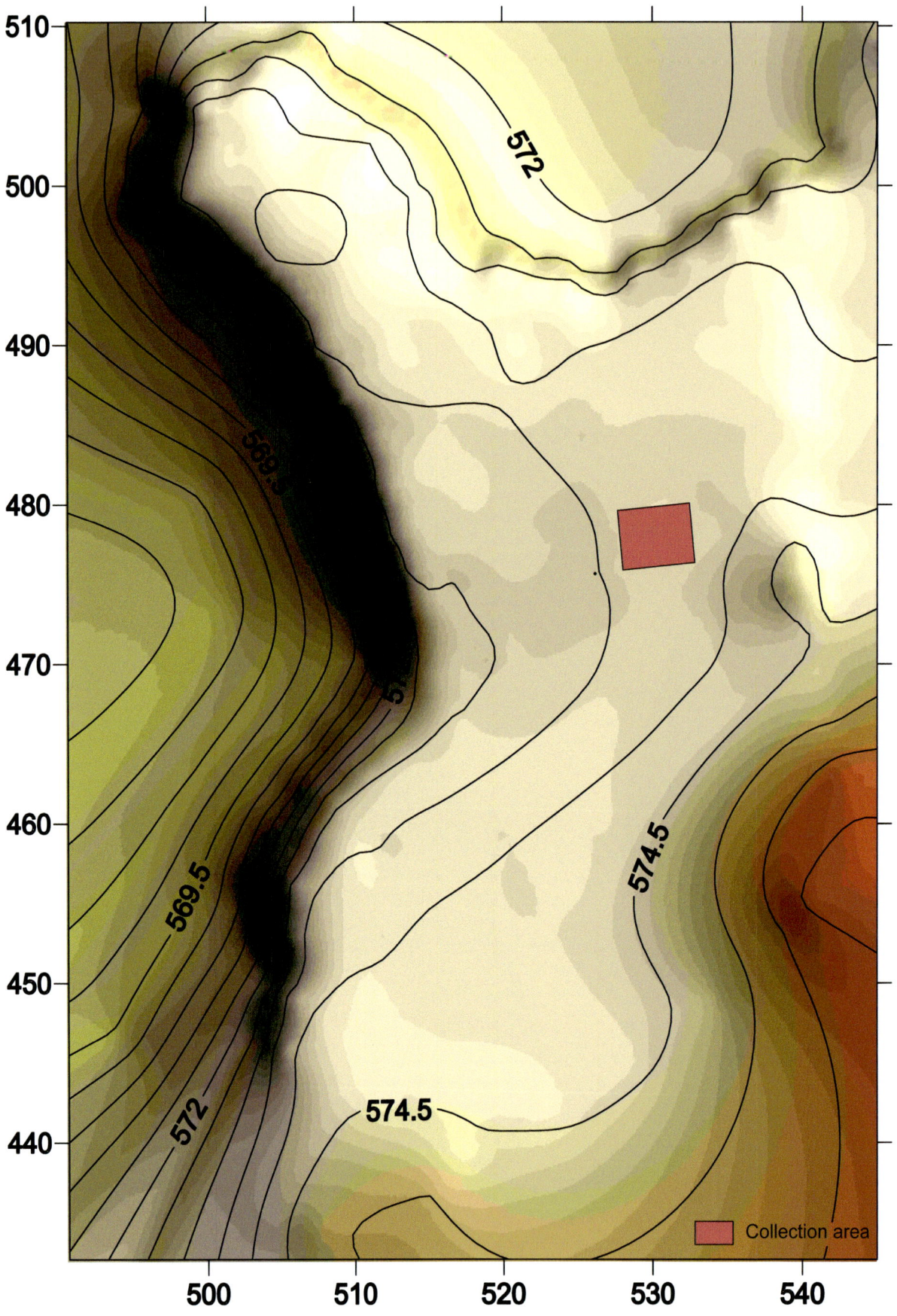

Figure 3.33. Topographic map of Jebel Najm showing the location of the TH.268 systematic collection area (figure plot by Y.H. Hilbert).

Table 3.6. Artifact counts from TH.268.

Jebel Koshab	N	Percent-age
Debitage	**444**	**65%**
Flake	*77*	*17%*
Blade	*24*	*5%*
Primary flake	*229*	*52%*
Primary blade	*49*	*11%*
Levallois preferential	*5*	*1%*
Débordant element	*52*	*12%*
Cortical débordant	*8*	*2%*
Cores	**220**	**32%**
Single platform flake core	*36*	*16%*
Single platform blade core	*48*	*22%*
Bidirectional opposed core	*30*	*14%*
Bidirectional Crossed	*2*	*1%*
Multi-Platform, Unrelated	*5*	*2%*
Orthogonal core	*2*	*1%*
Levallois Preferential Point	*2*	*1%*
Levallois Preferential core	*11*	*5%*
Nubian Levallois core	*48*	*22%*
Levallois early stage/ Facial core	*24*	*11%*
Precore	*12*	*5%*
Tools	**20**	**3%**
Awl	*2*	*10%*
Denticulate	*2*	*10%*
double-notched Levallois flake	*1*	*5%*
Notch	*3*	*15%*
End scraper	*4*	*20%*
Retouched piece	*7*	*35%*
Convex side scraper	*1*	*5%*
Total	**684**	**100%**

The typical Mudayyan recurrent bidirectional cores with faceted opposed platforms are also present within the assemblage. We observe an entirely separate reduction strategy characterized by single platform blade cores with unmodified striking platforms that exploit the narrow working surface. Like the diminutive Nubian Levallois cores, these volumetric blade cores are under 10 cm, significantly smaller than the locally outcropping Gahit chert nodules from which they were manufactured, which range between 20 and 50 cm in maximum dimension. The assemblage is likely to be palimpsest, indicated by a series of small bifacial foliates and biface thinning debitage superimposed over the Mudayyan scatter. Taphonomic studies indicate the bifacial component is younger than Nubian Levallois and other Mudayyan-type bidirectional reduction strategies. It is uncertain, however, whether the single platform blade cores belong to earlier or later industries (or both).

Figure 3.34. Jebel Najm. View of the site showing the location of the TH.268 collection area in the back adjacent to the dense chert outcrop (photograph by the authors).

Figure 3.35. Jebel Najm. View of the site showing the location of the TH.268 collection area (photograph by the authors).

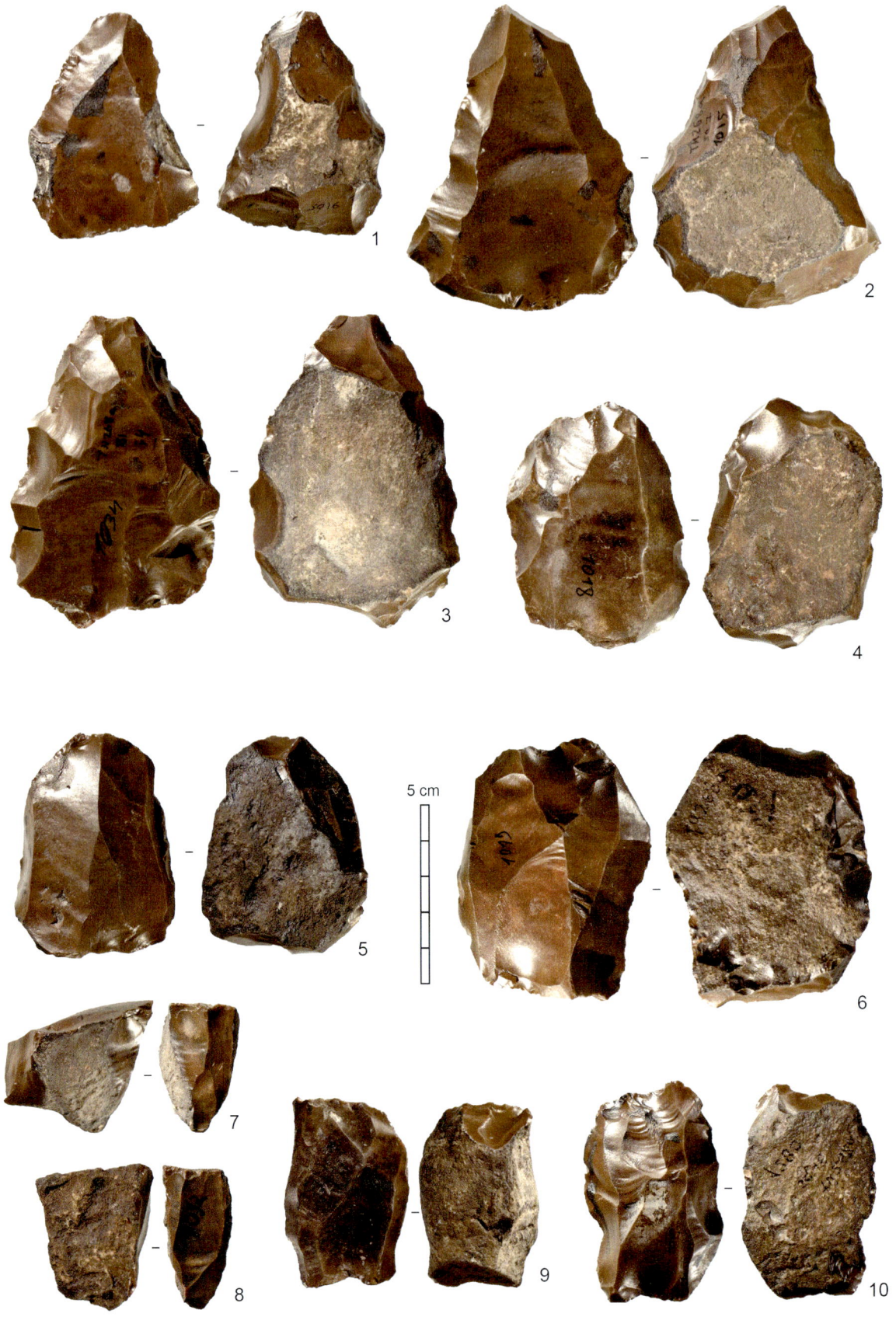

Figure 3.36. Middle Palaeolithic cores from TH.268: (1-3) Nubian Levallois cores, (4,6) bidirectional Levallois cores, (5) Nubian Levallois core during re-preparation, (7,8) single platform unidirectional blade cores on narrow surface of nodule, (9,10) bidirectional recurrent blade cores (photographs by Y.H. Hilbert).

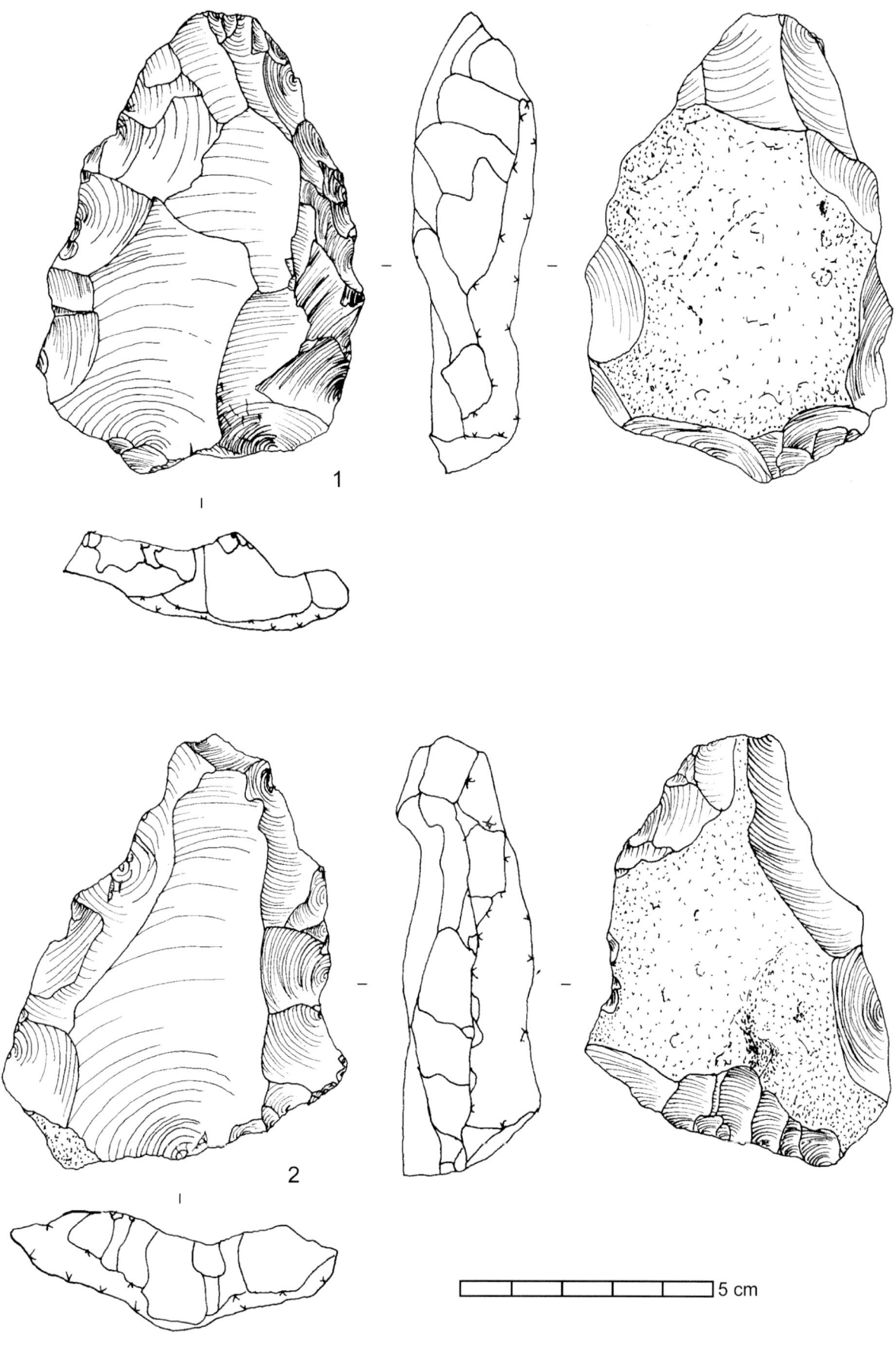

Figure 3.37. Small Nubian Type 2 Levallois cores from TH.268 (illustrations by Y.H. Hilbert).

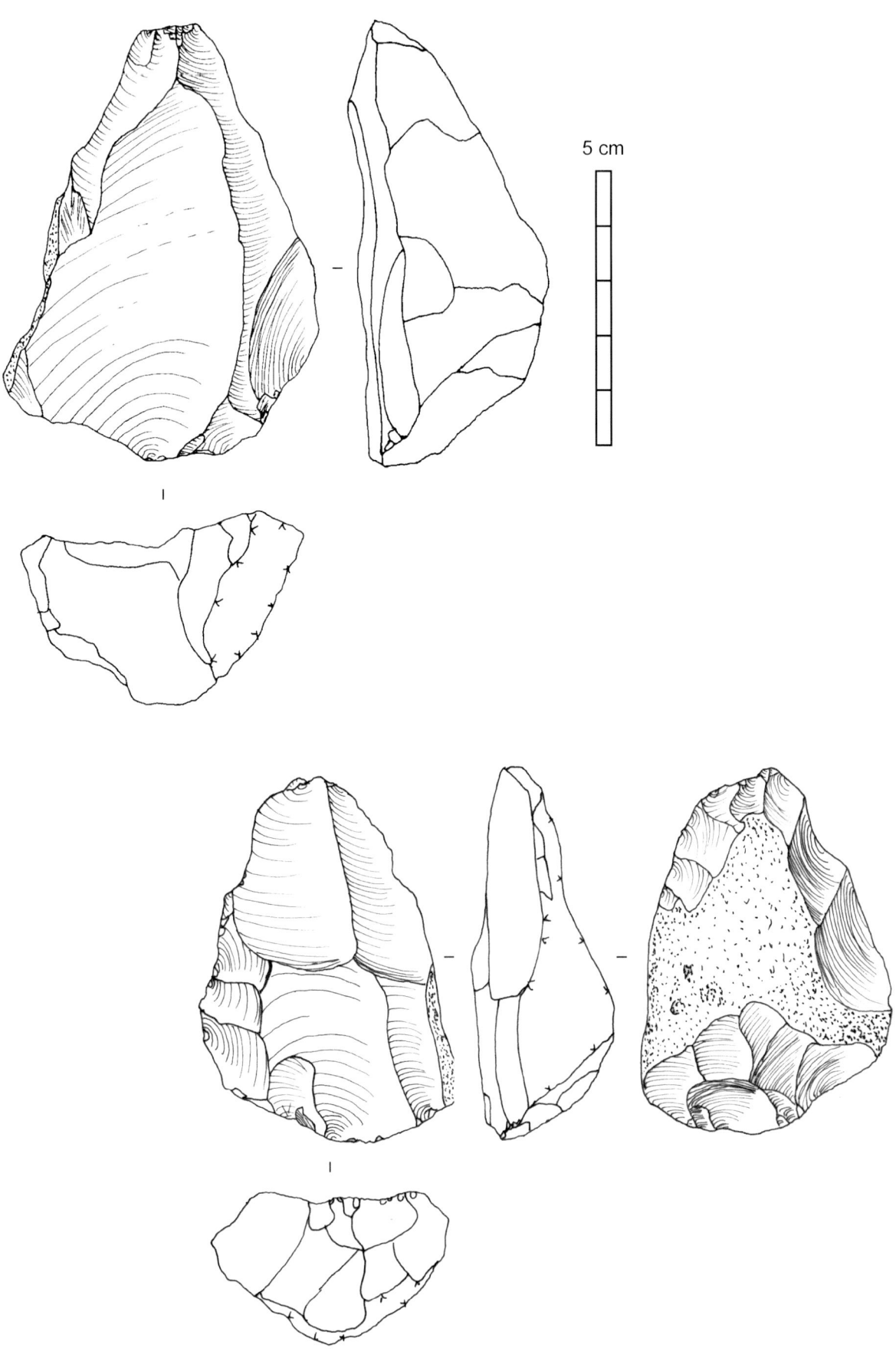

5 cm

Figure 3.38. Small Nubian Type 1 Levallois cores from TH.268 (illustrations by Y.H. Hilbert).

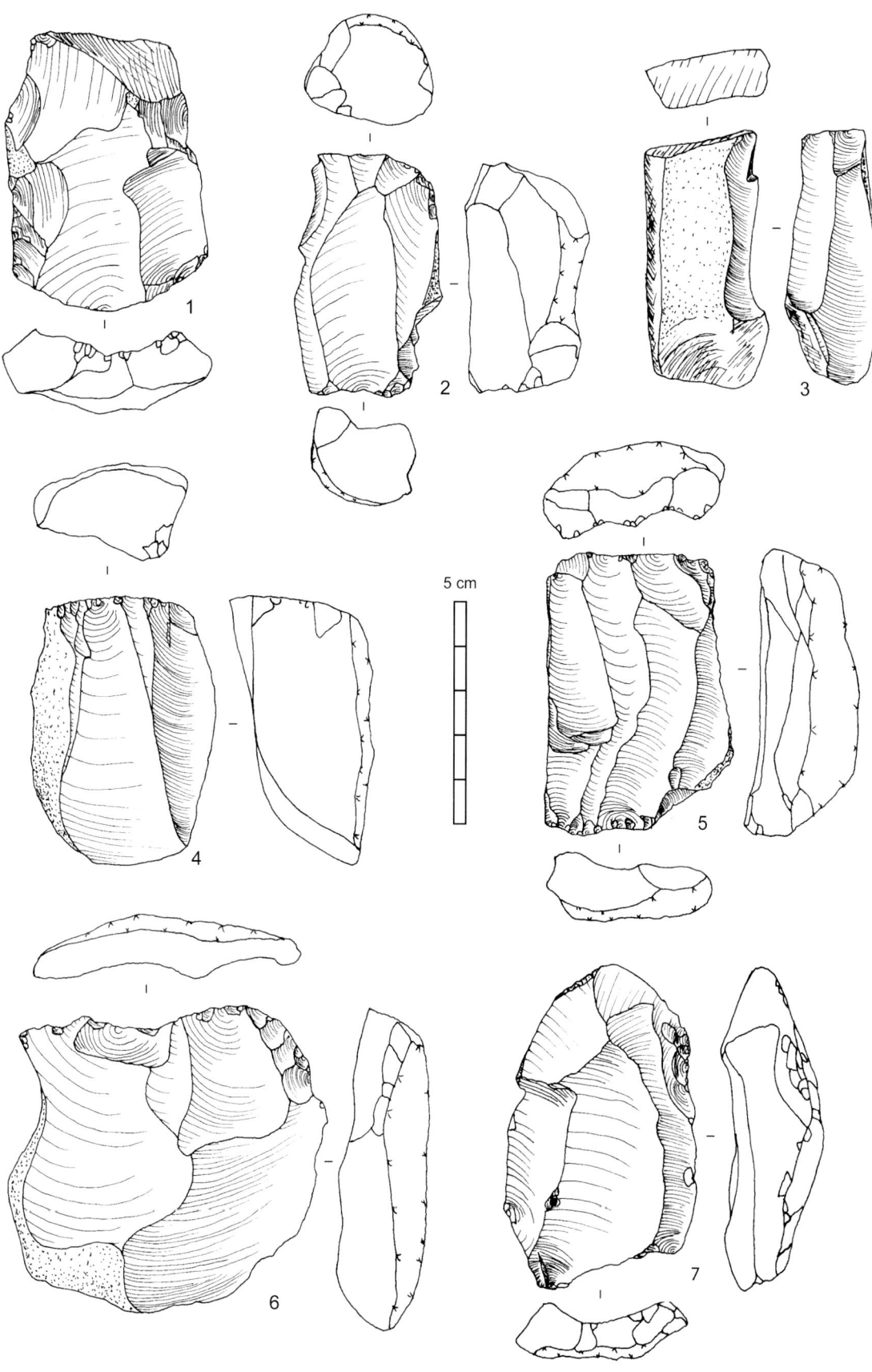

5 cm

Figure 3.39. Other Levallois and non-Levallois cores from TH.268: (1,2,7) Levallois cores, (3) single platform unidirectional-parallel core on narrow surface, (4) single platform unidirectional core, (5) bidirectional recurrent blade core with faceted platforms, (6) flat single platform unidirectional flake core (illustrations by Y.H. Hilbert).

Figure 3.40. Views of TH.191: top of the inselberg (photograph by the authors).

Figure 3.42. Views of TH.191: edge of site rising over the plain (photograph by the authors).

Figure 3.41. Views of TH.191: inselberg seen from a distance (photograph by the authors).

Table 3.7. Core counts from TH.191.

Cores from Nubi al Sagir	N	Percentages
Single platform unidirectional (broad)	72	0,27%
Single platform unidirectional (narrow)	43	16,10%
Double platform crossed	3	1,12%
Opposed 90' opposite	2	0,75%
Orthogonal core	12	4,49%
Bidirectional opposite core	30	11,24%
Single platform convergent	2	0,75%
Kombewa	1	0,37%
Recurrent radial core	8	3%
Levallois preferential core	2	0,75%
Nubian Levallois	31	11,61%
Precores	45	16,85%
Unidentified	16	5,99%
Total	**267**	**100%**

TH.191

Site TH.191 is located roughly two kilometers northwest of Jebel An-Najm on the high plateau between Wadis Amawt and Banawt. A series of moderate density lithic scatters were recorded along a chain of four low inselbergs (TH.191a-TH.191d) that rise up to 10 m above the undulating plain of weathered chert and limestone debris (Figure 3.39). Small (< 20 cm) and rounded chert pebbles outcrop from the flanks of the hill. Although diminutive, the raw material is homogenous and fine-grained with minimal inclusions.

Artifacts attributed to the Lower and earlier Middle Palaeolithic were observed on the plain below the hills, including handaxes and large, heavily weathered Nubian Levallois cores. On top of the mesas, we recorded Middle Palaeolithic artifacts exhibiting two different stages of weathering (Figure 3.40). The sample presented here comes from a 3 x 3 m systematic collection on inselberg TH.191a. The more weathered artifacts show moderate chemical dissolution and rounded edges, with a matte gray to black surface color. The less weathered artifacts range from light to dark brown in patina, with little to no chemical dissolution. In both clusters, the edges show moderate to heavy mechanical damage.

There were 267 cores in the TH.191a assemblage (Table 3.7), including early stage precores, single platform unidirectional cores exploiting the narrow working surface, Mudayyan-type bidirectional cores and Nubian Levallois cores (Figure 3.41). Two débordant blades and one flake were conjoined to a single platform core; in this case, the flake served as a core tablet to reprepare the striking platform (Figure 3.42: A1). A second refit shows a débordant blade with opposed dorsal scars reattached to a single platform core. After the first platform of the core was exhausted, the piece was turned around and reduction continued from the opposed platform. A few of the narrow working surface single platform cores have signs of crest preparation on the lateral edge; a technological feature that occasionally appears at other Mudayyan sites. While it is clear that there is a prominent Mudayyan component at TH.191a, the variable weathering suggests that the later Middle Palaeolithic assemblage is superimposed over an earlier Nubian occupation. As such, the frequency of core types represents a palimpsest of at least two separate Middle Palaeolithic occupations.

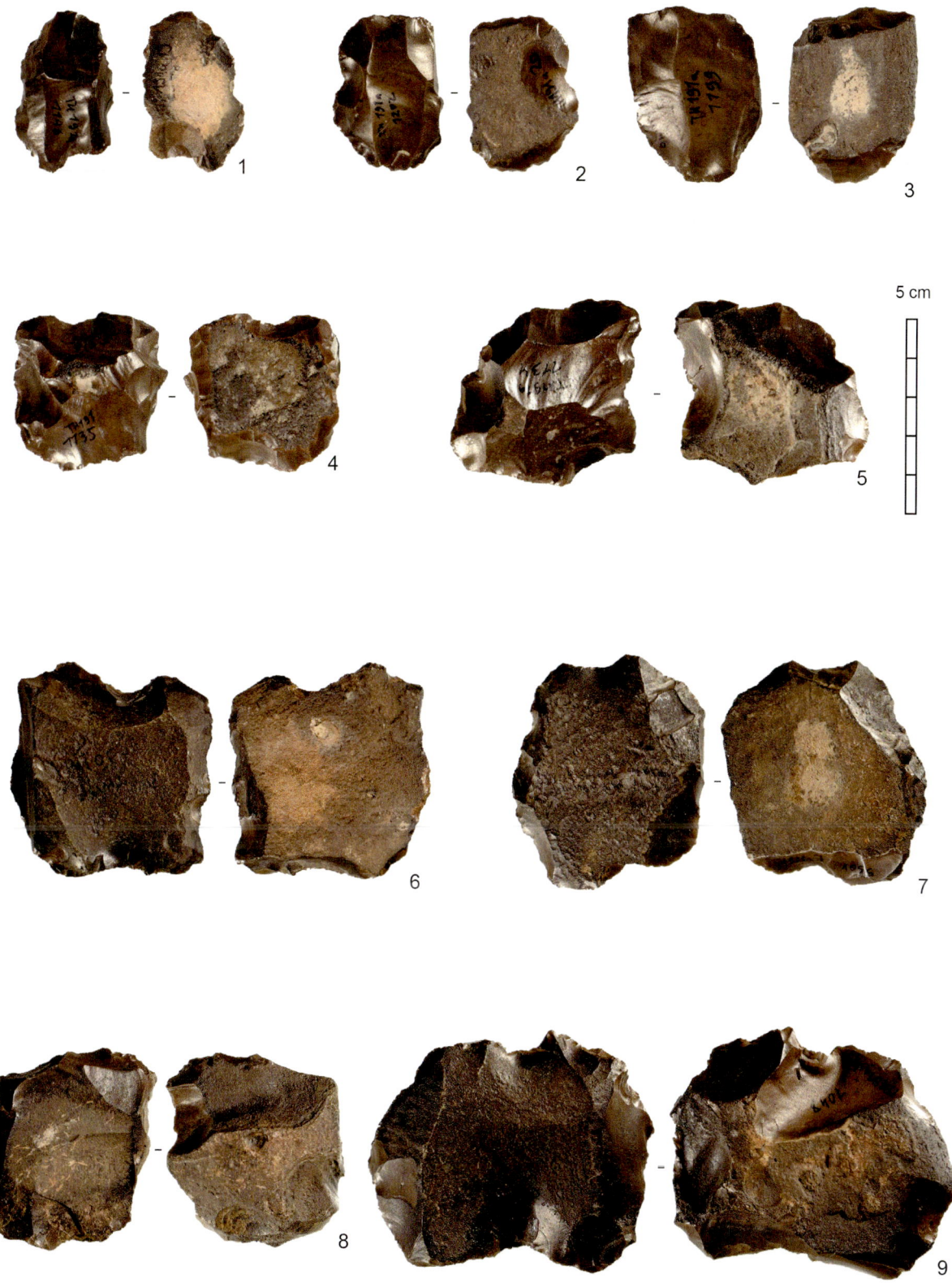

Figure 3.43. Flat bidirectional and exhausted Levallois cores from TH.191: (1-3) less heavily weathered small bidirectional Levallois cores, (4,5) less heavily weathered recurrent bidirectional and bidirectional lateral cores, (6-9) more heavily weathered bidirectional and bidirectional lateral exhausted Levallois cores (photographs by Y.H. Hilbert).

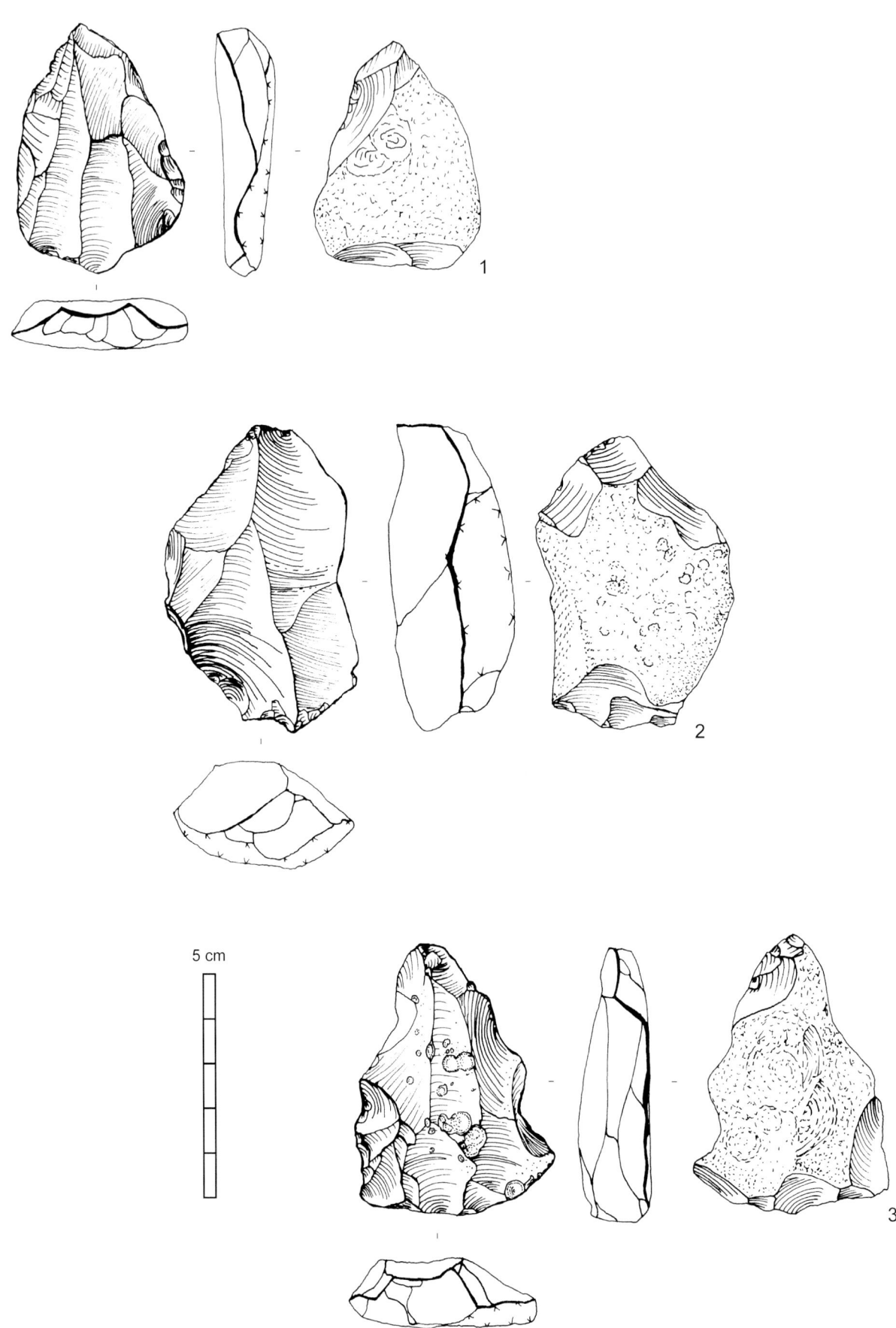

Figure 3.44. Nubian Levallois cores from TH.191 (illustrations by Y.H. Hilbert).

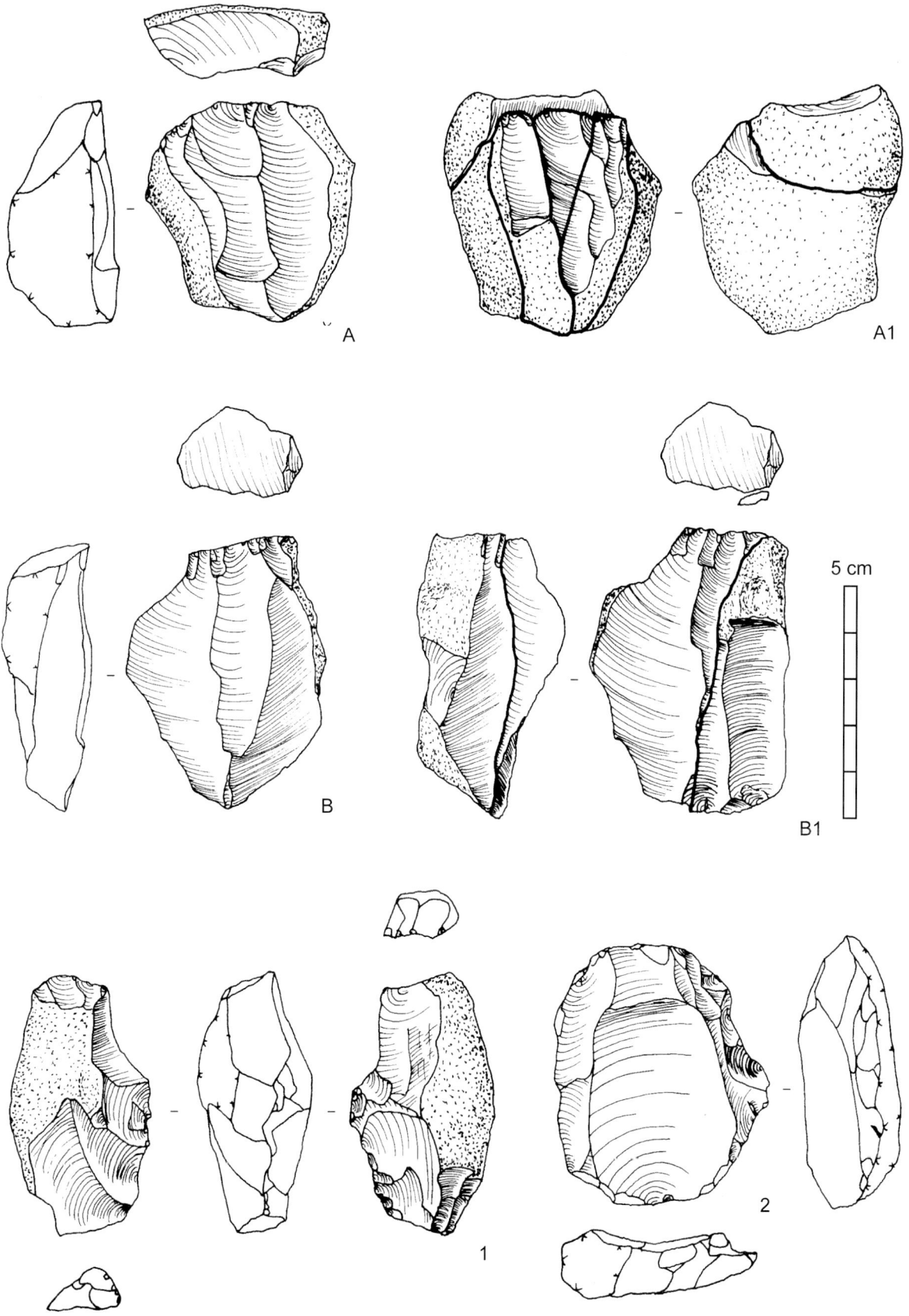

Figure 3.45. Artifacts and refittings from TH.191. A1 and B1 refittings: (1) single platform unidirectional core on narrow surface with crest preparation, (2) Levallois core with distal overpassed termination from which an additional rectangular preferential flake has been removed (illustrations by Y.H. Hilbert).

Summary of Middle Palaeolithic Findings

The Middle Palaeolithic of the Nejd Plateau appears to be almost exclusively characterized by Nubian and Nubian-derived reduction strategies. Between 2010 and 2013, DAP mapped over 250 surface sites with Nubian Levallois technology on the Nejd Plateau in southern Oman, ranging from large-scale workshops (>2000 artifacts) to isolated points and discarded Nubian Levallois cores. Beyond the Nejd Plateau, Nubian Complex assemblages have been reported on interdunal gravels in the Rub Al-Khali desert (Rose and Hilbert 2014), on ancient river terraces in northern Oman (Beshkani *et al.* 2017b), Al Kharj in central Saudi Arabia (Crassard and Hilbert 2016, 2013; Hilbert *et al.* 2016), Al-Jawf in northern Saudi Arabia (Hilbert *et al.* 2017), even as far north as the Negev desert (Goder-Goldberger *et al.* 2016). While chronological control over this lithic technocomplex is still poor, it is appears to be an MIS 5 archaeological phenomenon that stretches continuously from the eastern Sahara to the Arabian Peninsula and southern Levant.

In Dhofar, Nubian Complex sites are characterized by the standardized production of large, elongated points via preferential bidirectional Nubian Levallois core preparation, often comprising well over half the total cores. The only other type of reduction found in any significant amounts is a simple-unidirectional strategy for the production of elongated blanks. The classic centripetal Levallois strategy is extremely rare, comprising less than 3% of cores at most sites. Typologically, retouched tools are uncommon, but when found in reasonable numbers are weighted toward Middle Palaeolithic forms such as side scrapers.

The Nubian Levallois tradition endured in Dhofar for some time, encompassing at least two separate technological phases: the earlier "classic" Nubian Complex and its derivative, the Mudayyan industry. Although the Mudayyan has no absolute dates, these assemblages consistently exhibit less patination, chemical dissolution, rounding and edge damage than earlier Nubian Complex artifacts. The known distribution of the Mudayyan industry is limited around fossil springs on the western Nejd Plateau, as opposed to the earlier Nubian Complex that stretches across southern Arabia from the Ramlat As-Sabatayn to the Al-Hajar Mountains. Within the Mudayyan industry, the most prominent reduction strategy is Nubian Levallois reduction from diminutive cores, even when significantly larger raw material was available, as seen at TH.268. These small Nubian Levallois cores grade into a bidirectional Levallois variant, which has a flattened medial distal ridge and ranges in shape from sub-triangular to ovate, producing ovate endproducts. This type, in turn, grades into rectangular, opposed platform recurrent Levallois cores that enabled the serial production of elongated endproducts. Mudayyan assemblages consistently have a separate reduction strategy, in which elongated blanks were unidirectionally struck from the narrow working surface of the core. Crested blades, albeit rare, occasionally appear in these assemblages, associated with the preparation of single platform blade cores exploiting the narrow working surface.

The shift from classic Nubian Levallois to Mudayyan core reduction is characterized, in part, by a change from preferential Levallois to recurrent bidirectional point production systems. In the earlier Nubian Complex, toolmakers used the median distal ridge to shape the working surface and achieve one or two elongated points before having to rejuvenate the core. In later Mudayyan assemblages, recurrent bidirectional cores became increasingly common. Toolmakers began to use a flat working surface with equal opposed platforms, which enabled them to produce recurrent blanks from both ends of the prepared core. Consequently, rectangular-shaped cores replace the distinctive triangular/sub-triangular classic Nubian Levallois core shape. In both industries, the typical endproducts are Levallois points; however, Mudayyan points are categorically smaller. Mudayyan assemblages exhibit a higher percentage of tools and greater range of retouched tool types. The Mudayyan toolkit includes a variety of convex, nosed, straight and atypical endscrapers, as well as burins and perforators.

Chapter 4

The Upper and Late Palaeolithic in Dhofar

In Southwest Asia, cultural remains dating between approximately 45,000 and 15,000 years BP are classified within the Upper Palaeolithic archaeological phase. In Africa, this period is alternately referred to as the Late Stone Age. It was during this interval that our species spread into Australia and the Americas, drew pictures on cave walls, carved portable art objects and musical instruments; while at the same time, eradicated every other hominid species on earth. The roots of the Upper Palaeolithic behavioral "revolution" can be traced back to the Middle Palaeolithic (e.g., symbolism, burials, composite tools, increased mobility), but it was during this latter period that these elements blossomed into fruition.

The transition from Middle to Upper Palaeolithic stone tool technologies first occurred in Southwest Asia during early Marine Isotope Stage 3. Generally speaking, it was characterized by a shift from preferential prepared core reduction systems to the serial production of elongated points via opposed platform cores, seen in the Mudayyan industry of Dhofar, the Taramsan industry in the Nile Valley (Van Peer *et al.* 2010), the Bohunician industry of eastern Europe (Richter *et al.* 2008) and the Emiran industry in the southern Levant (Marks 1983). From a technological standpoint, these industries all appear to derive from the Nubian Levallois concept, namely the use of an opposed platform technique to maintain working surface convexity. Some have suggested that the catalyst for the Middle-Upper Palaeolithic transition in the southern Levant was the extirpation of late Middle Palaeolithic Nubian Complex toolmakers from Arabia, forced out of the Peninsula by increasing aridity (Rose and Marks 2014).

These transitional industries demonstrate similar technological trajectories from preferential to recurrent blank production methods. This shift brings about a change in the conceptual approach to the volume of raw material. Rather than using a single (or opposed) working surface to produce one preferential end product, toolmakers adopted a recurrent volumetric approach that enabled them to serially produce multiple blanks before rejuvenating or exhausting the core. Upper Palaeolithic blade technologies often employ a cresting technique to prepare the lateral edge of the working surface and remove core tablets to curate the striking platform.

Upper Palaeolithic toolmakers used materials other than stone to fashion their equipment, demonstrated by the increasing frequency of bone tools in the archaeological record. In Europe, where deep cave systems have preserved an exceptional record of Upper Palaeolithic organic remains, researchers excavated bone points, harpoons, needles, personal ornaments, musical instruments and ivory figurines (Conard 2003). During the latter half of the Upper Palaeolithic, architectural structures begin to appear at open-air sites in central and eastern Europe, large circular installations constructed of mammoth bones (Gladkih *et al.* 1984). The iconic cave paintings from sites such as Chauvet, Rouffignac, Lascaux, Altamira, Tito Bustillo, Santimamiñe, among others, were created during the latter half of the Upper Palaeolithic – representing the culmination of this cognitive revolution.

In the Oman Peninsula, a period known as the Late Palaeolithic succeeded the Upper Palaeolithic, falling between approximately 14,000 and 7,000 years ago. The Late Palaeolithic is a cultural unit distinct to South Arabia that is widespread from the Hadramawt Valley in central Yemen to the Al-Hajar Mountains in northern Oman.

(1) Jebel Faya NE-1

(2) Nad Al-Thamam
(Uerpmann *et al.* 2009)

(3) Jebel Faya 10
(Uerpmann *et al.* 2013)

(4) Wadi Wuttaya
(Uerpmann 1992)

(5) Natif Cave
(Charpentier *et al.* 2016)

(6) KR213
(Cremaschi and Negrino 2005)

(7) QG12
(Cremaschi *et al.* 2015)

(8) Ghazal
(Hilbert *et al.* 2012)

(9) Khamseen
(Hilbert *et al.* 2012)

(10) Al-Hatab
(Rose and Usik 2009;
Hilbert *et al.* 2015a)

(11) Meshed
(Amirkhanov 2006)

(12) Faw Well
(Edens 2001)

(13) Wadi at Tayyilah 3
(Fedele 2008)

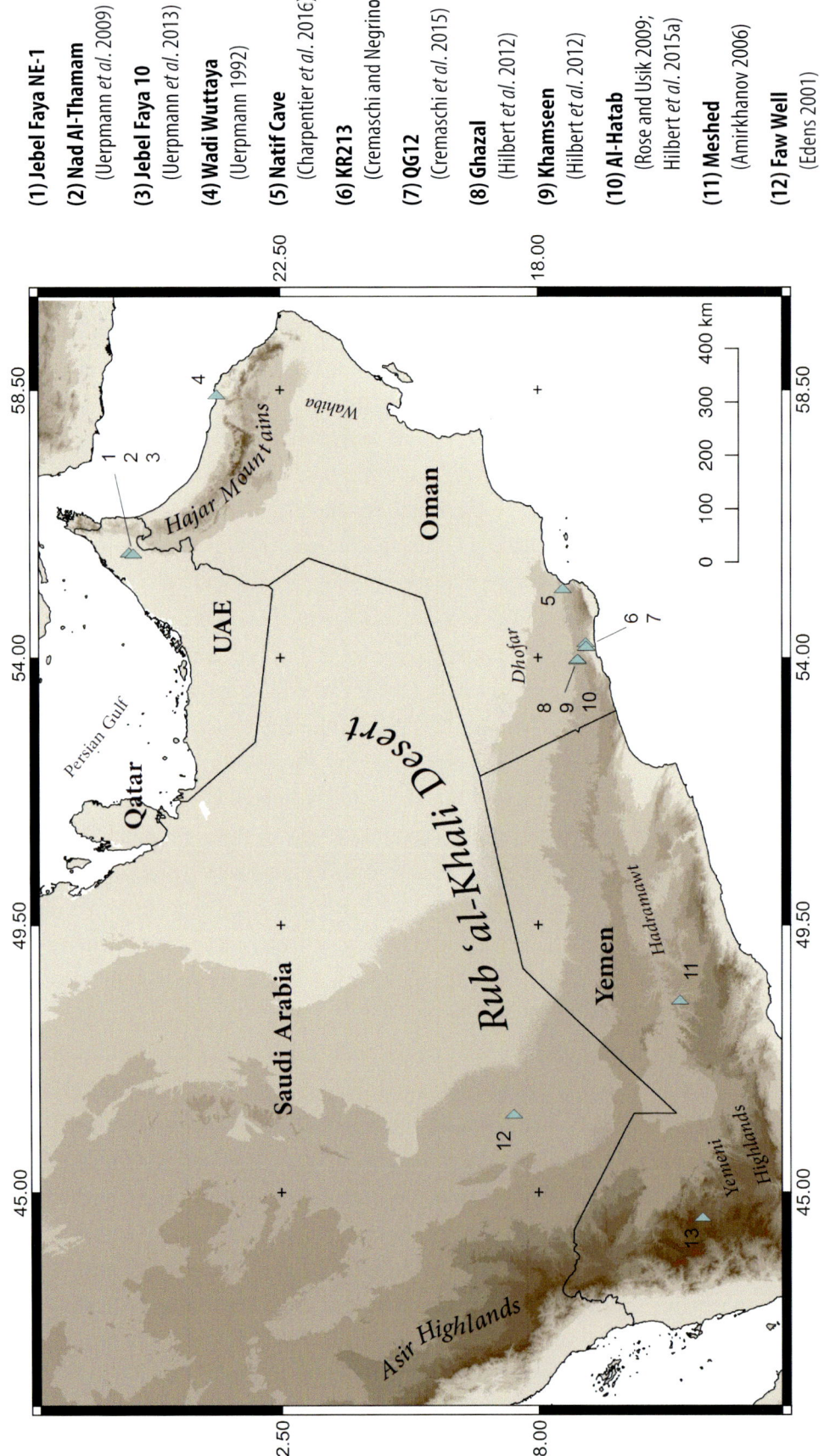

Figure 4.1. Map showing the location of dated Upper and Late Palaeolithic sites in southern Arabia (image by the authors).

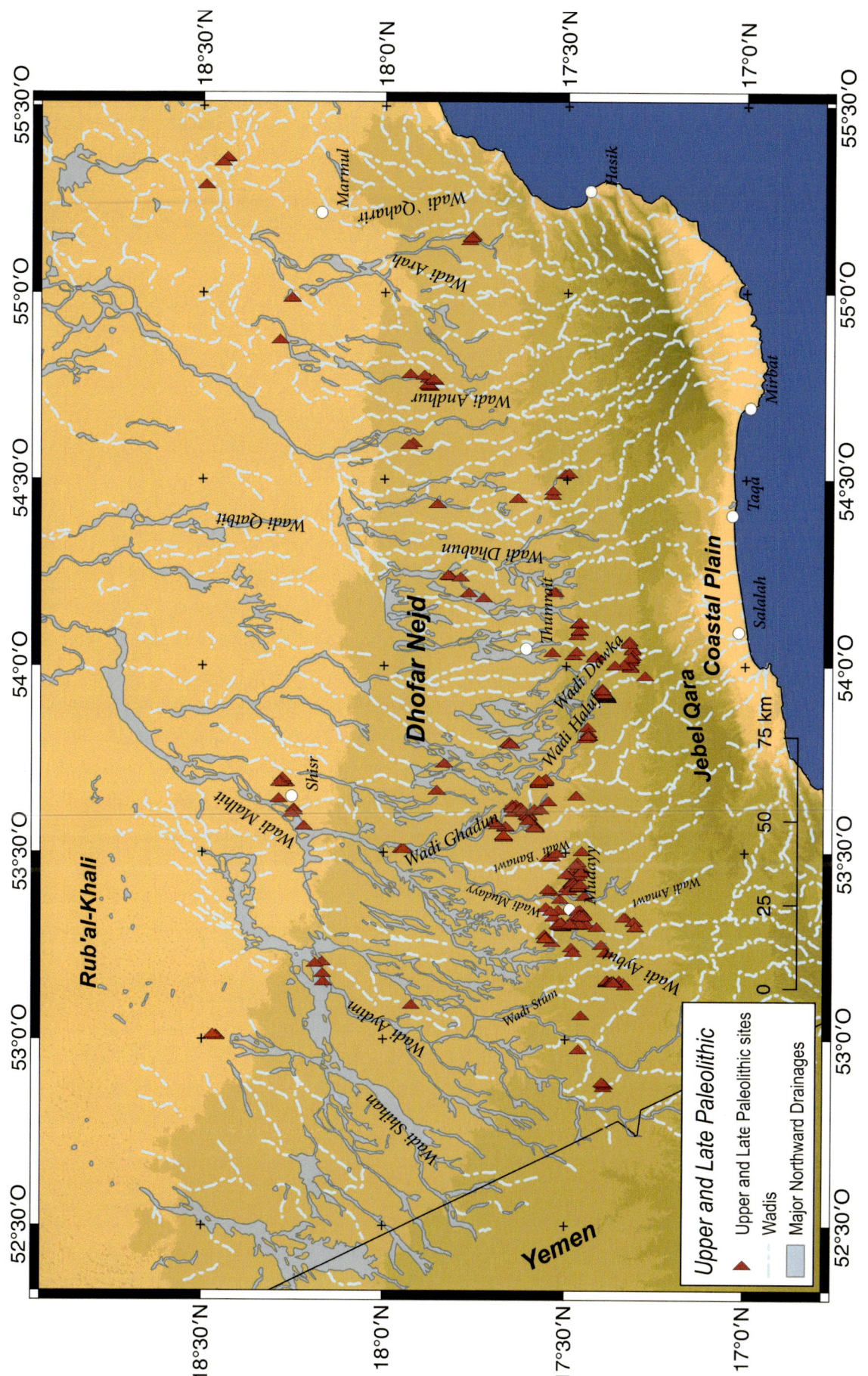

Figure 4.2. Map showing the location of Upper and Late Palaeolithic findspots recorded by the Dhofar Archaeological Project between 2002 and 2013 (image by the authors).

Genetic studies of indigenous Modern South Arabian-speaking populations in Dhofar have revealed deeply rooted mitochondrial lineages reaching as far back as 12,000 years old, which broadly correlate with the onset of the Late Palaeolithic. An analysis of mtDNA haplogroup R2 estimates the effective breeding population of Dhofar jumped from 1,000 to 10,000 individuals during this period (Al-Abri *et al.* 2012). Sometime between 8000 and 7000 years ago, domesticated cattle and goats were introduced to southern Arabia, heralding the Neolithic revolution. By 6,000 BP, the Holocene Climatic Optimum came to a close, punctuated by a millennium of drought and desiccation (Preston *et al.* 2015).

The Arabian Upper Palaeolithic

"Typical" Upper Palaeolithic sites are virtually absent in the Arabian Peninsula (Maher 2009; Rose and Usik 2009). The lone exception is a surface assemblage from the western Rub Al-Khali with typical Levantine late Upper Palaeolithic features including bladelets, crested blades, backed tools, burins and end scrapers (Edens 2001). The absence of Upper Palaeolithic sites may be partially due to our inability to recognize techno-typological features of local Arabian lithic industries, in addition to the steadily deteriorating climate from ca. 50,000 to 20,000 BP that rendered much of the Peninsula uninhabitable.

The only known stratified Upper Palaeolithic deposit in Arabia comes from Jebel Faya NE1 in Sharjah, UAE. From excavations on the scree slope outside the rockshelter, archaeologists unearthed Assemblage A with OSL dates around 40,000 BP (Armitage *et al.* 2011). Assemblage A technology is dominated by flake production from orthogonal, multiple platform cores with unfaceted platforms. Retouched tools include Middle Palaeolithic forms such as side scrapers and denticulates.

Inside the Faya NE1 rockshelter, archaeological horizon AH II was discovered overlying Assemblage A (Bretzke *et al.* 2014). AH II is bracketed between the underlying stratum dated to 40,000 BP and an overlying Neolithic layer dated to 9,500 BP. The AH II assemblage contains bidirectional opposed platform cores and elongated blanks with faceted platforms. The toolkit includes retouched blades and end scrapers.

Archaeological investigations in Hadramawt and Mahra documented a series of Upper Palaeolithic sites on the surface and in stratified contexts (Amirkhanov 2006). These assemblages are characterized by flat unidirectional-parallel and bidirectional blade cores associated with a variety of end scrapers. A time frame between 30,000 and 18,000 BP is proposed for these sites, based on radiocarbon ages from a corresponding geological context.

In the southern Yemeni highlands, Fedele (2008) reports a cultural horizon from the site of Wadi at Tayyilah 3 described as "pre-Neolithic." The toolkit contains burins, unifacial points, truncated pieces, foliates and retouched segments. A heavily fractured faunal assemblage was also recovered, including the remains of wild gazelle and wild cattle. The horizon is undated, but was found underlying a Neolithic level.

The South Arabian Late Palaeolithic

Within the last decade, researchers have articulated a lithic technocomplex unique to South Arabia, referred to as the Late Palaeolithic. Thousands of such sites have been identified across southern Arabia, from the Hadramawt Valley to the Huqf depression (Amirkhanov 1994; Crassard 2008a, 2008b; Hilbert 2014; Jagher and Pümpin 2010; Rose and Usik 2009), exhibiting a closely related suite of technological and typological characteristics.

The reduction strategy is strikingly homogenous: unidirectional-parallel blade blanks struck from frontal and semi-tournant cores with unfaceted platforms. The Late Palaeolithic toolkit includes burins, a variety of end and side scrapers, unifacial tanged points, occasional foliates, trifacial slugs and heavy bifacial implements.

Absolute dates for the Late Palaeolithic come from a series of collapsed rockshelters on the southern Nejd Plateau, near the headwaters of Wadi Dawkah (Figure 4.1). The assemblage from Al-Hatab is associated with numeric ages between 14,000 and 10,000 BP (Hilbert *et al.* 2015b). At Khamseen rockshelter, workers documented a multi-occupation sequence spanning the Early and Middle Holocene (Hilbert 2013). The lowest horizon, AH V, contained a Late Palaeolithic assemblage dating around 9,500 BP. The youngest Late Palaeolithic site was found at Ghazal rockshelter, with upper and lower horizons dating to 8,600 and 7,200 BP, divided by a layer of sterile aeolian sand (Hilbert *et al.* 2012, 2015a).

South of the Dhofar rainfall divide, archaeologists report similar assemblage types found within rockshelters on the high grasslands, where Late Palaeolithic assemblages were excavated from deposits dating between 10,000 and 8,700 BP (Cremaschi *et al.* 2015; Cremaschi and Negrino 2002). Recent work along the coast of Dhofar near Hacik has uncovered a Late Palaeolithic assemblage with exceptional preservation inside a seaward-facing cave. In addition to the characteristic blade blanks and unifacial tanged points, researchers report fish bones, shellfish, fish hooks and other fishing equipment dating to around 10,000 BP (Charpentier *et al.* 2016). Although possessing a homogenous core reduction strategy, Late Palaeolithic sites are found across a diverse range of ecosystems and demonstrate a range of subsistence strategies from hunting to gathering to fishing.

DAP Upper and Late Palaeolithic Sites

The Dhofar Archaeological Project mapped over 300 Upper and Late Palaeolithic findspots between 2010 and 2013. Sites with Upper Palaeolithic technological features are extremely rare (n=7), while Late Palaeolithic assemblages are the most common occurrence in Dhofar (n=303). The few Upper Palaeolithic sites were discovered in different settings: wadi tributaries and hilltops on the western Nejd and interdunal gravels in the southern Rub Al-Khali. Sites dating to the Late Palaeolithic are distributed across the entire Nejd Plateau, with particularly dense concentrations in the southwest around Wadi Haluf and Wadi Dawkah, on the eastern side of the plateau around Wadis Arah, Andhur and Mahwis and on the central-western portion of the plateau between Wadi Ghadun and Wadi Aybut (Figure 4.2).

Late Palaeolithic sites are typically found on low wadi terraces associated with chert outcrops. Only 33 sites (11%) have been found away from raw material outcrops. While Lower and Middle Palaeolithic workshop sites are often found together, Late Palaeolithic quarries are frequently found in isolation or in proximity to later Neolithic occupations. This suggests either different settlement patterns and/or the raw material outcrops exploited by Late Palaeolithic populations had not yet been exposed in the preceding Middle and Lower Palaeolithic periods.

Late Palaeolithic sites are classified as lithic workshops, habitation areas exhibiting later stages of stone tool manufacture and higher numbers of tools and woodworking sites. Woodworking sites are specialized activity zones comprised of dense concentrations of burins on truncations. These were typically made on large elongated blanks struck from classic Late Palaeolithic blade cores (Figure 4.3). They are highly standardized, which is perhaps a function of the hafting element. Functional and traceological analyses suggest that these tools were utilized intensively and applied with great force on hard wood (Figure 4.4).

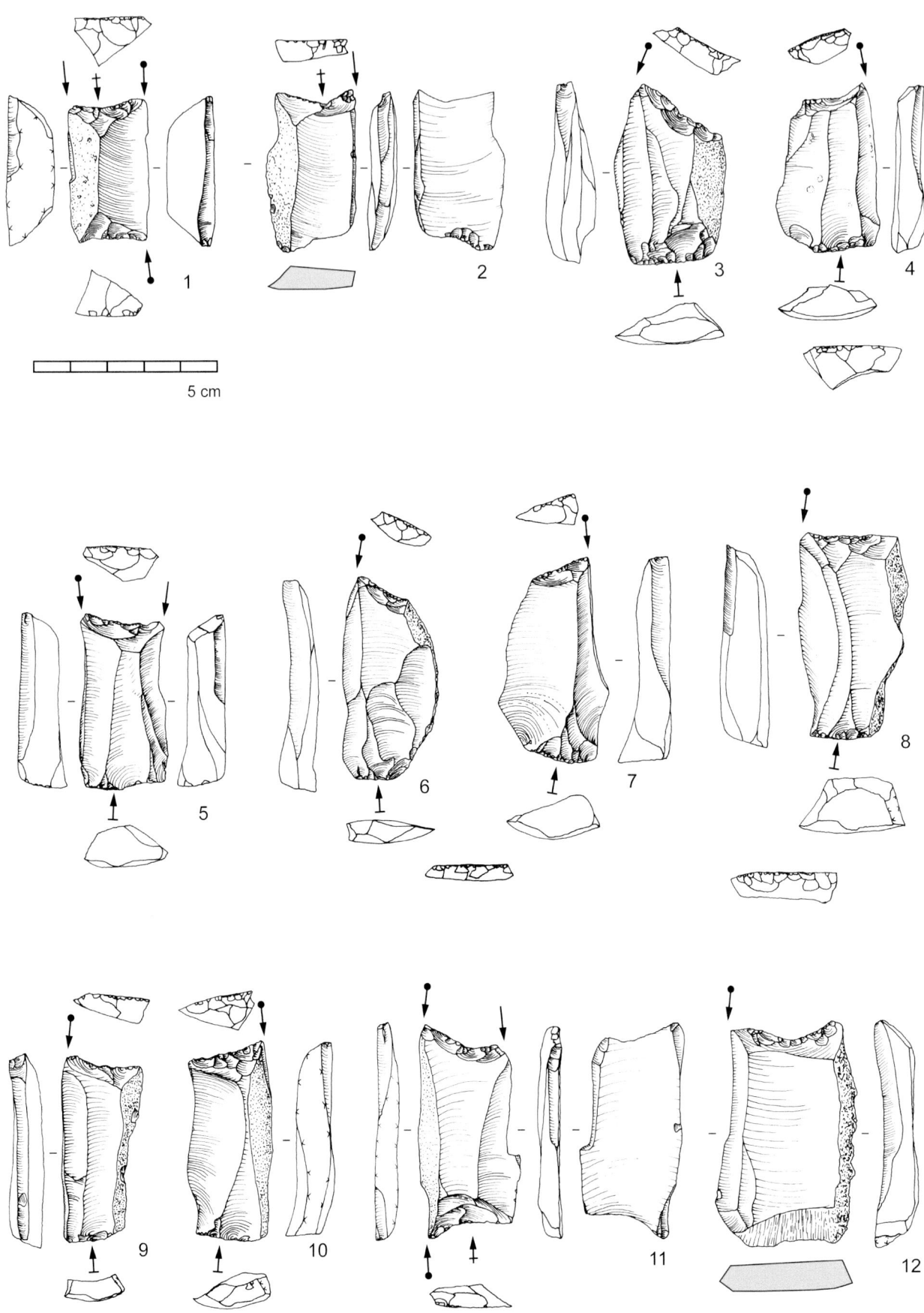

5 cm

Figure 4.3. Burins from Late Palaeolithic sites on the southern Nejd Plateau (after Hilbert *et al*. 2018).

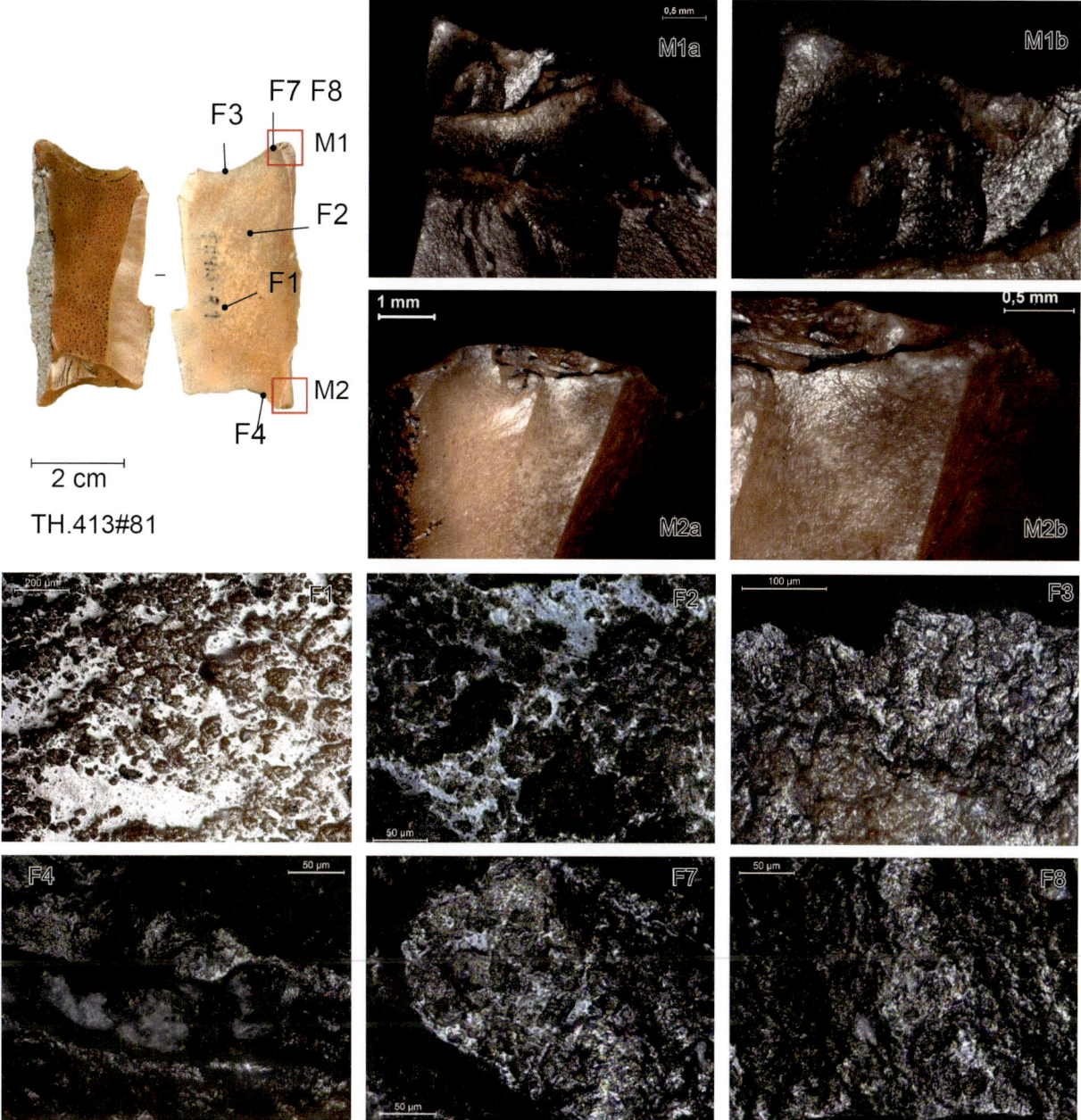

Figure 4.4. Use-wear traces on burins from TH.413 (after Hilbert *et al.* 2018).

In each case, the working edge was found to be along the truncation rather than the burin blow. Hence, the application of the burin blow seems to be a technical step to stabilize the truncated working edge.

Upper and Late Palaeolithic Sample Assemblages

The following is a description of technological and typological variability from a sample of Upper and Late Palaeolithic sites on the Nejd. The older sites are characterized by backed bladelets, crested blades, carinated pieces, unifacial points, bifacial and partly-bifacial points and end scrapers, while later sites are recognized by large blades, burins on truncation, bifacial foliates and unifacial tanged points. Whether these assemblages belong to a single cultural continuum is yet to be determined.

Figure 4.5. View of Jebel Kareem (photograph by the authors).

Figure 4.6. Terraces at the foot of Jebel Kareem (photograph by the authors).

TH.68

Findspot TH.68 is a dense surface scatter (500 pieces per square meter) located on top of a high inselberg overlooking the floodplain west of Wadi Aybut (Figures 4.5 and 4.6). The hill, which we dubbed "Jebel Kareem" for its rich and distinct lithic assemblage, is about 30 m in height and has a narrow top and wide slopes with low terraces at its base. Jebel Kareem is composed of Umm er Raduhma limestone beds, with large, high quality Mudayy chert nodules outcropping from its flanks and on the lower terraces. The TH.68 scatter occurs in a small but dense concentration atop the inselberg (Figures 4.7 to 4.9). Taphonomic and technological studies, as well as refittings suggest the assemblage is largely homogenous and does not include a successive Late Palaeolithic component. We identified a low number of more heavily weathered Middle Palaeolithic artifacts, many of which were recycled. A total of 3437 lithic artifacts were collected from seven square meters (Table 4.1), which includes 440 chunks and 1712 chips. There were four different collection areas, designated Areas 1 to 4. Area 1 was a 2 x 2 m grid placed at the densest part of the scatter. Areas 2 and 3 were half-meter squares situated at the periphery and Area 4 was a 4.0 x 0.5 m transect at the edge of the scatter (Figure 4.10). There was no discernable variability in assemblage composition between the collection areas.

Most of the assemblage was made from local Mudayy chert (n=1730), with nine specimens made from non-local Gahit chert. It is noteworthy that among the Gahit artifacts, five are bifacial tools and the remaining four are biface thinning flakes. There are an additional ten specimens manufactured from an unidentifiable chert source. Some of the older Middle Palaeolithic artifacts were recycled into diagnostic Upper Palaeolithic tools that exhibit two separate stages of surface weathering (Figure 4.11), indicating that the TH.68 toolmakers also used more ancient artifacts on or near the site as raw material. There is only minor variation in artifact patination, which exhibit uncommon features. The specimens have a luminous manganese oxide gloss (Figure 4.12), as if painted with clear varnish. The colors range from dark brown to reddish-brown. Some of the pieces demonstrate two phases of patination, with a heavier black varnish associated with the Middle Palaeolithic objects.

Core reduction strategies were aimed at fabricating blades, bladelets and small flake segments with thick cross-sections. Blades and bladelets predominantly exhibit unidirectional dorsal scars, followed by bidirectional and crested patterns (Table 4.2). Blank shapes show that nearly half the blades have parallel edges, bladelets have parallel and convergent edges and flakes are often transverse with expanding edges (Table 4.3). Blank midpoint cross-sections, longitudinal profiles and distal terminations are summarized in Table 4.4. The blanks from TH.68 are most often trapezoidal and triangular in cross-section with feathering terminations. Striking platforms tend to be straight and unfaceted, with a small number of blades and bladelets exhibiting dihedral and punctiform platforms (Table 4.5). Nearly half of the blades and majority of bladelets show some evidence of abrasion at the interface of the dorsal surface and striking platform. There are a few carinated cores that may have used indirect percussion to produce small twisted bladelets (Figure 4.13).

The TH.68 débitage is small to medium in size (Table 4.6). Blades are relatively small and bladelets tend to be narrow and elongated. Cortical pieces and core trimming elements are larger than the blades and bladelets. One blade outlier measures 12 cm in length, which is the largest piece of débitage found at the site. Blank types are mostly elongated blanks, core trimming elements, crested blades, core tablets and débordant elements (Figure 4.14). There are 79 cores in the assemblage (Table 4.7), most of which are unidirectional-parallel blade (Figure 4.15) and bladelet cores (Figure 4.16). Opposed platform cores with bidirectional scar patterns also make up a significant percentage of core types, as well as cores-on-flakes. The cores are small in relation to the local chert nodules.

Figure 4.7. Surface of the top of Jebel Kareem (photograph by the authors).

Figure 4.8. The DAP team making systematic collections from TH.68 (photograph by the authors).

Figure 4.9. View from the top of the inselberg (photograph by the authors).

Table 4.1. Artifacts counts from TH.68.

Jebel Kareem 1 (TH.68)	N	Percentages
Débitage	**1089**	**63%**
Blades	*324*	*19 %*
Bladelets	*91*	*5 %*
Flakes	*371*	*21 %*
Primary Débitage	*155*	*9 %*
Core Trimming Elements	*64*	*4 %*
Bifacial Trimming Elements	*84*	*5 %*
Cores	**79**	**5 %**
Kareem segments	**260**	**15 %**
Tools	**297**	**17 %**
Total	**1725**	**100 %**

Table 4.2. Débitage scar patterns from TH.68.

Scar pattern	Flake	Blade	Bladelet	Cortical pieces	Débordant elements
Unidirectional	210	166	50	79	17
Unidirectional Crossed	37	14	2	3	2
Parallel	4	35	14		
Convergent	17	45	18	4	
Bidirectional	36	39	4	1	
Radial	3	1			
Transverse crested		1			
Opposed	8	3		3	
Unidirectional crested	9	11			1
Transverse	10	4	1	6	
Bidirectional crested		1			

Table 4.3. Débitage shapes from TH.68.

Shape	Flake	Blade	Bladelet	Cortical pieces	Débordant elements
Parallel	100	142	46	41	3
Expanding	121	43	3	35	5
Convergent	41	56	30	7	3
Lateralized	51	57	10	16	8
Ovoid	33	8		38	2
Irregular	23	16	1	16	

A significant component of TH.68 are pieces we refer to as "Kareem segments," comprising nearly 15% of the assemblage. Kareem segments were produced using a specific core-on-flake method that detached small transverse segments from blanks. Refittings enable us to reconstruct how these segments were produced (Figure 4.17), similar to a chef cutting a carrot into small discs. In four cases, large débordant blades and cortical elements were used as Kareem segment cores, knapped along their longitudinal axis. The segments tend to be similar in shape and size (Figure 4.18), which is a function of the flake-core's cross-section. The majority are triangular and trapezoidal in shape. Kareem segment reduction typically follows the orientation of the blank perpendicular to its technological axis, using either dorsal or ventral surfaces as the striking platform and commencing from either the proximal or distal end of the blank.

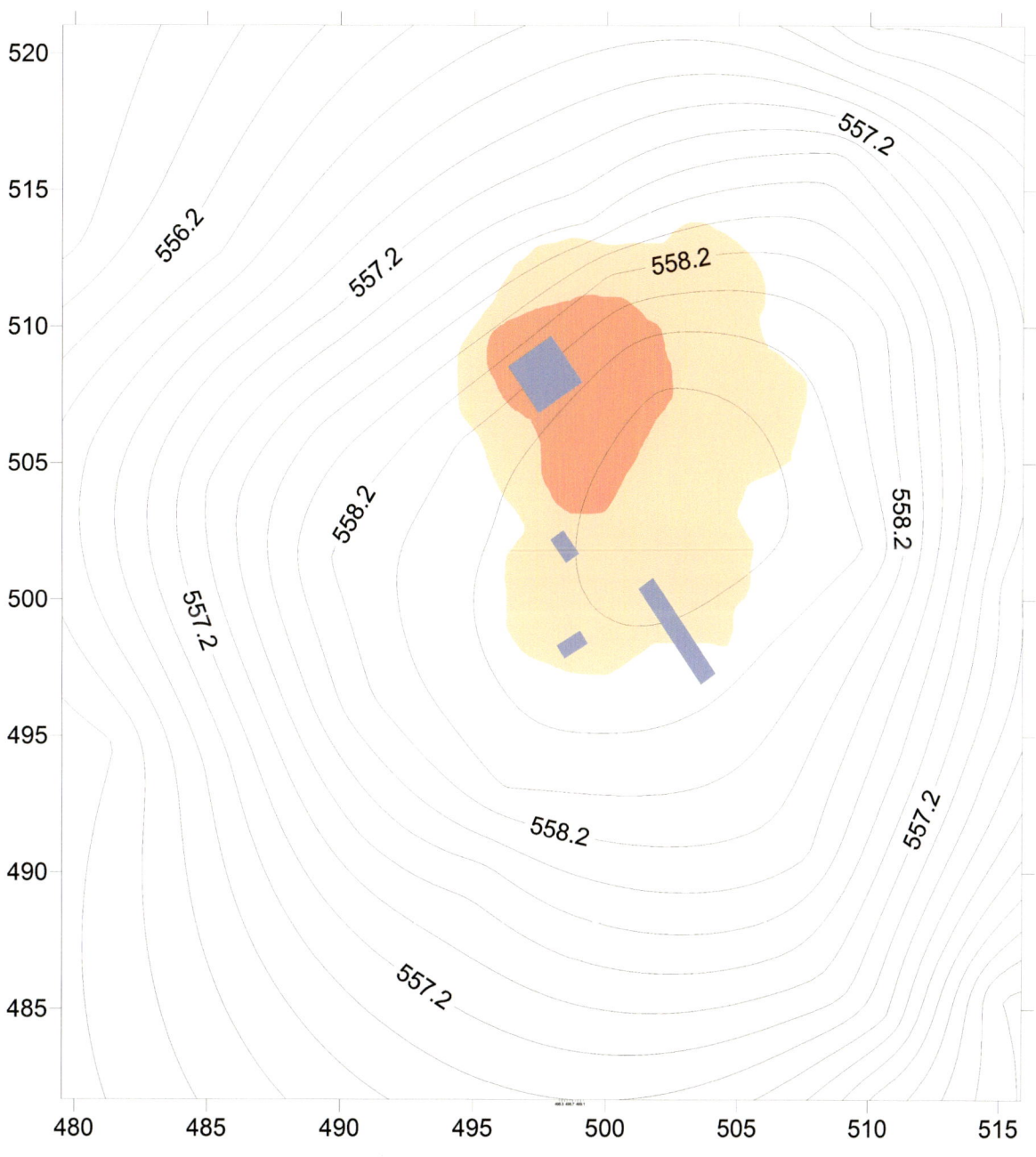

Figure 4.10. Topographic map of TH.68 showing the higher density area (red), lower density area (yellow) and collection areas (blue) (figure plot by Y.H. Hilbert).

Table 4.4. Débitage midpoint cross sections, distal terminations and longitudinal profiles from TH.68.

Midpoint cross section	Flake	Blade	Bladelet	Cortical pieces	Débordant elements
Flat	8	1		5	1
Triangular	81	92	33	39	6
Lateral step	75	40	11	36	5
Trapezoid	142	140	37	15	7
more 3 vectors	37	32	8	2	2
Rectangular	22	14	1	7	
Convex				47	
House	2	2			
Distal Termination					
Feathered	179	111	48	16	8
Hinged	93	66	21	10	4
Overpassed	77	59	6	9	9
Absent	21	87	14	119	
Longitudinal Profile					
Flat	132	105	32	12	1
Incurvate	111	80	23	12	4
Twisted	111	105	31	9	16
Concave	17	34	4	121	

Figure 4.11. Middle Palaeolithic artifacts from TH.68: (1-3) Levallois blanks into tools retouched during a subsequent phase of usage, (4,5) Middle Palaeolithic cores (photographs by Y.H. Hilbert).

Figure 4.12. Upper Palaeolithic tools from TH.68: (1) Composite end scraper and burin on truncation, (2-4) backed bladelets, (5) plano-convex bifacial point, (6) unifacial point, (7) partly-unifacial point, (8) preform, (9) shouldered end scraper (photographs by Y.H. Hilbert).

Table 4.5. Débitage striking platforms from TH.68.

Platform type	Flake Platforms	Blade Platforms	Bladelet Platforms	Cortical Pieces	Débordant elements
Cortical	22	14	2	17	1
Unfaceted	243	166	35	103	19
Dihedral	25	18	2	3	1
Punctiform	4	16	11	1	
Faceted	11	3	1		
Crushed	22	33	22	13	
Absent	14	11	3	1	
Transverse faceted	5	1		2	
Platform abrasion					
Not Abraded	202	112	21	109	12
Partially Abraded	97	76	25	20	8
Abraded	23	51	21	3	
Inverse abraded	9	4	2		1

5 cm

Figure 4.13. Carinated core from TH.68 (photograph by Y.H. Hilbert).

Table 4.6. Débitage metric data from TH.68.

Max Length	Flake	Blade	Bladelets	D Blades	D flakes	C Flakes	C Blades	BTF
MAX	104,31	120	67,32	87,51	60	76,61	93,27	50,91
MIN	14,15	30,26	18,65	42,57	28,63	17,87	21	9,83
AVERAGE	37,97248503	53,58623656	33,48	60,35368421	44,315	46,82347826	52,34333333	29,89213333
STD	11,65167235	14,05996324	8,620611365	12,07602731	22,18193973	12,60894471	13,9100256	9,141538591
n	334	186	68	19	2	92	39	75
Max Width								
MAX	75,2	47,65	11,97	33,07	36,67	73,82	44,98	40,83
MIN	4,77	12	3,57	12,32	31,09	11,67	9,21	5,02
AVERAGE	30,41218487	20,78651316	8,877083333	23,37157895	33,88	37,24377358	23,64222222	22,78975904
STD	9,858525783	5,975775107	2,110522967	5,653768913	3,945655839	11,56858673	6,791649582	8,174863611
n	357	308	96	19	2	106	45	83
Thickness								
MAX	23,45	31,44	10	24,13	18,41	33,27	18,84	11,62
MIN	2,56	2,68	1,05	7,6	5,25	3,75	3,73	1,48
AVERAGE	9,257073171	8,133601286	3,596421053	13,77157895	11,83	12,88111111	10,77244444	4,845662651
STD	4,05276544	3,61734485	1,723564414	4,534895887	9,30552524	6,235114061	3,864707537	2,194335942
n	369	311	95	19	2	108	45	83
Weight								
MAX	138	85	12	55	45	116	63	18
MIN	2	1	1	6	6	2	3	1
AVERAGE	13,76986301	11,15081967	2,264150943	26	25,5	25,80392157	18,06976744	5,777777778
STD	13,3198881	10,09055419	1,902942493	13,60963711	27,57716447	19,66755343	12,96588077	3,957208386
n	365	305	53	19	2	102	43	63

Table 4.7. Core classifications from TH.68.

Core type	No
Single platform convergent cores	5
Single platform parallel	25
Opposed platform core	14
Two unopposed platform core	7
Core on flake	16
Multiple platform core	3
Pre-core	3
Broken	4
Radial	2
Total	**79**

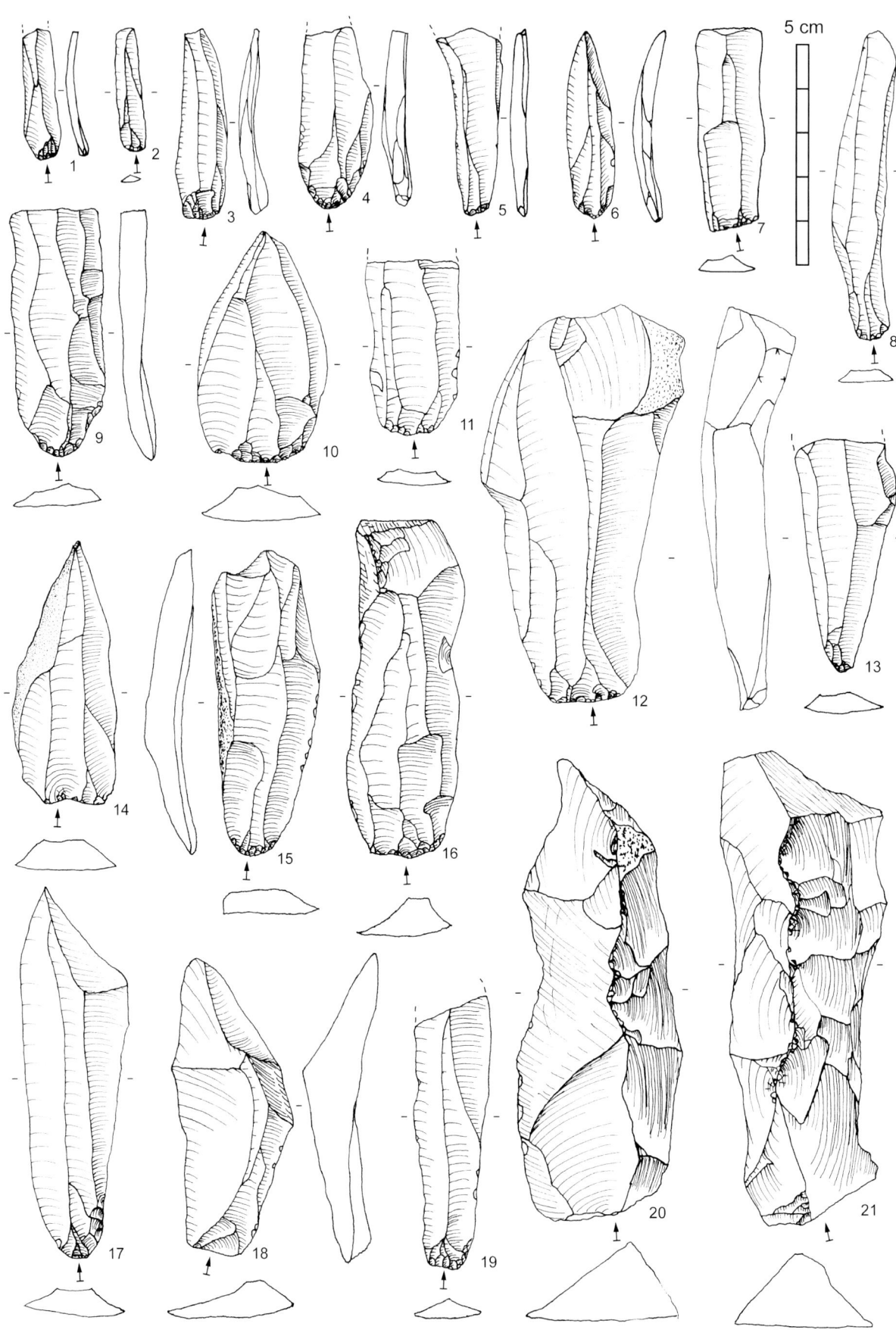

Figure 4.14. Blade debitage from TH.68 (illustrations by Y.H. Hilbert).

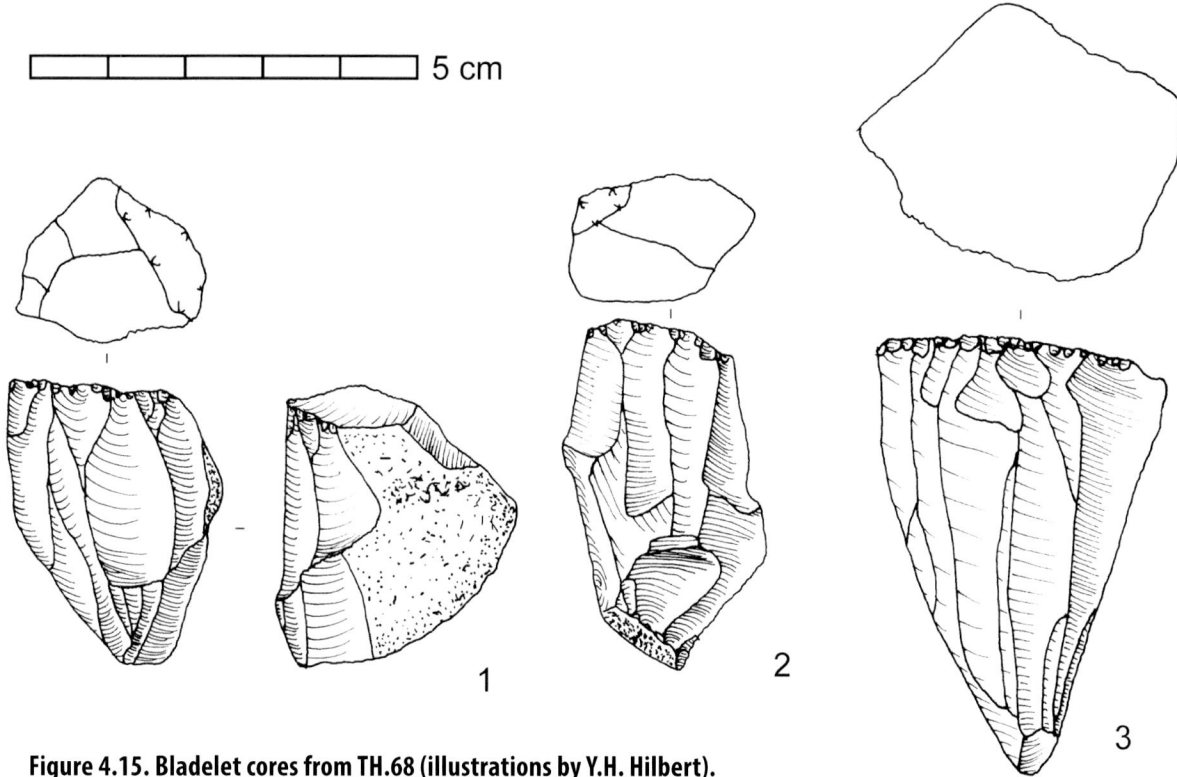

5 cm

1

2

3

Figure 4.15. Bladelet cores from TH.68 (illustrations by Y.H. Hilbert).

TH.68 includes nearly 300 tools, accounting for 17% of the total assemblage. There is an extraordinarily high frequency and diversity of tools in comparison to other surface sites we encountered on the Nejd Plateau. The toolkit includes different types of burins (Figure 4.19), end scrapers, bifacial points, backed bladelets and other retouched tools (Table 4.8). Many of the Kareem segments exhibit retouch in the form of a burin blow (n=57). Not larger than 3 cm, it is possible the segments were used as hafted elements on composite tools.

Bifacial tools (Figure 4.20) are classified as early and late stage preforms, unifacial points, bifacial and partly-bifacial points and "trifaces". Trifaces are a common type in both Upper and Late Palaeolithic assemblages from Dhofar. They are elongated, bi-pointed tools with a thick triangular cross-section. The unifacial and bifacial points were typically made on flakes, exhibiting remnants of the ventral face and plano-convex cross-sections. Some are symmetric (Figure 4.20: 2,4,8), while others are asymmetric leaning to either the left or right (Figure 4.20: 1,3). Bifaces were manufactured on site, indicated by the presence of various stages of preforms and biface thinning flakes (n=84).

End scrapers are predominantly simple with convex working edges. Shouldered variants and nosed end scrapers are present but less common (Figure 4.21). The end scrapers are made on blades or elongated flakes. The bifacial scrapers, which may have been used as hafted knives, have ventral thinning on the back of the tool. These are generally larger than the bifacial points and exhibit less invasive retouch. Additional cutting tools include denticulated sidescrapers that have finely retouched teeth, notches, retouched blanks, awls and perforators. Of particular interest are six backed bladelets, which in some contexts are diagnostic of the Upper Palaeolithic. Two types can be discerned based on size: larger backed bladelets approximately 5 cm in length and smaller backed microblades roughly 1 cm in length. Backing is always abrupt and in three cases was administered from both ventral and dorsal faces.

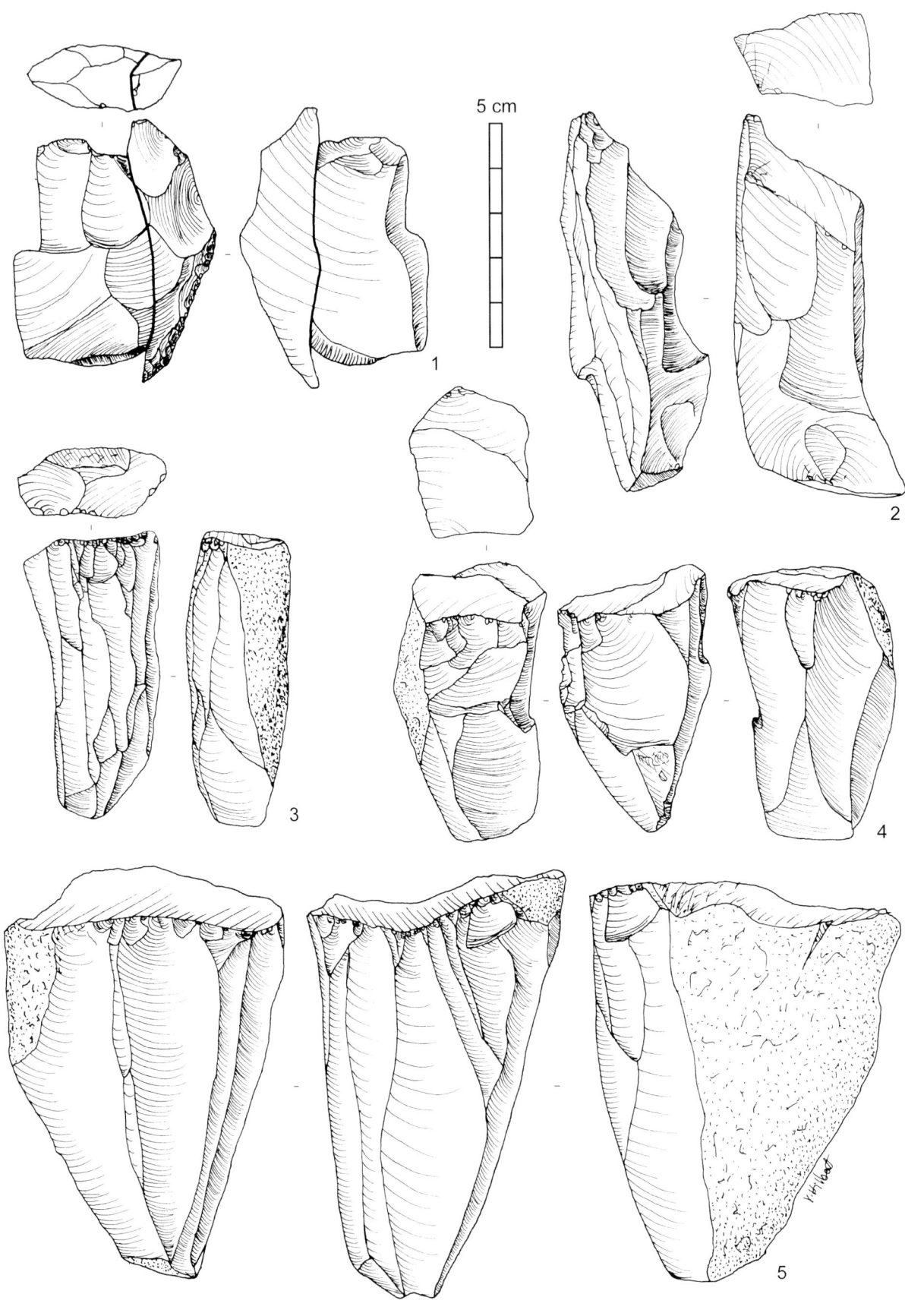

5 cm

Figure 4.16. Upper Palaeolithic cores from TH.68: (1) refit core on flake (2) core on flake, (3) unidirectional single platform bladelet core, (4,5) unidirectional single platform blade cores (illustrations by Y.H. Hilbert).

5 cm

Figure 4.17. TH.68 segment refittings (photographs by Y.H. Hilbert).

TH.262

Findspot TH.262 is located 200 m to the north of Jebel Kareem, found on a limestone terrace at the foot of the inselberg (Figure 4.22). To the east of the terrace, some minor wadis and gullies meander across an anastomosing gravel plain. The scatter is low-medium density and artifacts were systematically collected within a 5 x 8 meter grid. The lithics were all manufactured from a fine-grained, dark yellow chert often covered in a manganese oxide gloss. The nearest source of raw material is the slopes of Jebel Kareem. Both TH.68 and TH.262 assemblages were manufactured from these nodules; however, the former exhibits different weathering. We cannot be certain if this is the result of temporal or taphonomic differences.

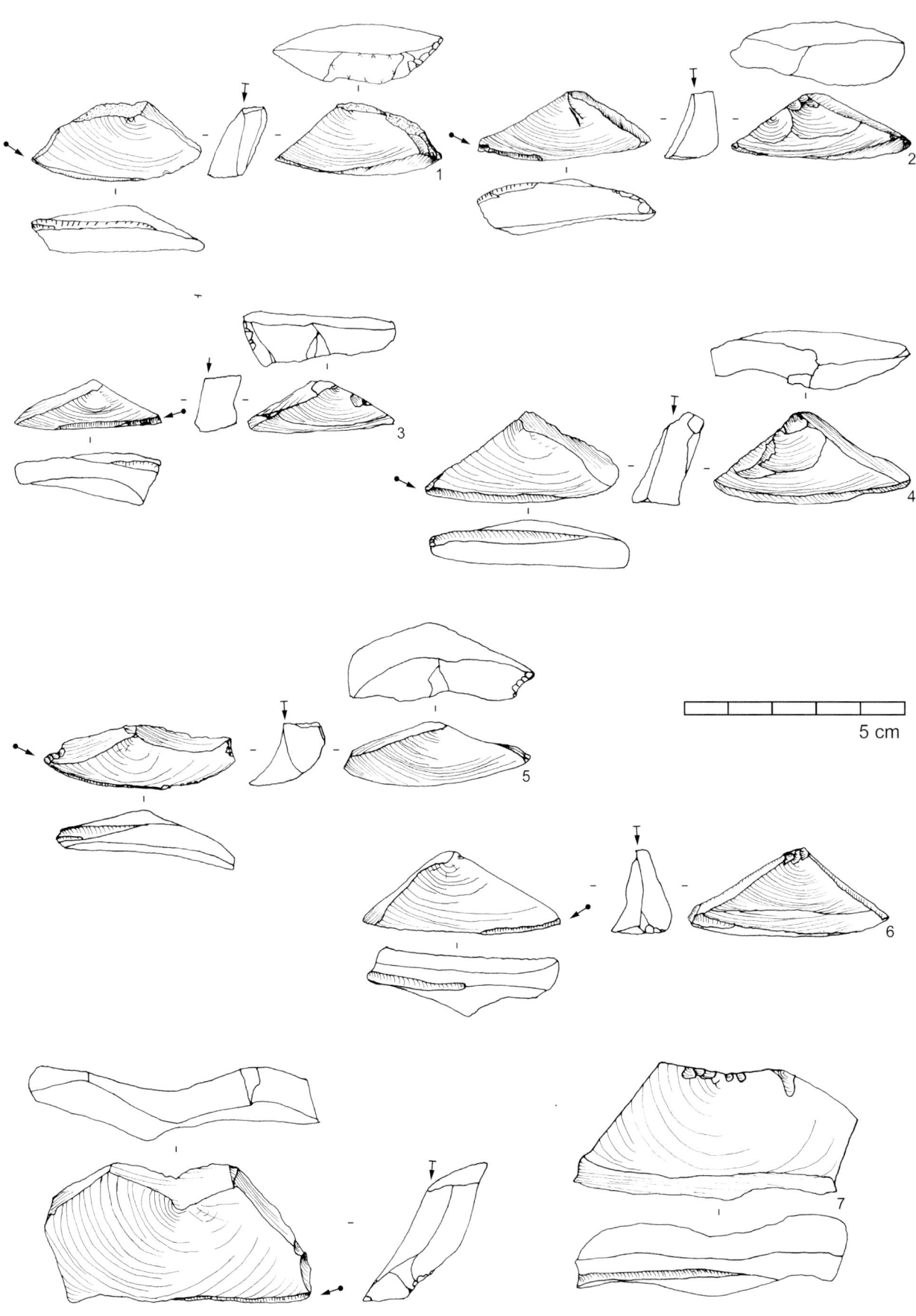

Figure 4.18. TH.68 burins made on snapped segments (illustrations by Y.H. Hilbert).

Table 4.8. Tool classifications from TH.68.

Endscrapers	n	Bifaces	n
Simple end scraper	17	Biface	14
Shouldered end scraper	5	Bifacial preform	8
Single shouldered end scraper	6	Bifacial scraper	5
Nosed end scraper	1	Bifacial point	9
Endscraper with lat. retouch	2	Triface	3
		Partially unifacial/bifacial point	7
Scrapers	**n**		
Denticulated side scraper	3	**Burins**	**n**
Side scraper	10	Single burin on nat. surface	5
Backed side scraper	1	Single burin on snap	1
Bilateral side scraper	3	Single burin on truncation	61
		Kareem burin	57
Other	**n**	Dihedral burin	5
Piercer	1	Multiple burin on truncation	3
Perforator	4		
Limace	4	**Retouched Pieces**	**n**
Notch	13	Retouched blanks	31
Double Notch	1	Backed bladelet	6
Denticulate	1	Partially retouched point	1
Multi function tool	3	Truncated piece	6

The lithic assemblage includes 138 artifacts (Table 4.9). Débitage is predominantly comprised of elongated flakes and blades struck from unidirectional, single platform cores. Among the blades, dorsal scar patterns are typically unidirectional-parallel and unidirectional-convergent, three have bidirectional scar patterns (Table 4.10). Flake scar patterns are slightly more variable, many of which were likely core trimming elements. A single crested blade was found. Bifacial preforms are also found in the assemblage; hence, some of the flake debitage may include waste from biface thinning activities. The relatively high frequency of cortical débitage, 27% of the assemblage, suggests that primary stages of raw material processing were carried out on site. Striking platforms are typically flat and unfaceted, created by a single blow to remove a core tablet. Unlike TH.68, there is minimal striking platform abrasion. The débitage from TH.262 is characterized by small to medium sized pieces (Table 4.11). While débitage length and width are relatively variable, shown by the high standard deviation, débitage thickness is homogenous.

There are 18 cores, comprising 12% of the total assemblage. These are predominantly unidirectional-parallel and unidirectional-convergent blade cores struck from a narrow working surface on the side of a nodule or plaquettes (Figure 4.23). Some cores have multiple striking platforms that produced haphazardly arranged working surfaces. These surfaces seldom intersect, which is to say they do not function to shape the volume, as is the case in Middle Palaeolithic technology. While there is some variability in core size, the length to width proportions show that they are longer than they are wide, which is expected given the elongated products.

Refittings confirm that blank production occurred in situ. Most are reconstructions of unidirectional-parallel blades struck from single platform cores. Four of the cores have associated debitage conjoins. One group of refits shows a core-on-flake technique for producing blanks (Figure 4.24).

Tools are rare and include thin ovate and pointed bifaces, end scrapers, side scrapers, a retouched flake and a perforator (Figure 4.25). The end scrapers are made on blades and one has been retouched at both ends with ogival working edges. The bifaces include two preforms, one in advanced stages of manufacture. Despite being located at the base Jebel Kareem just 200 m away from TH.68, the TH.262 toolkit stands out in contrast. The assemblage lacks Kareem segments, burins, backed bladelets and backed points. The bifacial preforms are morphologically closer to those excavated at Al-Hatab, which are associated with a Late Palaeolithic context, rather than the plano-convex retouched points from TH.68. This may also be a function of low sample size and different activities performed at TH.262 (the base of Jebel Kareem) versus TH.68 (the top of Jebel Kareem).

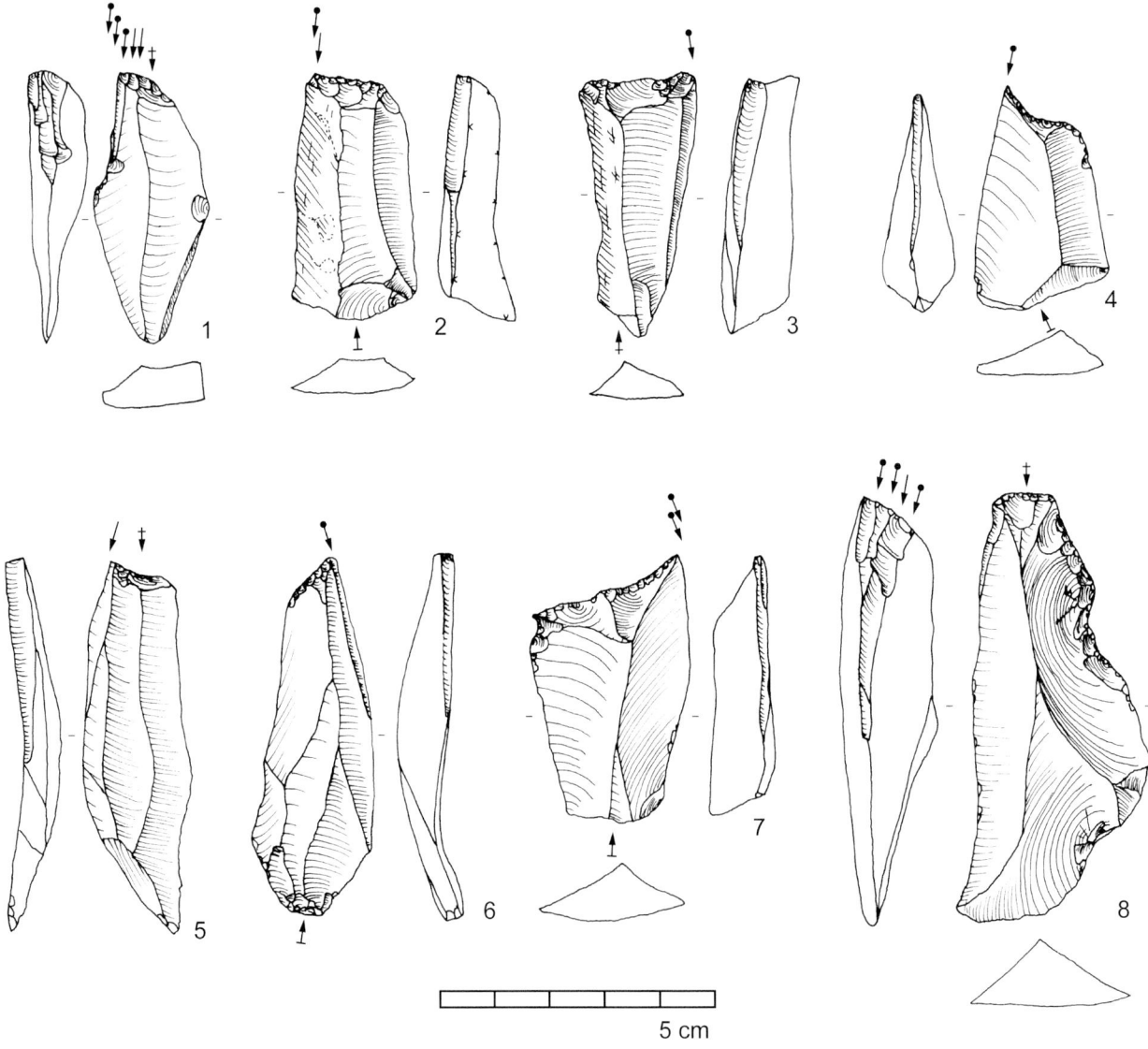

5 cm

Figure 4.19. Multiple and single burins on truncation from TH.68 (illustrations by Y.H. Hilbert).

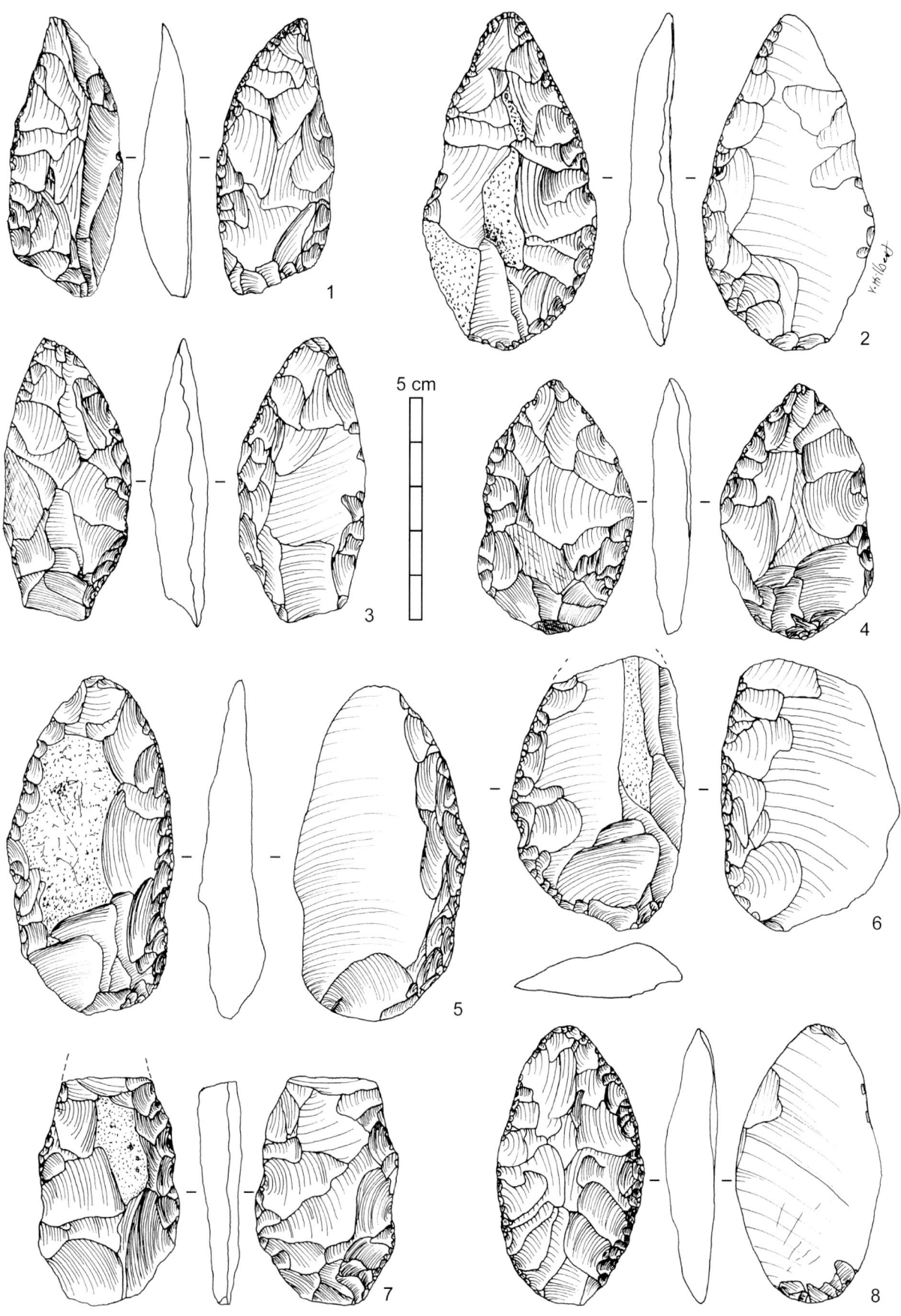

5 cm

Figure 4.20. Bifacial and unifacial tools from TH.68 (illustrations by Y.H. Hilbert).

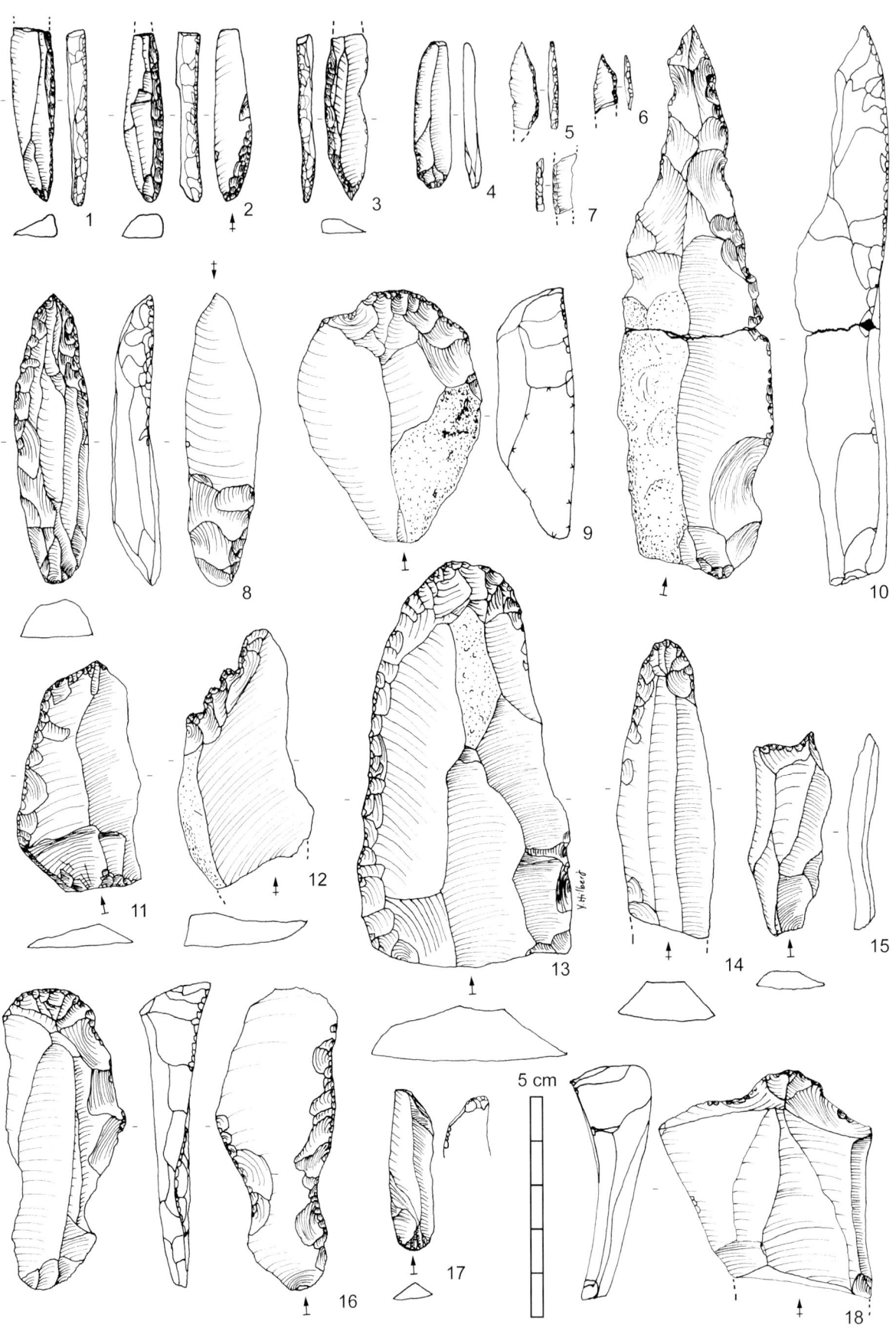

Figure 4.21. Upper Palaeolithic tools from TH.68: (1-7) backed bladelets, (8) unifacial point, (9,13,14,16,18) end scrapers, (10) awl, (11) laterally retouched blade, (12) denticulate, (15) piercer, (17) retouched bladelet (illustrations by Y.H. Hilbert).

Figure 4.22. DAP team systematically collecting findspot TH.262 (photograph by J.M. Geiling).

TH.143a

The previous two chapters presented Lower and Middle Palaeolithic assemblages collected from findspot TH.143 on the Jebel Sanoora terraces. During the 2011 fieldwork campaign, a separate and distinct knapping area away from Lower and Middle Palaeolithic artifacts was identified at the back of the terrace, associated with a chert seam actively eroding from the scarp (Figure 4.26).

The artifacts were manufactured on fine-grained Mudayy chert nodules eroding from the soft bioclastic matrix comprising the scarp. The nodules are medium-sized relative to other outcrops on the Nejd, up to 30 cm in maximum dimension. The patination of the lithic material is variable; some pieces have a manganese oxide gloss, some have no gloss, while others are whitish in color, possibly from having been buried at one time. The artifacts exhibit mild chemical dissolution, in contrast to the heavy dissolution of the Middle Palaeolithic assemblage and the nearly eradicated surfaces of Lower Palaeolithic blades at the edge of the terrace.

A total of 197 artifacts were systematically collected from 2 square meters (Table 4.12). The majority of the assemblage is composed of débitage, blades and flakes being the most common type of blanks. Cortical elements are also relatively common, which is expected given the location of the assemblage on a raw material outcrop. Among the débitage, 7% included biface thinning flakes. Only five tools were discovered, including two retouched blades, a large hammerstone and a biface. It is evident the two main reduction strategies at TH.143a were the production of elongated blanks and the production of bifacial tools.

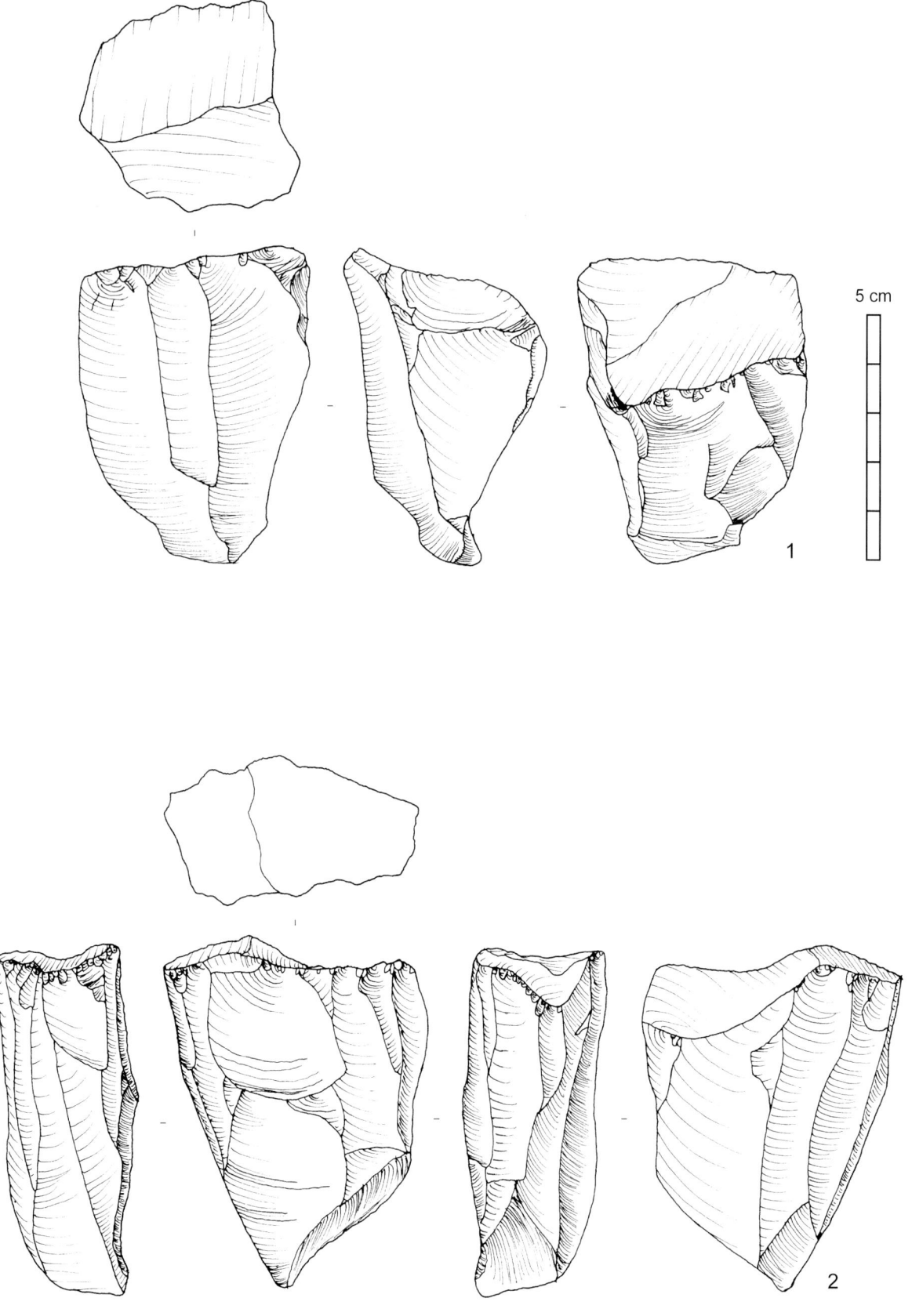

5 cm

Figure 4.23. TH.262 blade cores (illustrations by Y.H. Hilbert).

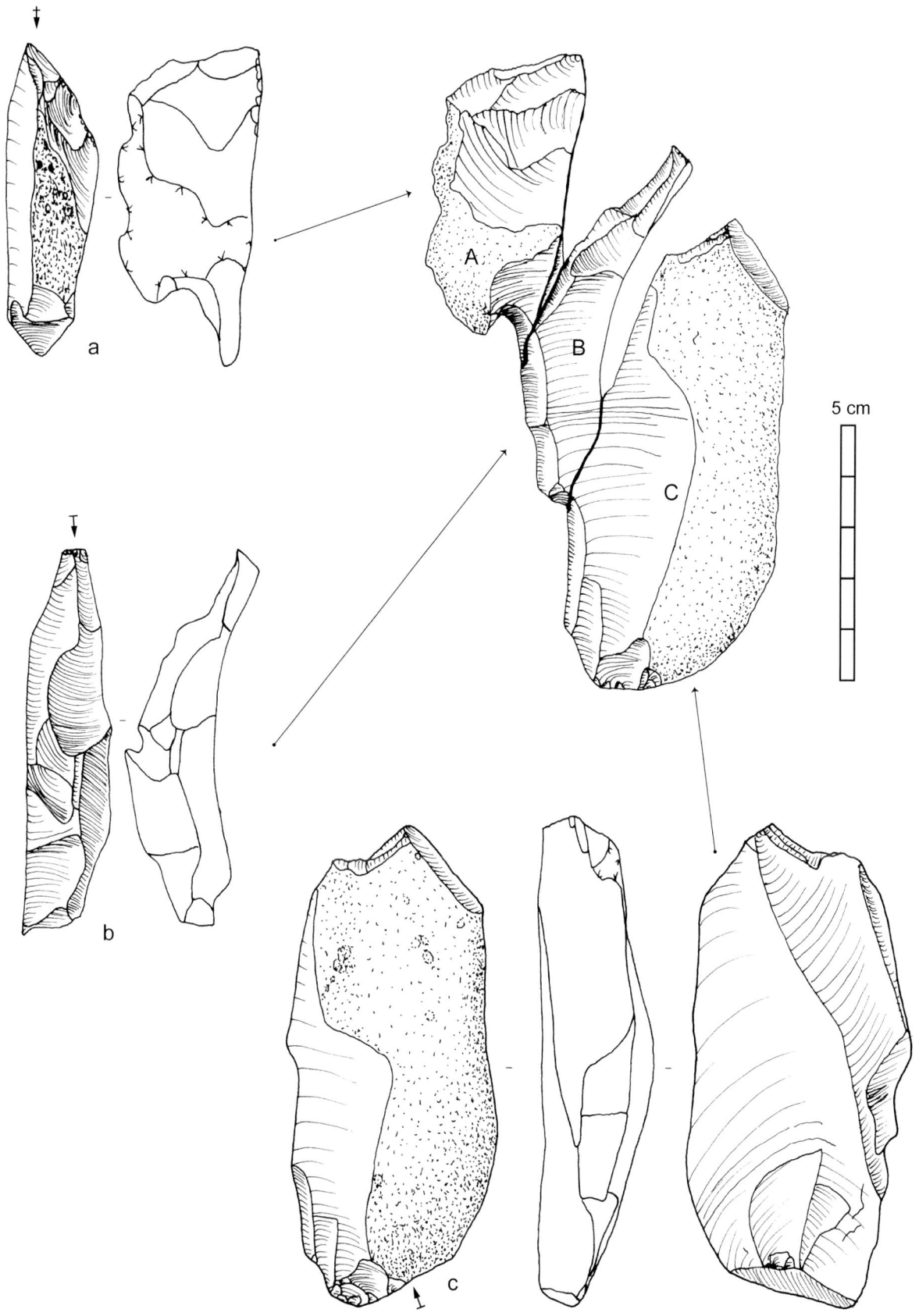

Figure 4.24. TH.262 core-on-flake refittings (illustrations by Y.H. Hilbert).

Table 4.9. Artifact counts from TH.262.

Artifact type	N	Percentage
Débitage	**119**	**82%**
Flakes	*45*	*30%*
Blades	*28*	*18%*
Bladelet	*1*	*1%*
Cortical flake	*27*	*18%*
Cortical blades	*13*	*9%*
Débordant flake	*1*	*1%*
Débordant blade	*4*	*3%*
Knapping debris	*28*	*19%*
Crested blade	*1*	*1%*
Cores	**18**	**12%**
Single platform convergent cores	*1*	*6%*
Single platform parallel	*8*	*44%*
Opposed platform core	*2*	*11%*
Two unopposed platform core	*2*	*11%*
Multiple platform cores	*2*	*11%*
Perpendicular core surface	*1*	*6%*
Core on flake	*2*	*11%*
Tools	**9**	**6%**
End Scraper	*1*	*11%*
Biface	*3*	*34%*
Side Scraper	*3*	*33%*
Perforator	*1*	*11%*
Retouched flake	*1*	*11%*
Total	**138**	**100%**

Cores make up 7% of the total lithic assemblage; most are either exhausted blade cores or early stage cores that have been discarded after a maximum of three removals. The number of cores is low relative to the surrounding débitage. Scar patterns, blank shape and striking platforms are summarized in Table 4.13. Blades and flakes typically have unidirectional dorsal scars, with some variants showing bidirectional, convergent and unidirectional-crested patterns. Débordant flakes and blades are present in low numbers. Flakes have predominantly expanding edges, while blades typically exhibit parallel and convergent edges, resulting in an elongated pointed shape (Figure 4.27).

Débitage striking platforms are mostly straight, however, a low percentage of specimens show faceting. These are primarily bifacial thinning flakes, where the faceting is an incidental feature of bifacial reduction. There are no lipped striking platforms and bulbs of percussion are prominent, suggesting hard hammer percussion. A large 435 g hammerstone was found within the collection area, perhaps one of the percussors used to produce this assemblage. Several blades (n=27) show evidence of partial or full platform abrasion, as do five of the biface thinning flakes.

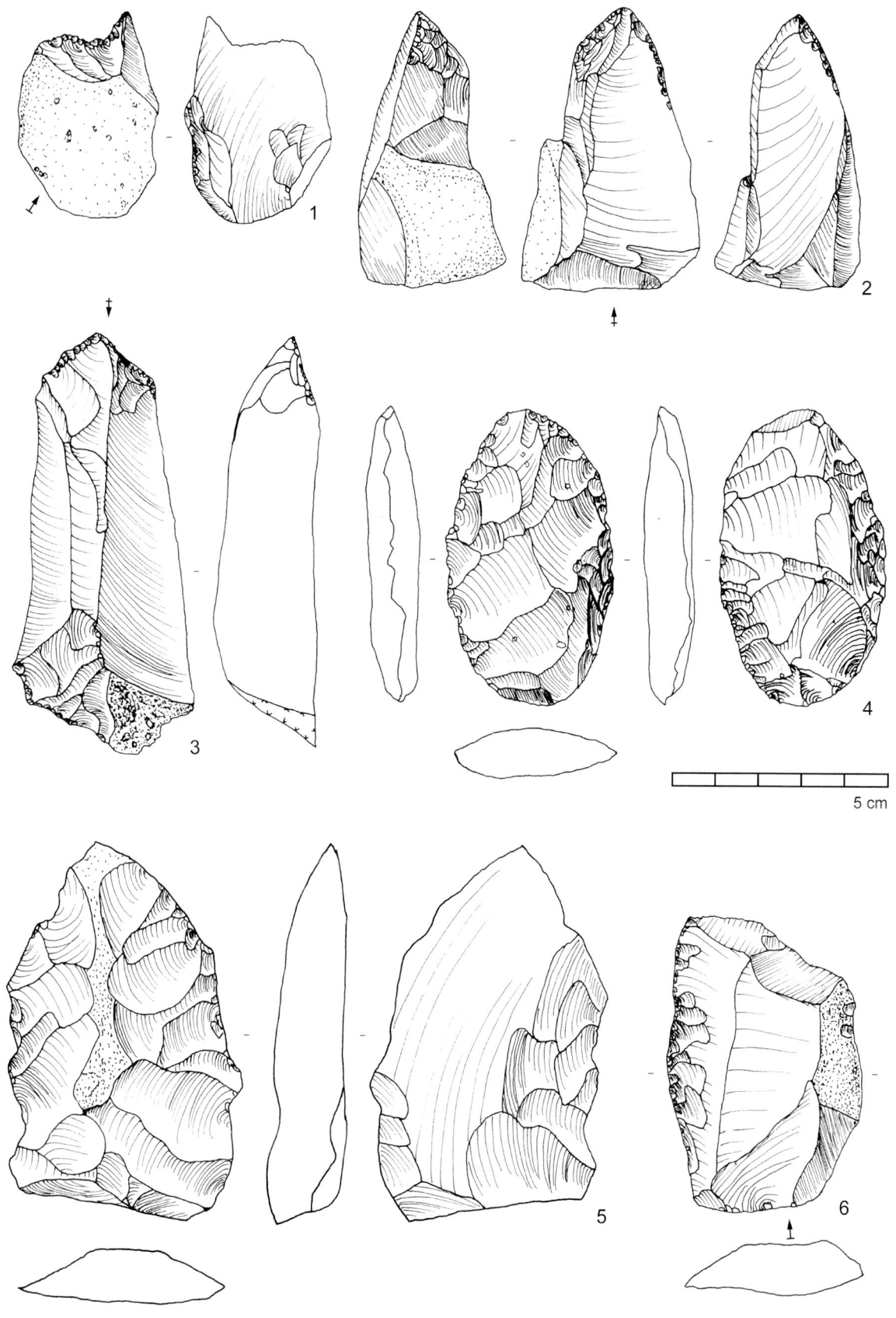

Figure 4.25. TH.262 tools: (1) piercer, (2,3) ogival end scrapers, (4) bifacial foliate, (5) bifacial preform, (6) retouched blade (illustrations by Y.H. Hilbert).

Table 4.10. Débitage attributes from TH.262.

Scar pattern	Flake	Blade	Cortical blade	Cortical flake	Crested blade	Débordant blade	Débordant flake
Opposed	1						
Transverse	2						
Unidirectional crested	2						
Bidirectional	4	3				1	
Convergent	3	1					
Crested					1		
Parallel	2	5					
Unidirectional	27	17	10	14		3	1
Unidirectional Crossed	4	3					

Blank shape	Flake	Blade	Cortical blade	Cortical flake	Crested blade	Débordant blade	Débordant flake
Convergent	2	2	1	1	1		
Lateral	7	4	4	1		2	
Expanding	13	6	2	6			
Irregular	5	1	2	6			
Ovoid	7	1	2	11			
Parallel	13	16	3	3		2	1

Striking platform	Flake	Blade	Cortical blade	Cortical flake	Crested blade	Débordant blade	Débordant flake
Absent/ unidentifiable	2	1		2			
Cortex	8	4	1	3		1	
Crushed	3	3				1	
Dihedral	1	2		1	1		
Faceted	1						
Punctiform		1					
Unfaceted	27	14	10	18		2	1

Figure 4.26. TH.143 Late Palaeolithic collection area (photograph by the authors).

Table 4.11. Débitage metric data from TH.262.

Length (mm)	Max Length	Min Length	Avg Length	StDev Length	Count
Flake	89,69	20,84	47,29842105	14,04412112	38
Blade	95,57	16,25	63,7147619	20,01043168	21
Cortical flake	92,83	33,02	56,79952381	14,93041308	21
Cortical blade	108,01	24,24	74,69083333	24,02815298	12
Débordant flake	87,54	87,54	87,54		1
Débordant blade	102,9	62,74	78,4875	17,43552958	4
Width (mm)	Max Widths	Min Widths	Avg Widths	StDev Widths	Count
Flake	60,97	14,17	37,55340909	10,01783942	44
Blade	42,21	4,32	23,89444444	9,613689892	27
Cortical flake	64,43	22,45	39,07777778	9,521478284	27
Cortical blade	53,05	12,21	35,83384615	11,57247059	13
Débordant flake	48,39	48,39	48,39		1
Débordant blade	38,25	15,15	24,3025	10,20308899	4
Thickness (mm)	Max Thickness	Min Thickness	Avg Thickness	StDev Thickness	Count
Flake	29,62	4,38	10,67066667	4,933999116	45
Blade	26	4,83	11,31285714	5,979760219	28
Cortical flake	26,09	5,58	14,24703704	5,027650327	27
Cortical blade	33	8,72	18,08076923	8,135903414	13
Débordant flake	19,83	19,83	19,83		1
Débordant blade	17,35	11,54	14,53	3,253623621	4
Weight (g)	Max Weight	Min Weight	Avg Weight	StDev Weight	Count
Flake	154	2	23,95454545	24,68023835	44
Blade	109	4	26,5	25,23110572	24
Cortical flake	110	11	32,7037037	27,74168595	27
Cortical blade	162	12	57,5	48,61256852	12
Débordant flake	117	117	117		1
Débordant blade	50	17	32,25	17,7270979	4

Table 4.12. Artifact counts from TH.143 Late Palaeolithic component.

Artifact type	N	Percentage
Débitage	**179**	**91%**
Flakes	*49*	*27%*
Blades	*54*	*30%*
Cortical flakes	*17*	*9%*
Cortical blades	*22*	*12%*
Débordant elements	*19*	*11%*
Bifacial thinning element	*13*	*7%*
Chip	*3*	*2%*
Knapping debris	*1*	*1%*
Crested blade	*1*	*1%*
Cores	**13**	**7%**
Unidirectional parallel blade cores	*6*	*46%*
Unidirectional convergent blade core	*2*	*16%*
Opposed Platform core,	*2*	*15%*
Tested nodule	*3*	*23%*
Tools	**5**	**2%**
Retouched blades	*2*	*40%*
Biface	*1*	*20%*
Hammerstone	*1*	*20%*
Notch	*1*	*20%*
Total	**197**	**100%**

The size of blanks is relatively variable (Table 4.14). The largest four blades, all more than 20 cm in length, exhibit a darker patina than the rest of the assemblage. It is noteworthy that among these aberrant pieces was the crested blade; a technological feature that is not found in the Late Palaeolithic and is presently only known locally in low frequencies from Mudayyan late Middle Palaeolithic assemblages and the TH.68 Upper Palaeolithic findspot. The rest of the blade débitage averages 7 cm in length, which is consistent with the size of the cores. The limited number of tools is typical of Late Palaeolithic workshop sites, producing retouched blades and a plano-convex ovate biface (Figure 4.28).

In sum, the TH.143a assemblage appears to be a typical Late Palaeolithic blade and biface workshop. Four anomalously large blanks, including a crested blade, suggest that there is an older Upper Palaeolithic component present as well. An expanded collection area around this findspot may be useful for studying the composition of a palimpsest Upper and Late Palaeolithic surface scatter to examine spatial, taphonomic and technological variability between the two phases.

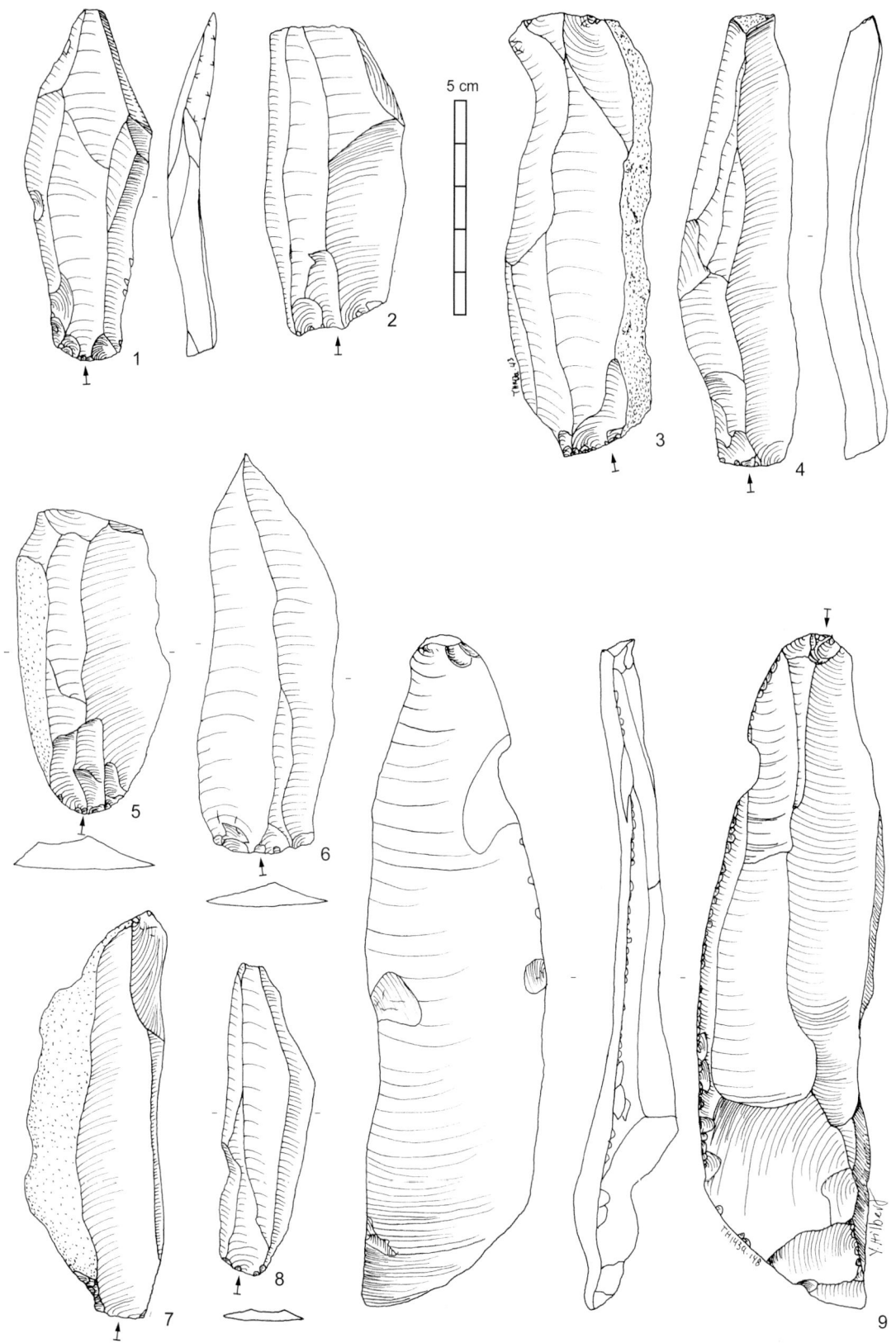

5 cm

Figure 4.27. TH.143 artifacts: (1-8) Late Palaeolithic blade debitage, (9) retouched blade (illustrations by Y.H. Hilbert).

Table 4.13. Débitage attributes from TH.143 Late Palaeolithic component.

Scar pattern	Flake	BTE	Blade	Cortical blade	Cortical flake	Crested blade	Débordant blade	Débordant flake
Bidirectional	5	2	3		1		4	
Convergent	3	1	9				2	
Opposed		1		1				
Parallel	1		5				2	1
Radial		2						
Transverse					1			
Unidirectional	30	5	32	8	2		8	
Unidirectional Crested	1		3			1	1	
Unidirectional Crossed	8	2	2					

Blank shape	Flake	BTE	Blade	Cortical Blade	Cortical Flake	Crested blade	Débordant blade	Débordant flake
Convergent	3	2	12	3	1		1	
Lateral	4		11	6	2		8	
Expanding	16	5	3	1	2		2	1
Irregular	7	5	4	6	4		1	
Ovoid	7	1	1	2	3			
Parallel	11		22	5	3	1	5	
Sinuous			2					

Striking Platform	Flake	BTE	Blade	Cortical Blade	Cortical Flake	Crested blade	Débordant blade	Débordant flake
Absent	3	1						
Cortex	2		1	2	2			
Crushed	3	1	6	1	1			
Dihedral	1				1			
Faceted	2	4	1					
Punctiform	1		1					
Transverse	1		2		1			
Unfaceted	31	7	38	17	10	1	17	1

TH.38

Findspot TH.38 is located just over five kilometers east of the village of Shisr, on the northern-central Nejd. The local landscape is a lifeless, gently undulating gravel plain covered in a thin veneer of surface sands. Beneath the surface is a petrogypsic soil horizon typical of xeric environments. Weathered chert nodules are found eroding from the low hills 500 m to the north of the site. The material is a medium-grained grayish-brown chert with fossil impurities.

Artifacts were systematically collected within a 5 x 8 m grid (Figure 4.29). The assemblage shows minimal wind abrasion, minor edge damage and no gloss or patina. In contrast, a handful of older Middle Palaeolithic Levallois cores were found at the site (Figure 4.30: 7) with moderate to heavy chemical dissolution and a yellow-brown patina.

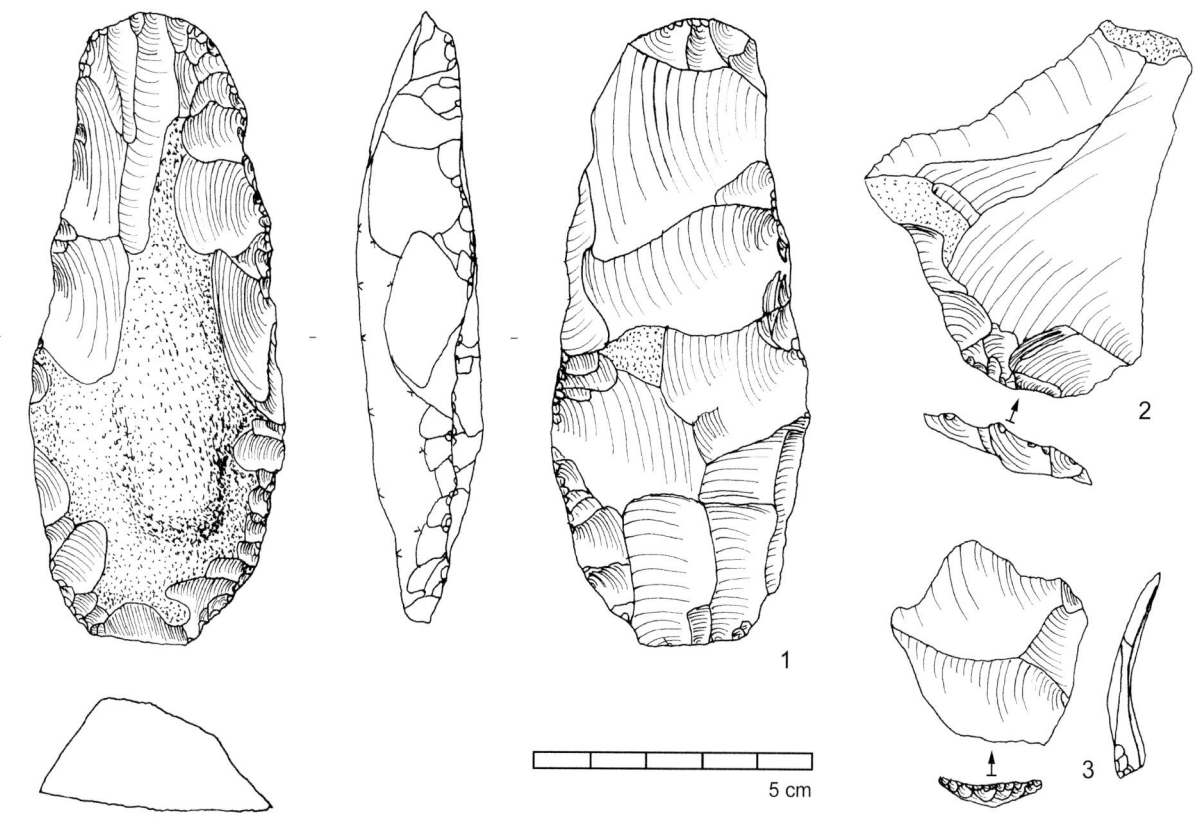

Figure 4.28. TH.143 Late Palaeolithic biface and bifacial thinning elements (illustrations by Y.H. Hilbert).

The assemblage comprises 748 artifacts including primarily débitage (94%), while cores and tools are rare (Table 4.15). Among the débitage, 17% are under 2 cm, indicating there has been minimal post-depositional disturbance. The low percentages of débordant elements, which are typical in the Late Palaeolithic for maintaining the core's working surface, may indicate some variability in blade blank production systems and/or may be a function of the distance to the raw material source (i.e., stage of reduction).

Débitage attributes are summarized in Table 4.16. Blades and flakes most commonly exhibit unidirectional and unidirectional-parallel scar patterns (Figures 4.31 and 4.32), while a low percentage have bidirectional scars. Débordant elements are variable, demonstrating unidirectional-crested, transverse-crested, opposed and bidirectional scar patterns. The crested débitage was not produced by a classic cresting technique; rather, they are the byproducts of core rejuvenation. After one working surface was exhausted, Late Palaeolithic flintknappers sometimes turned the core and began removing elongated blanks from an adjacent surface. The first few blanks removed from the intersection of the striking platform and the old working surface exhibit crested scars morphologically similar, but unrelated to the *lame à crete* technique.

The flakes show some variability in shape, including expanding, lateral, ovate and parallel edges. Blades typically have parallel and convergent edges. Striking platforms are almost exclusively straight and unmodified. Of the 501 extant platforms, only nine specimens were faceted and 19 dihedral. Platform abrasion is almost entirely absent (n=8). Analysis of blank sizes indicates that blades are smaller that cortical elements. These larger cortical elements provide an indication of the maximum core length (Table 4.17). The longest blade measures 16 cm, suggesting large blocks of raw material were reduced on site.

Figure 4.29. Late Palaeolithic collection area near Shisr Farms (photograph by the authors).

The assemblage includes 27 cores, typically exhibiting single platform unidirectional-parallel reduction systems (Figures 4.33 and 4.34), with a low percentage of opposed platform cores (Figure 4.35). Refittings on the opposed platform cores indicate that the platforms were not used simultaneously, differing from the Mudayyan Middle Palaeolithic bidirectional reduction system. In this case, the second platform did not serve to correct or shape the working surface of the core. There is a portion of the debitage with complex dorsal scar patterns (Figure 4.36) that is consistent with this variant of opposed platform reduction.

The cores are medium in size, averaging 9 cm in length, 8 cm in width and 6 cm in thickness. Working surfaces are typically on the broad face of the nodule, which may be one explanation for the relatively low percentage of débordant elements. Débordant reduction from the lateral edges of the core is still present, however and appears to have been the only strategy for maintaining convexity as illustrated by the refittings in Figures 4.37, 4.38 and 4.39.

There are 19 tools in the assemblage, of which 12 are classified as bifaces and bifacial preforms. The seven preforms are from early stages of manufacture and appear to have been discarded due to knapping errors, while four of the more complete bifaces were fragments. Other retouched tools include an end scraper, perforator, side scraper made on an elongated cortical blank and four retouched pieces (Figure 4.40).

The artifacts from TH.38 fall outside the metric range of other Late Palaeolithic sites on the southern Nejd Plateau (Al-Hatab, Khamseen and Ghazal rockshelters). This may simply be due to the large chert nodules available in the nearby hills, some of which exceed 50 cm. The technological, typological and taphonomic characteristics, however, fit comfortably within the Late Palaeolithic.

TH.34

Findspot TH.34 was found on a low erosional terrace just above the Al-Hatab collapsed rockshelter. The artifacts were collected from a 5 x 6 m grid (Figures 4.41 and 4.42), for the purpose of comparing stratified and surface assemblages to test whether the buried Al-Hatab assemblage had originated on the terrace and fallen into secondary position as the gully cut downward during the Early Holocene.

The raw material used at the site is almost exclusively local banded Gahit chert with a thin dark cortex. Gahit nodules are found eroding from the scarp immediately below. The weathering of the artifacts is also fairly homogenous and lithics are patinated a light brown color, with little to no chemical dissolution.

A total of 915 artifacts were collected, including 84% débitage, 11% cores and 5% tools (Table 4.18). Flakes and cortical flakes are the most common débitage, followed by blades are débordant blades that together make up 25% of the total blanks. Despite excavating and sieving the surface layer, chips were found in low numbers. The collection area was positioned on a low gradient slope, which may explain their absence due to post-depositional transport from gravity and surface wash. The TH.34 artifacts show minimal edge damage, suggesting that the larger pieces have remained undisturbed and are in a good state of preservation. The ratio of cores and pre-cores to débitage is relatively high, indicating that nodules were tested and discarded on site.

Attribute analyses on the TH.34 assemblage is summarized in Table 4.19. Dorsal scar patterns are mostly unidirectional; the number of blanks showing non-unidirectional scar patterns accounts for 13% of the total debitage. Blades and flakes have similar scar patterns, although the latter exhibit greater variability.

Table 4.14. Débitage metric data from TH.143 Late Palaeolithic component.

Length (mm)	Max Length	Min Length	Avg Length	StDev Length	Count
Flake	99,74	22,34	48,68444444	18,8638515	45
Blade	201,65	34,95	75,9215	34,28734472	40
Cortical flake	110,58	22,65	57,432	24,36003495	15
Cortical blade	218,54	38,18	100,0721053	35,98211756	19
Débordant flake	64,57	64,57	64,57		1
Débordant blade	123,84	65,58	96,84941176	15,86445062	17
BTE	64,1	26,9	42,51307692	12,91302404	13
Width (mm)	Max Widths	Min Widths	Avg Widths	StDev Widths	Count
Flake	96,08	19,59	38,86770833	16,92633504	48
Blade	60,86	9,79	26,15788462	9,747222095	52
Cortical flake	100,93	20,25	43,69	19,260676	16
Cortical blade	55,51	14,45	31,26454545	11,35944446	22
Débordant flake	43,18	43,18	43,18		1
Débordant blade	47,49	20,08	32,41176471	7,092344672	17
BTE	63,94	18,32	36,00461538	14,099998	13
Thickness (mm)	Max Thickness	Min Thickness	Avg Thickness	StDev Thickness	Count
Flake	24,98	3,24	9,398571429	4,316211205	49
Blade	29,04	4,04	9,005849057	5,439267992	53
Cortical flake	28,03	5,06	13,86470588	7,62145419	17
Cortical blade	55,44	5,73	18,41681818	10,9154174	22
Débordant flake	14,12	14,12	14,12		1
Débordant blade	24,08	10,11	16,63764706	4,245173037	17
BTE	7,15	3,48	5,456153846	0,985110302	13
Weight (g)	Max Weight(g)	Min Weight(g)	Avg Weight(g)	StDev Weight(g)	Count
Flake	228	3	27,32653061	41,80380154	49
Blade	247	3	27,47169811	43,03067053	53
Cortical flake	235	4	46,52941176	58,83145167	17
Cortical blade	740	3	87,85714286	153,9614516	21
Débordant flake	45	45	45		1
Débordant blade	110	23	66,52941176	23,64084825	17
BTE	20	3	9,769230769	5,890017631	13

Figure 4.30. Artifacts from TH.38 (photographs by Y.H. Hilbert).

Table 4.15. Artifact counts from TH.38.

Artifact type	N	Percentage
Débitage	**702**	**94%**
Flake	*242*	*35%*
Blade	*164*	*23%*
Cortical flake	*98*	*14%*
Cortical blade	*30*	*4%*
Débordant flake	*15*	*2%*
Débordant blade	*35*	*5%*
Chip	*118*	*17%*
Cores	**27**	**4%**
Single platform convergent core	*1*	*4%*
Single platform parallel core	*20*	*74%*
Opposed platform core	*2*	*7%*
Two unopposed platform core	*1*	*4%*
Multiple platform core	*1*	*4%*
Perpendicular core	*2*	*7%*
Tools	**19**	**2%**
End scraper	*1*	*5%*
Retouched piece	*4*	*22%*
Piercer	*1*	*5%*
Biface	*12*	*63%*
Side scraper	*1*	*5%*
Total	**748**	**100%**

In terms of shape, the flakes have parallel, expanding, or convergent edges. Blades and débordant blades are mostly parallel or irregular in shape, while convergent edges are rare (Figure 4.43).

Striking platforms are mostly straight and unmodified. Of the 754 blanks analyzed, only 37 specimens had evidence of partial platform abrasion. There was minimal platform lipping and blanks have prominent bulbs of percussion, indicative of hard hammer percussion. Blanks are medium in size and homogenous in length, width and thickness (Table 4.20).

Most of the cores are single platform with parallel or convergent scars (Figure 4.44). These are generally small and exhausted, with flat working surfaces. Hinge fractures are common on the working surfaces. Some of the cores can be classified as Wa'shah (Crassard 2008b), which produced pointed blades and bladelets that are notably absent within the TH.34 assemblage. Striking platforms have received little preparation and are mostly set up by a single blow, or strategically placed on a natural fracture plain. Other core types include a discoid (Figure 4.45), multiple platform cores, flat unidirectional-convergent cores, perpendicular cores that have removals from two independent striking platforms arranged at a right angle to one another and opposed platform cores. The opposed platform cores are similar to TH.38, where the platforms have been used separately to produce blanks from adjacent working surfaces.

Table 4.16. Débitage attributes from TH.38.

Scar pattern	Flake	BTE	Blade	Cortical blade	Cortical flake	Débordant blade	Débordant flake
Bidirectional	7		6			4	1
Convergent	15		25			3	
Opposed	4		2		2	2	
Parallel	12		15			1	
Radial	4	2					
Transverse	5			1	3	2	
Traverses crested							2
Unidirectional	164		100	17	19	21	7
Unidirectional Crested	1					2	3
Unidirectional Crossed	18		15		1	2	1

Blank shape	Flake	BTE	Blade	Cortical blade	Cortical flake	Débordant blade	Débordant flake
Convergent	46		38	4	10	8	1
Lateral	20	1	12	10	6	9	1
Expanding	87		36	3	29	8	8
Irregular	7	1			6	1	1
Ovoid	28		1	2	14		2
Parallel	51		75	9	12	11	1

Striking Platform	Flake	BTE	Blade	Cortical blade	Cortical flake	Débordant blade	Débordant flake
Absent	22		9	5	7		2
Cortex	18		2	3	14	6	1
Crushed	25		9	2	5	2	3
Dihedral	13		2	1	2		
Faceted	3	2	2		1	1	
Punctiform	2		2		3	1	
Unfaceted	141		102	17	43	21	7

There were 16 conjoins in the assemblage, three of which are illustrated in Figure 4.46. Refitting A includes two débordant elements reattached to a core. The core bears a series of successive débordant removals that created a central ridge to guide the subsequently detached blanks. The blades and elongated flakes struck from this ridge had convergent edges, typical of the Wa'shah method. Two débordant blades were refitted to the core, making it possible to identify a second ridge on the cores main plane of removal. The subsequent hinged negative along this second ridge may be the failed attempt to remove a pointed blade. Refitted blanks were struck from both edges of the core. Refitting B shows a débordant flake reattached to a core. The core is classified as a Wa'shah type based on the scar pattern on its frontal plane and the reduction system seen in the refitting. The core has a single platform from which convergent blanks were struck. The refitted blank is a débordant flake detached from the edge of the core's plane of removal. The refit exhibits negatives of two unidirectional removals, the latter overlaps the earlier detached blank. Although unidirectional, the removal does not show a parallel scar pattern.

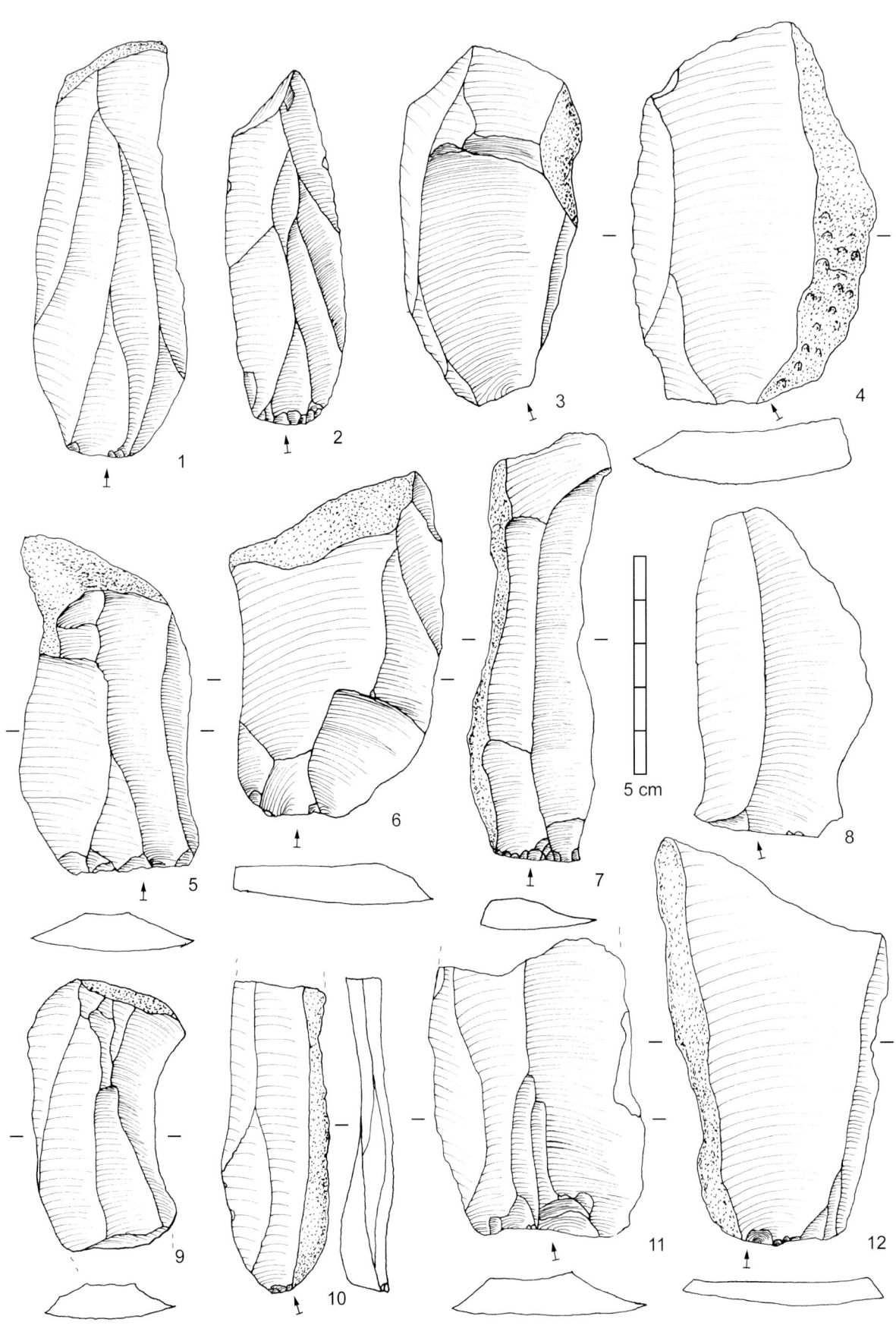

Figure 4.31. Debitage from TH.38 (illustrations by Y.H. Hilbert).

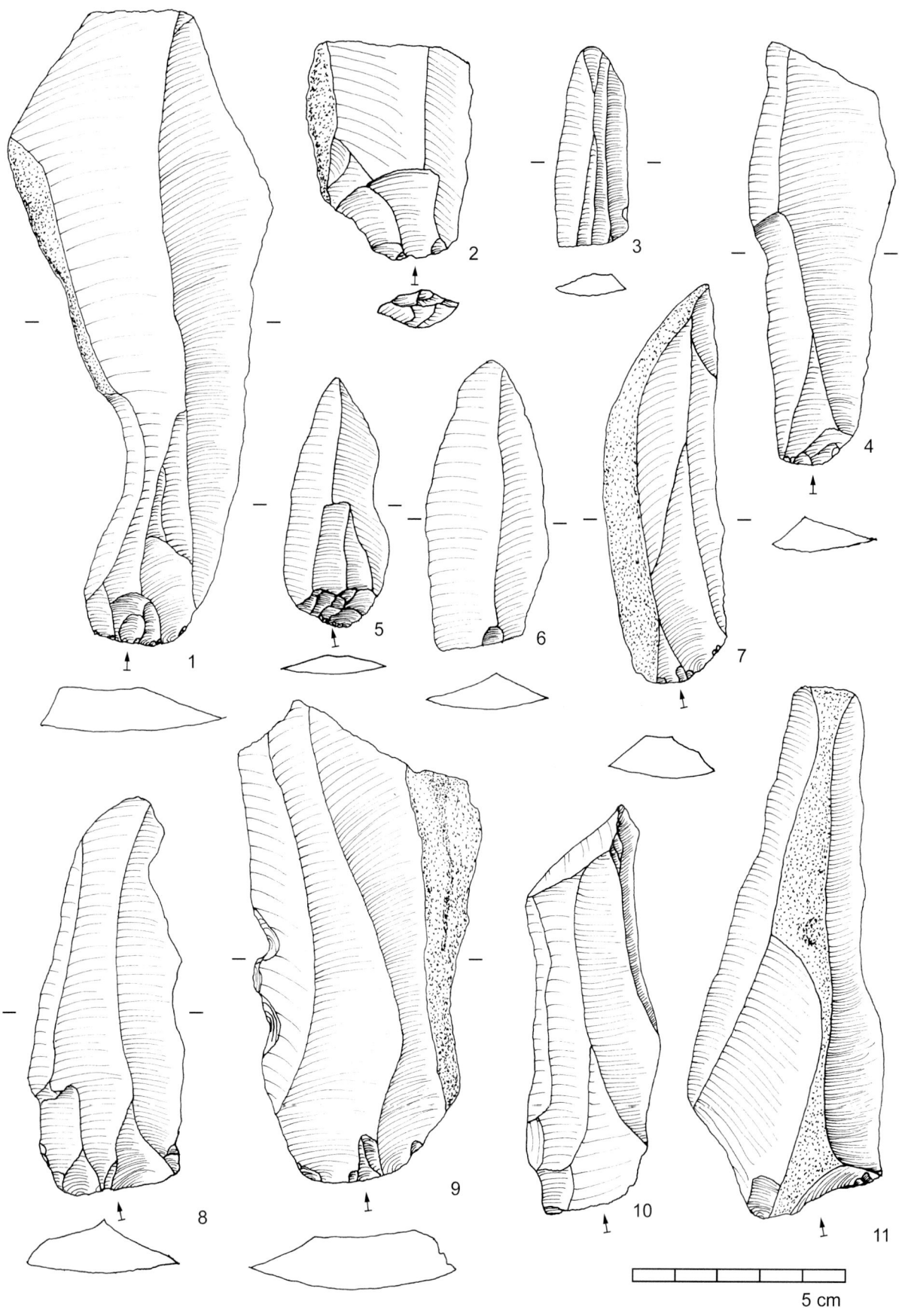

Figure 4.32.Debitage from TH.38 (illustrations by Y.H. Hilbert)

Table 4.17. Débitage metric data from TH.38.

Length (mm)	Max Length	Min Length	Avg Length	StDev Length	Count
Flake	144,69	22,96	56,6526943	19,57691144	193
Blade	161,28	34,39	71,09360825	22,96708393	97
Cortical flake	141,64	26,06	64,58115942	23,83155271	69
Cortical blade	151,76	47,66	93,37384615	26,77853425	26
Débordant flake	126,62	41,96	67,74230769	22,03247798	13
Débordant blade	140,94	60,5	91,34125	19,99008621	32
BTF	66,12	53,33	59,725	9,043895731	2
Width (mm)	Max Widths	Min Widths	Avg Widths	StDev Widths	Count
Flake	127,73	14,61	42,13915612	15,87049913	237
Blade	50,47	4,29	26,6368323	7,92203552	161
Cortical flake	120,45	21,5	52,96101266	19,68924141	79
Cortical blade	66,98	15,17	34,35178571	11,61872246	28
Débordant flake	69,51	24,25	43,99357143	13,8762307	14
Débordant blade	85	15,55	33,33810811	12,92177573	37
BTF	63,21	42,06	52,635	14,95530842	2
Thickness (mm)	Max Thickness	Min Thickness	Avg Thickness	StDev Thickness	Count
Flake	52,75	2,61	13,33620253	7,832993232	237
Blade	27,93	3,56	9,700123457	4,193236937	162
Cortical flake	142	3,85	17,90443038	16,37667124	79
Cortical blade	25,6	4,74	14,5775	5,44150825	28
Débordant flake	54,65	6,63	23,575	13,09751165	14
Débordant blade	63,45	7,62	17,10055556	9,679366846	36
BTF	25,42	12,08	18,75	9,432804461	2
Weight (g)	Max Weight(g)	Min Weight(g)	Avg Weight(g)	StDev Weight(g)	Count
Flake	922	4	52,99122807	87,28292097	228
Blade	373	3	27,10967742	38,16719332	155
Cortical flake	408	5	83,51282051	85,94391762	78
Cortical blade	326	3	72,89285714	74,91790039	28
Débordant flake	377	12	92,5	98,54928482	14
Débordant blade	597	11	73,94444444	98,14186363	36
BTF	67	37	52	21,21320344	2

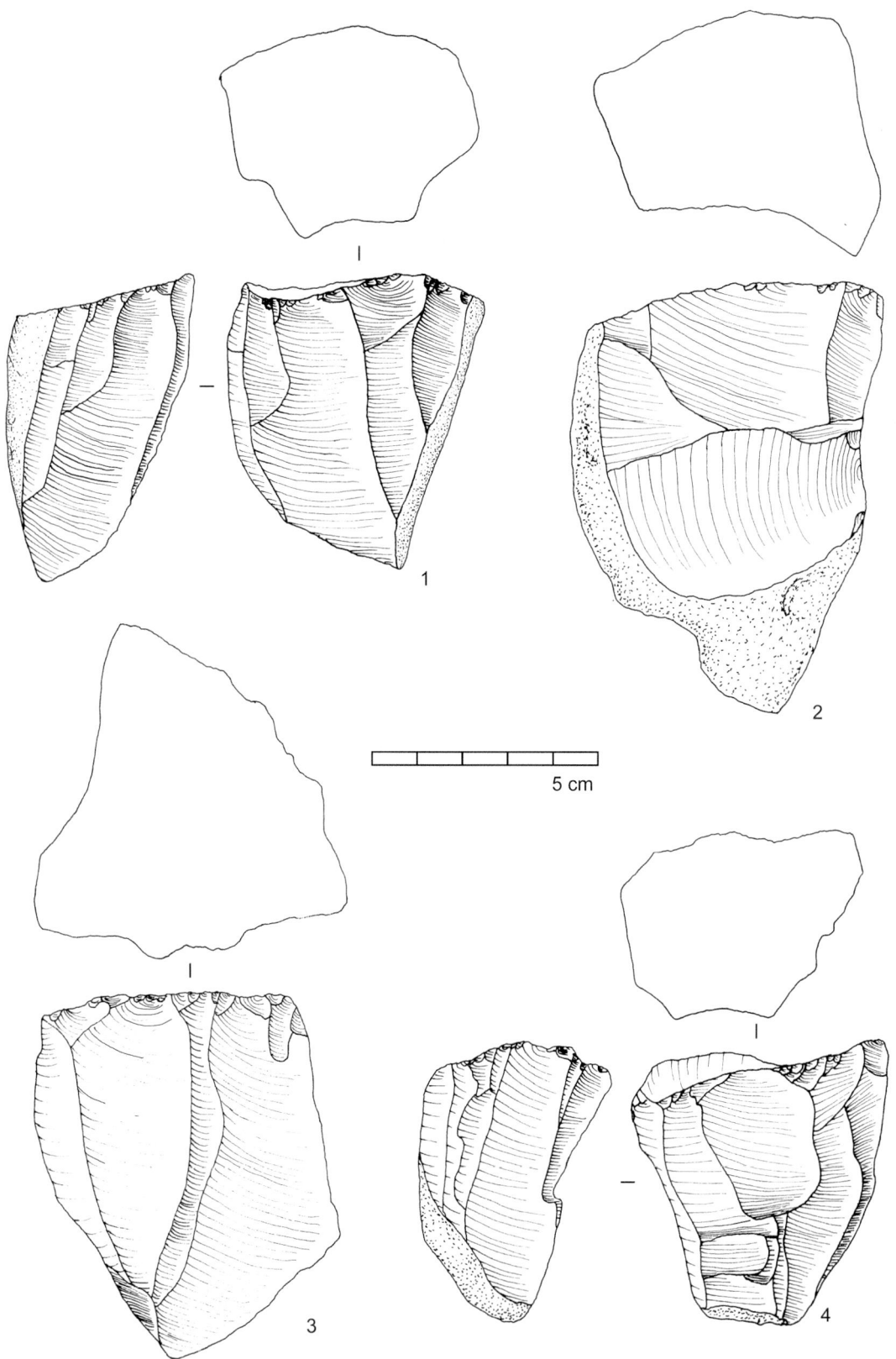

5 cm

Figure 4.33. Cores from TH.38: (1,3,4) single platform unidirectional cores, (2) perpendicular core (illustrations by Y.H. Hilbert).

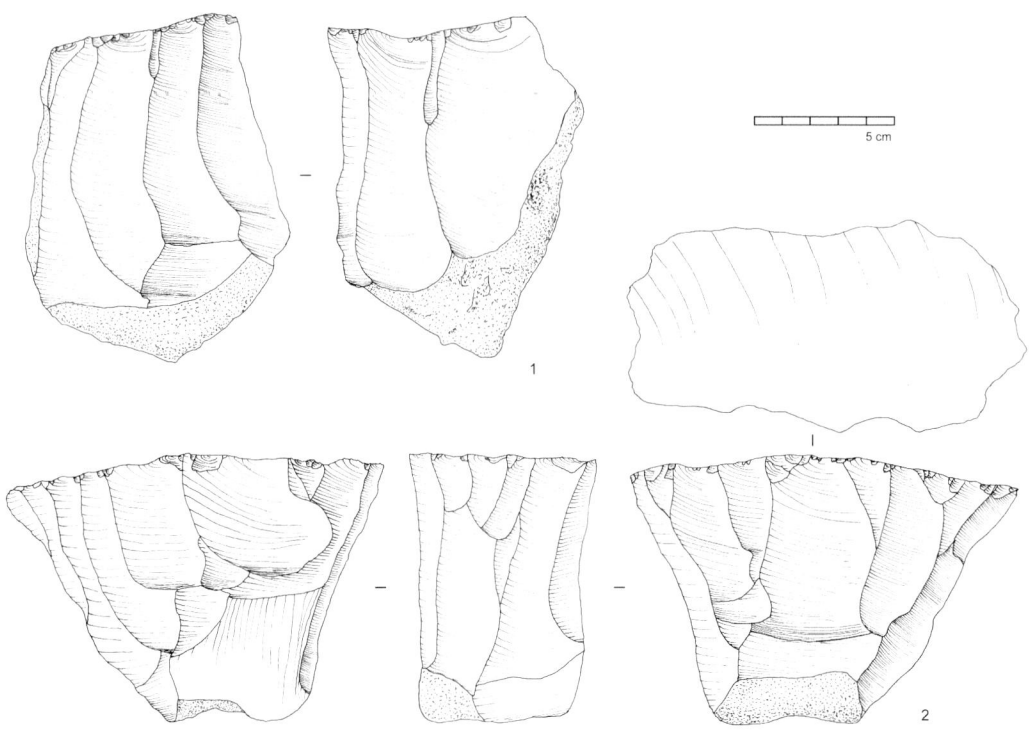

Figure 4.34. Large flake cores from TH.38 (illustrations by Y.H. Hilbert).

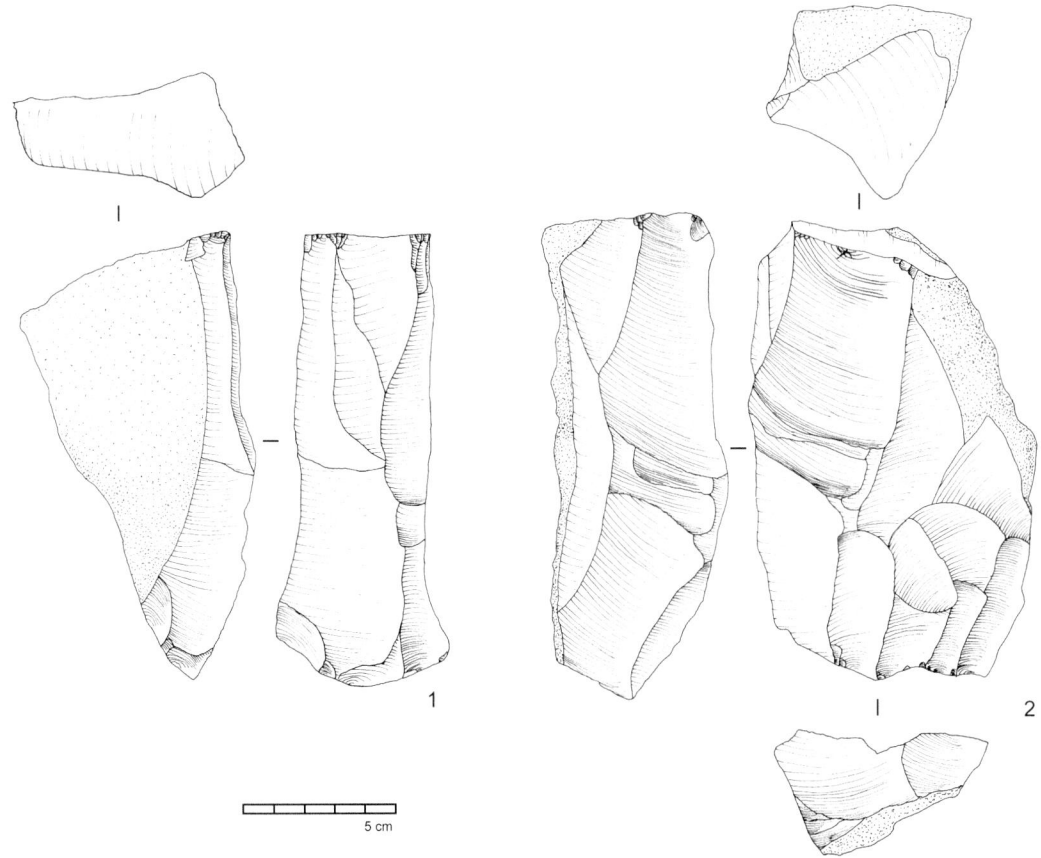

Figure 4.35. Large bidirectional opposed platform cores from TH.38 (illustrations by Y.H. Hilbert).

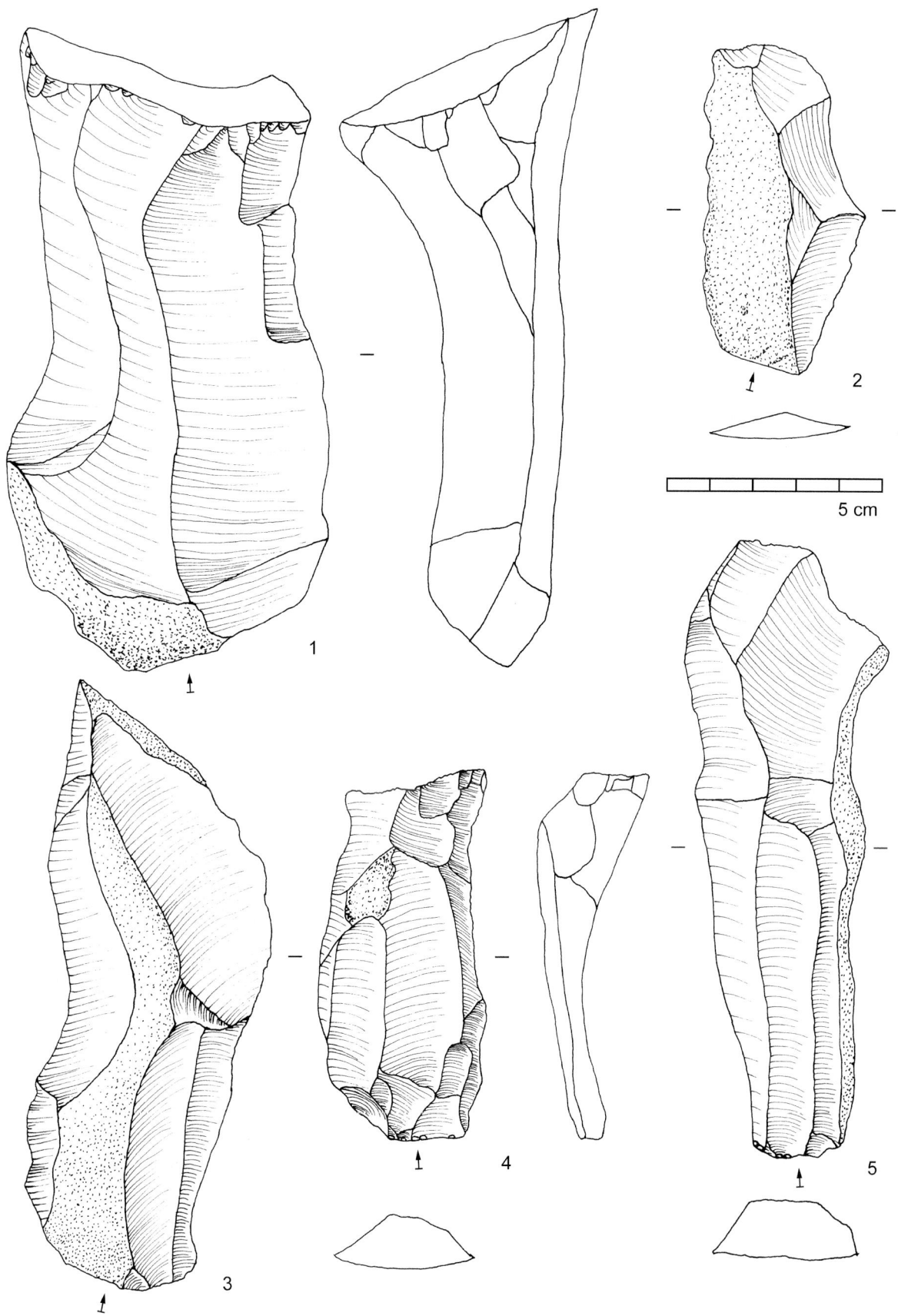

Figure 4.36. Debitage from TH.38 with complex scar patterns (illustrations by Y.H. Hilbert).

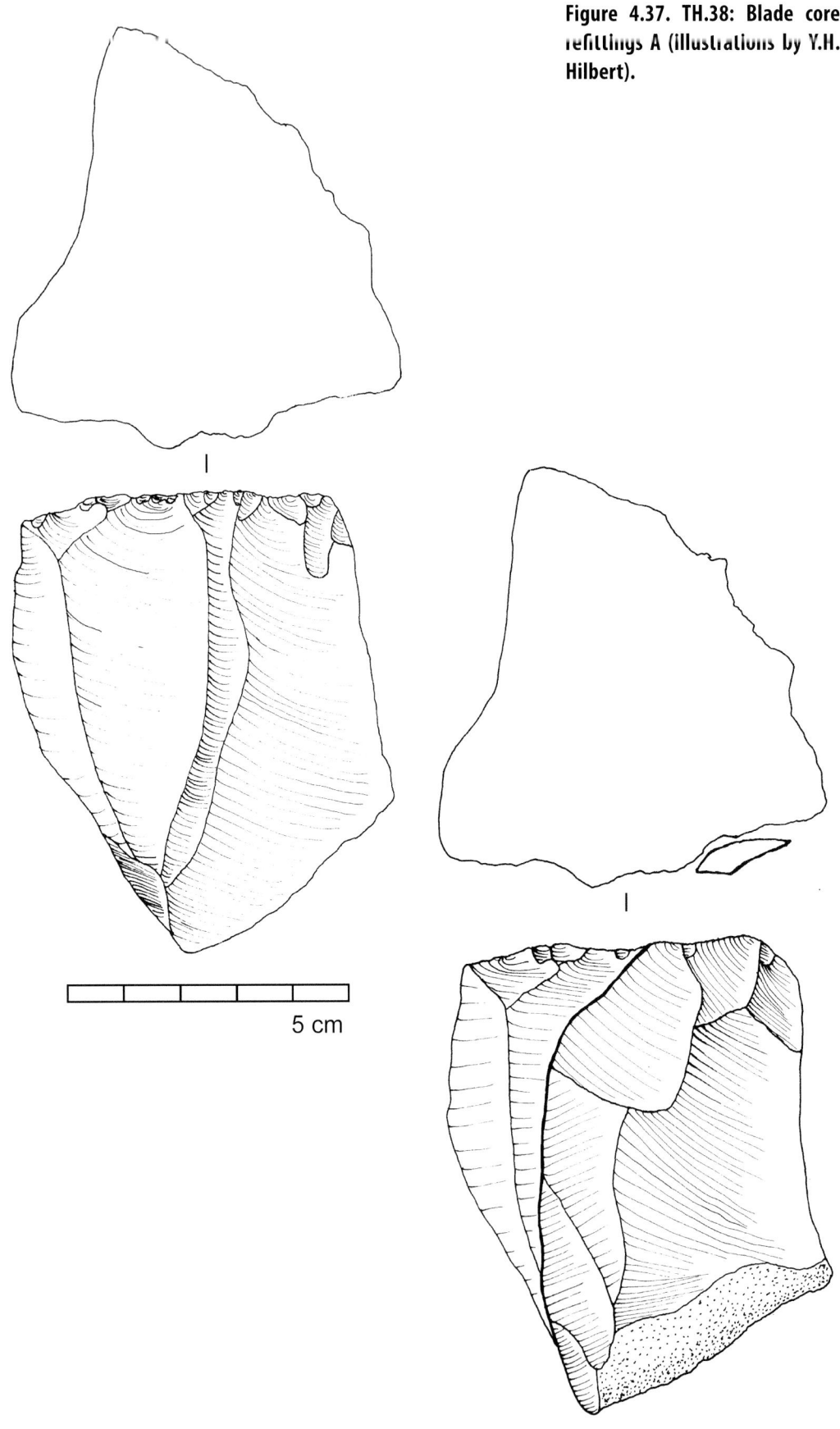

5 cm

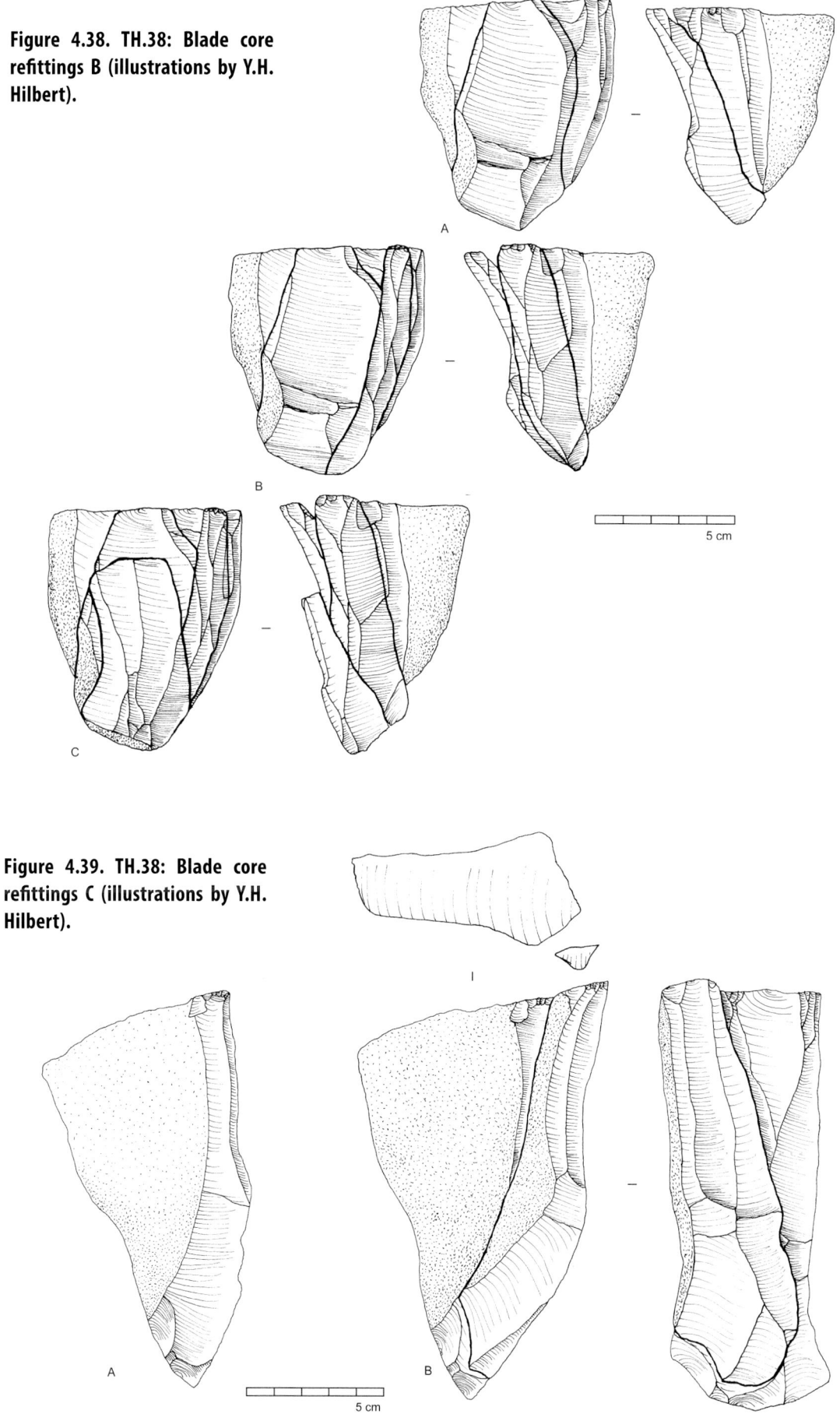

Figure 4.38. TH.38: Blade core refittings B (illustrations by Y.H. Hilbert).

Figure 4.39. TH.38: Blade core refittings C (illustrations by Y.H. Hilbert).

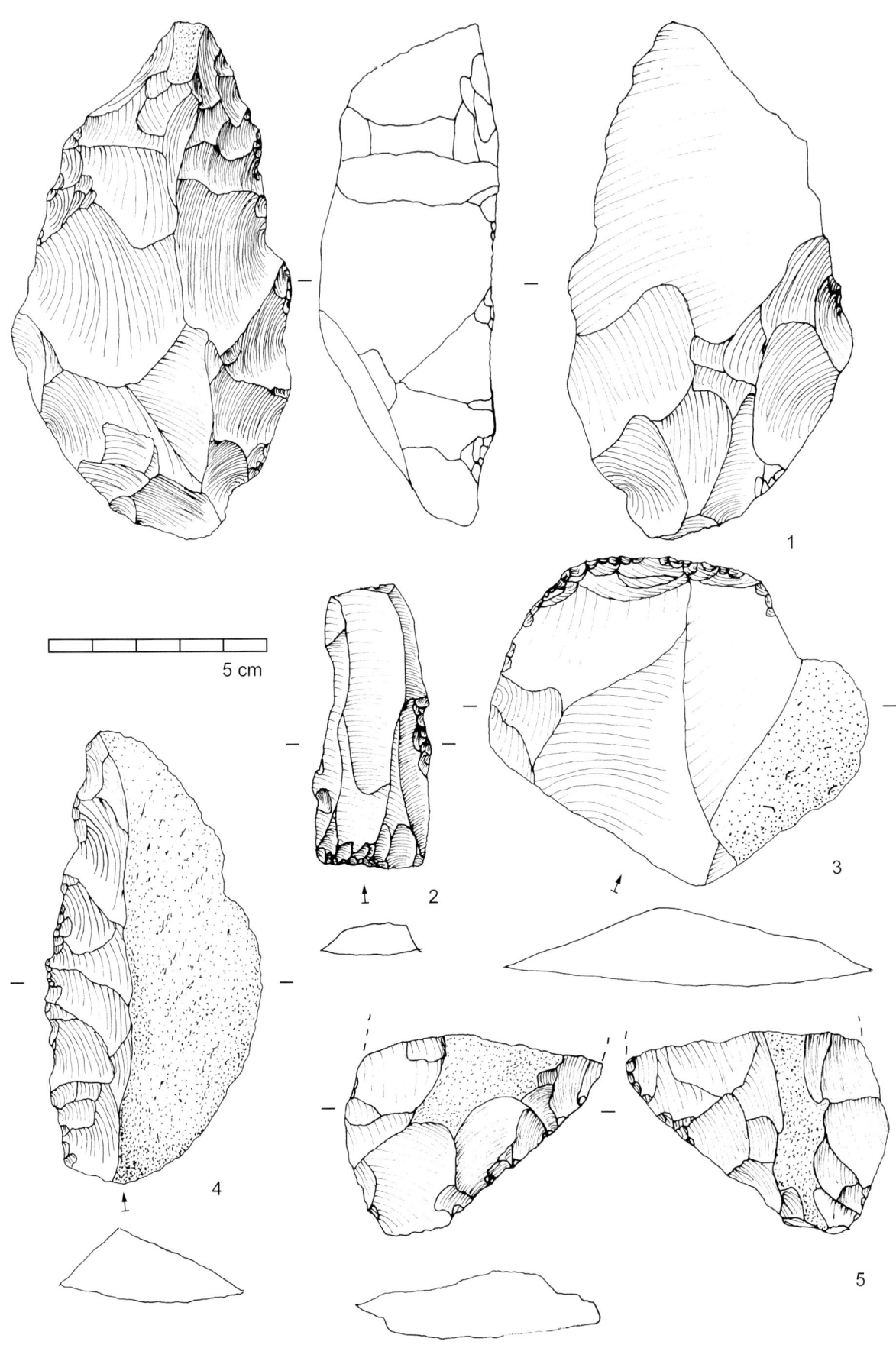

Figure 4.40. Tools from TH.38: (1) bifacial preform, (2,3) retouched blanks, (4) side scraper, (5) bifacial fragment (illustrations by Y.H. Hilbert).

Figure 4.41. View towards the south from the Al-Hatab Rockshelter (photograph by the authors).

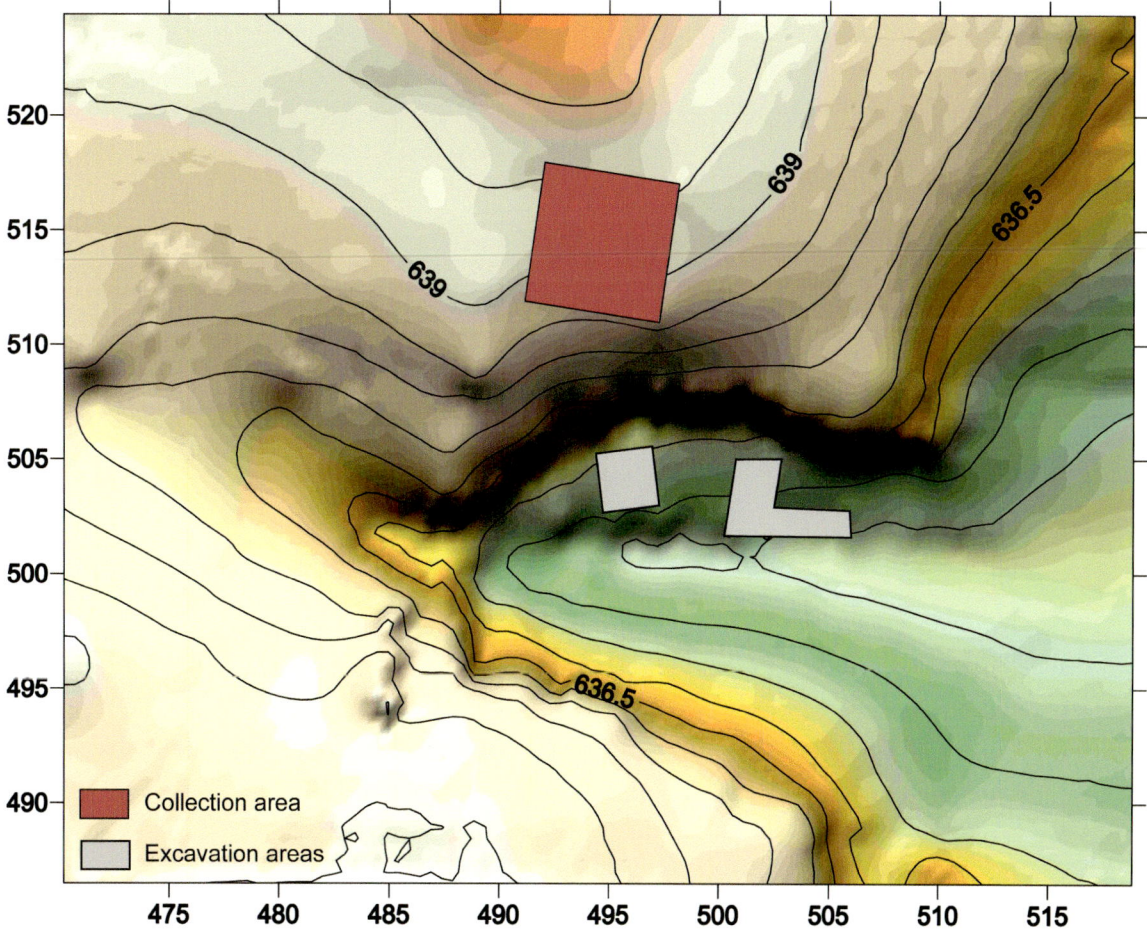

Figure 4.42. Surface plot of Al-Hatab showing the location of TH.29 excavation areas and TH.34 surface collection area (figure plot by Y.H. Hilbert).

Table 4.18. Artifacts counts from TH.34.

Artifact type	N	Percentage
Débitage	**766**	**84%**
Flake	318	41%
Blade	91	12%
Cortical flake	155	20%
Cortical blade	36	5%
Débordant flake	59	8%
Débordant blade	98	13%
Cores	**105**	**11%**
Single platform convergent cores	22	21%
Single platform parallel core	35	33%
Opposed platform core	2	2%
Two unopposed platform core	6	5%
Multiple platform cores	4	4%
Perpendicular core	5	5%
Preform core	24	23%
Broken core	6	6%
Discoid	1	1%
Perpendicular core	2	7%
Tools	**44**	**5%**
End scraper	7	16%
Retouched piece	6	14%
Side scraper	3	7%
Denticulated scraper	1	2%
Notch	2	5%
Truncated piece	5	11%
Dihedral burin	4	9%
Multiple burin on truncation	2	5%
Single burin on natural surface	3	7%
Single burin on snap	5	12%
Single burin on truncation	5	12%
Total	**915**	**100%**

Refitting Ab shows two blanks exhibiting unidirectional-crested dorsal scar patterns that have been conjoined atop one another. Removals of the two blanks might have taken place consecutively. The blank detached first shows multiple negatives on its dorsal face, bearing unidirectional-crossed scars. Likely this kind of pattern represents a shift in the orientation of the striking platform, which is a common rejuvenation technique in the Dhofar Late Palaeolithic. The majority of tools are burins, including burins on truncations, dihedral and multiple burins (Figure 4.47). Most were manufactured on blades and likely inserted in a haft. The toolkit also includes ogival and simple end scrapers, which are also typical of the Late Palaeolithic.

Table 4.19. Débitage attributes from TH.34.

Scar pattern	Flake	Blade	Cortical blade	Cortical flake	Débordant blade	Débordant flake
Bidirectional	7	1		1	7	2
Convergent	13	6		1	2	1
Opposed	6		1	3		1
Parallel	11	11		1	1	
Radial	4			1		
Transverse	8		1	10	2	3
Traverses crested			1			
Unidirectional	172	60	15	44	68	45
Unidirectional Crested	1	1	1	4	6	3
Unidirectional Crossed	38	5	1	3	8	3

Blank shape	Flake	Blade	Cortical blade	Cortical flake	Débordant blade	Débordant flake
Convergent	54	6	2	12	13	3
Lateral	13	7	9	10	37	18
Expanding	80	8	5	36	7	16
Irregular	33	6	3	7	3	2
Ovoid	43	1	1	40	3	6
Parallel	83	63	13	28	34	11

Striking Platform	Flake	Blade	Cortical blade	Cortical flake	Débordant blade	Débordant flake
Absent	12	2		7	4	
Cortex	13	5	4	15	3	
Crushed	20	4	3	6	6	5
Dihedral	22	1	1	7	3	3
Faceted	4	2		7	1	1
Punctiform	24	4	2	12	2	1
Transverse	7	2		3	1	1
Unfaceted	170	58	20	70	63	40

Comparing TH.34 and the stratified assemblage from Al-Hatab, there can be little doubt that the two findspots are technologically related. At Al-Hatab Area 1, a similar concentration of burins on truncations was excavated from the Late Palaeolithic horizon in Sondage 1 (Rose and Usik 2009). One significant difference is the presence of bifacial tools and biface thinning flakes within the Al-Hatab assemblage, while TH.34 has no evidence for bifacial reduction among the debitage or tools. Hilbert (2014) recognizes a later facies within the Late Palaeolithic that consistently lacks bifacial technology, which he terms the Khashabian industry. Consequently, we can infer that TH.34 is chronologically later than Al-Hatab rockshelter. Given the absence of chips, it is likely that smaller elements of the surface scatter washed into the gully and contributed to the Al-Hatab deposit.

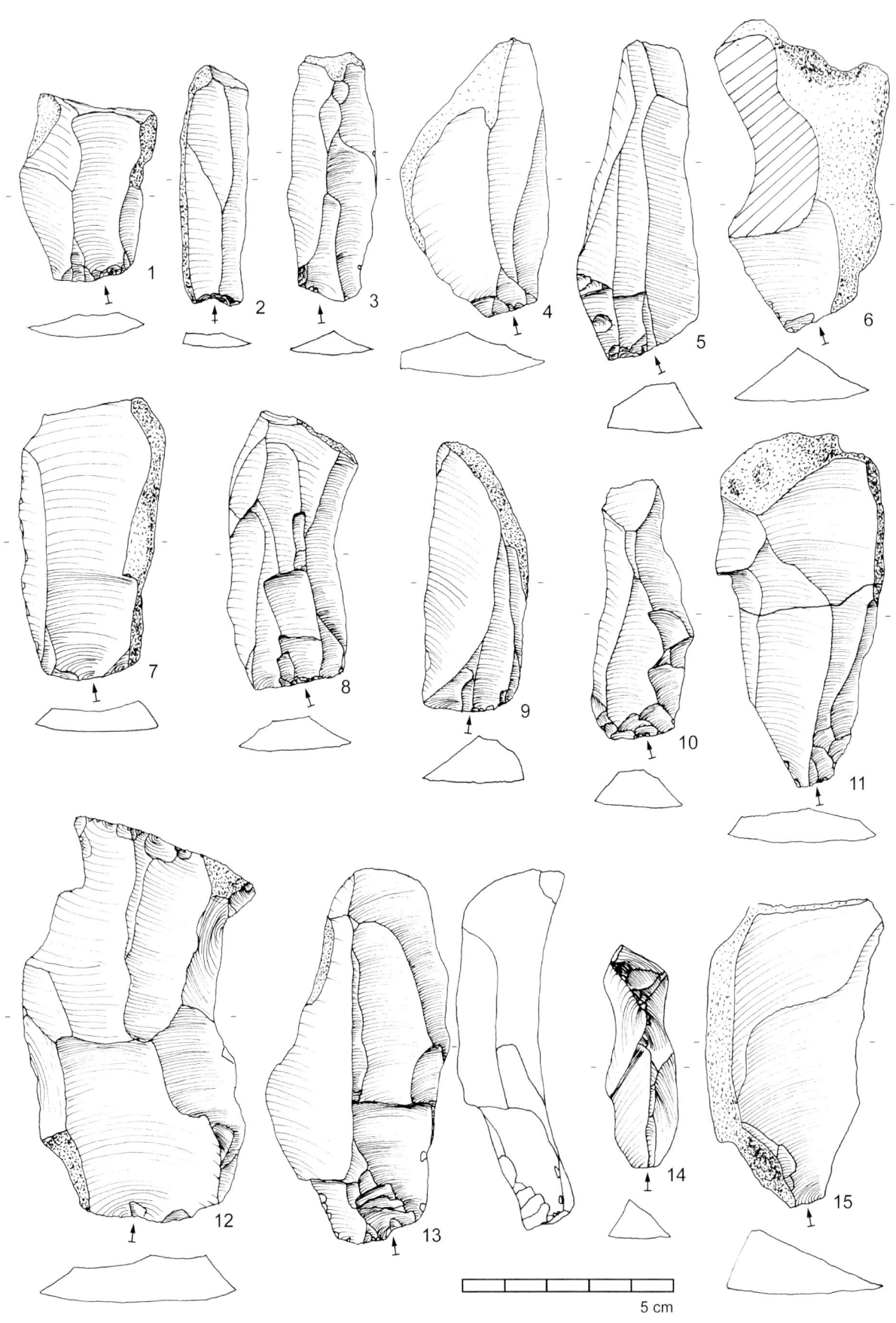

Figure 4.43. Debitage from TH.34 (illustrations by Y.H. Hilbert).

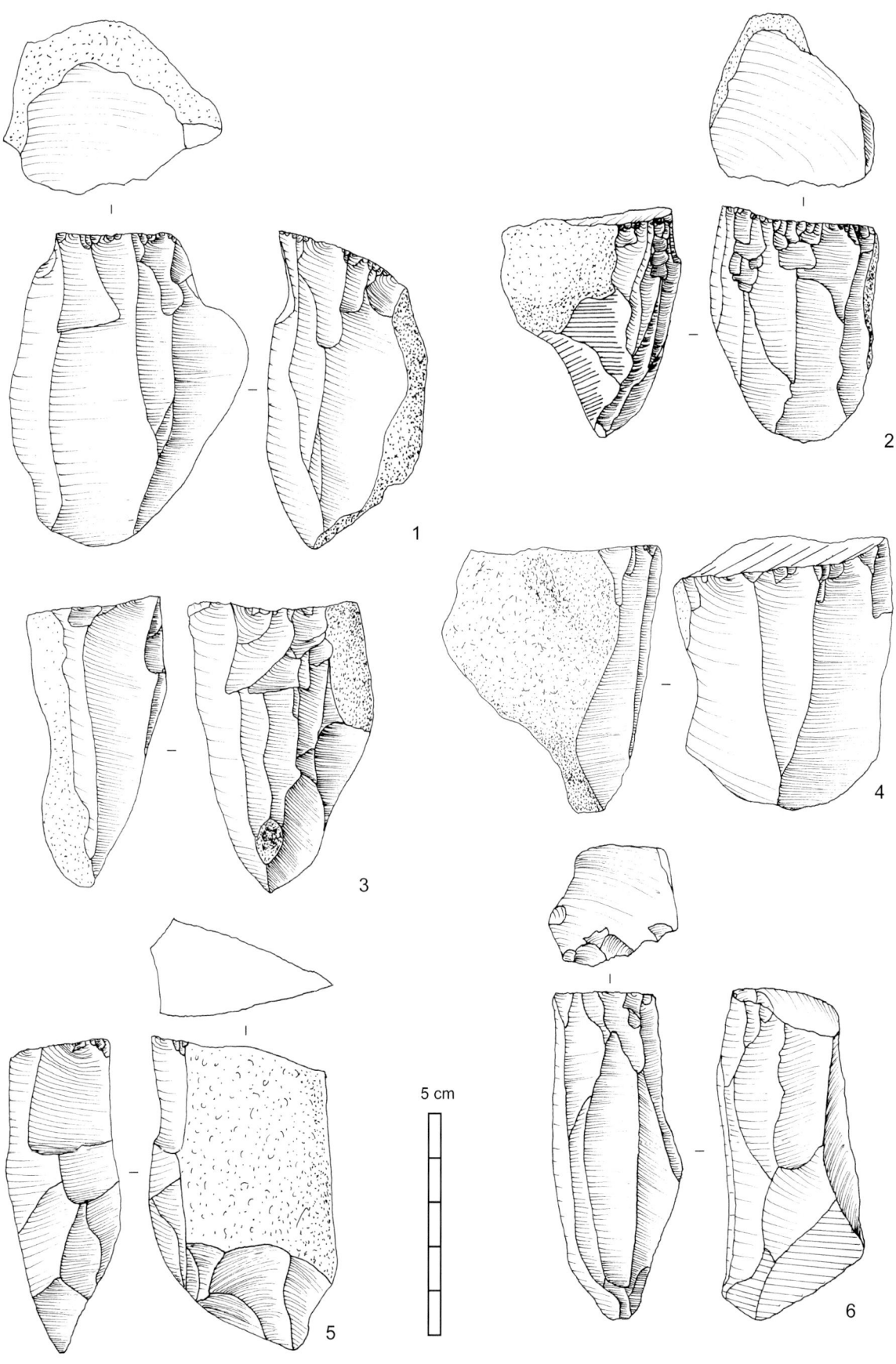

Figure 4.44. Blade cores from TH.34 (illustrations by Y.H. Hilbert).

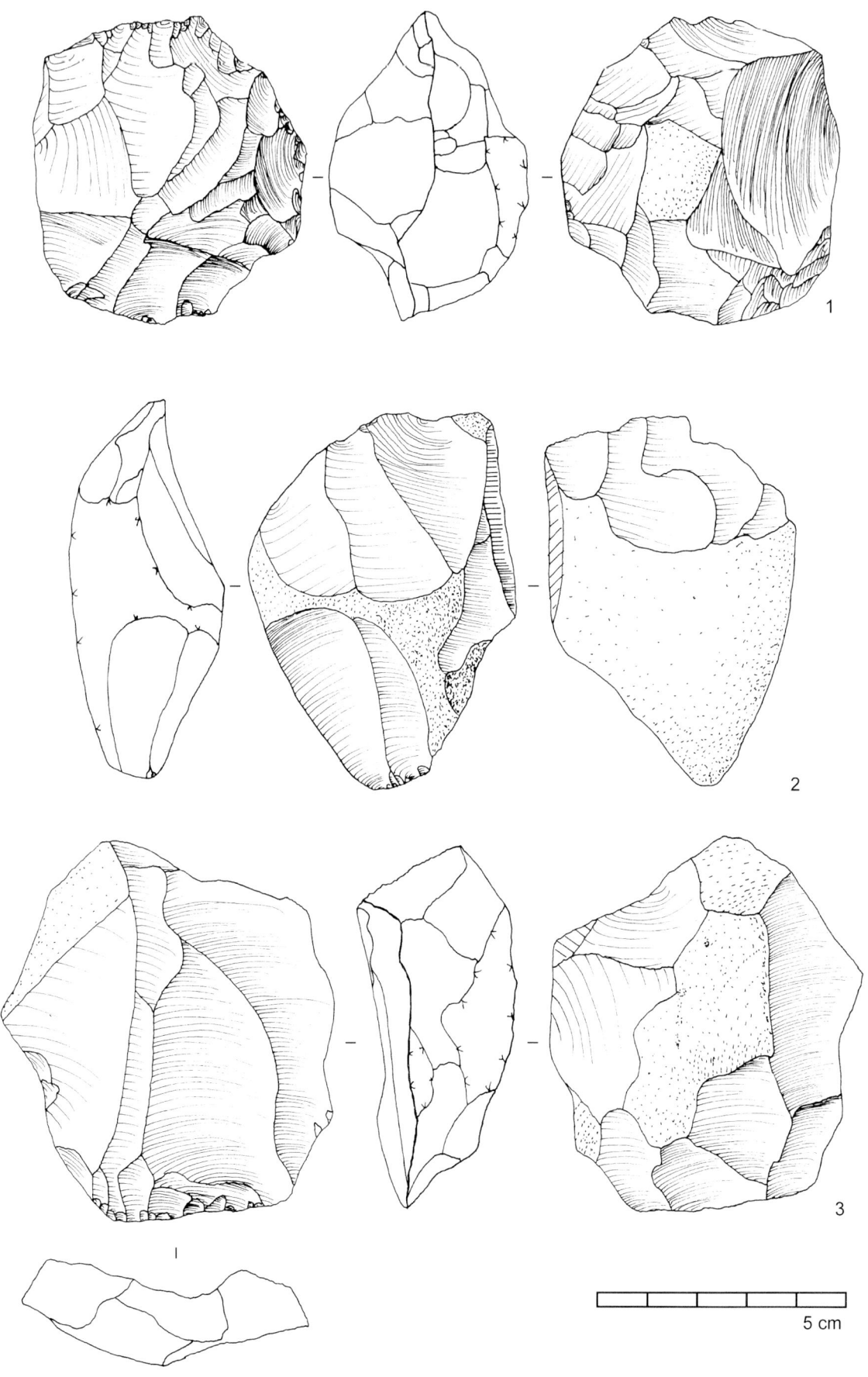

Figure 4.45. Multiple platform cores from TH.34 (illustrations by Y.H. Hilbert).

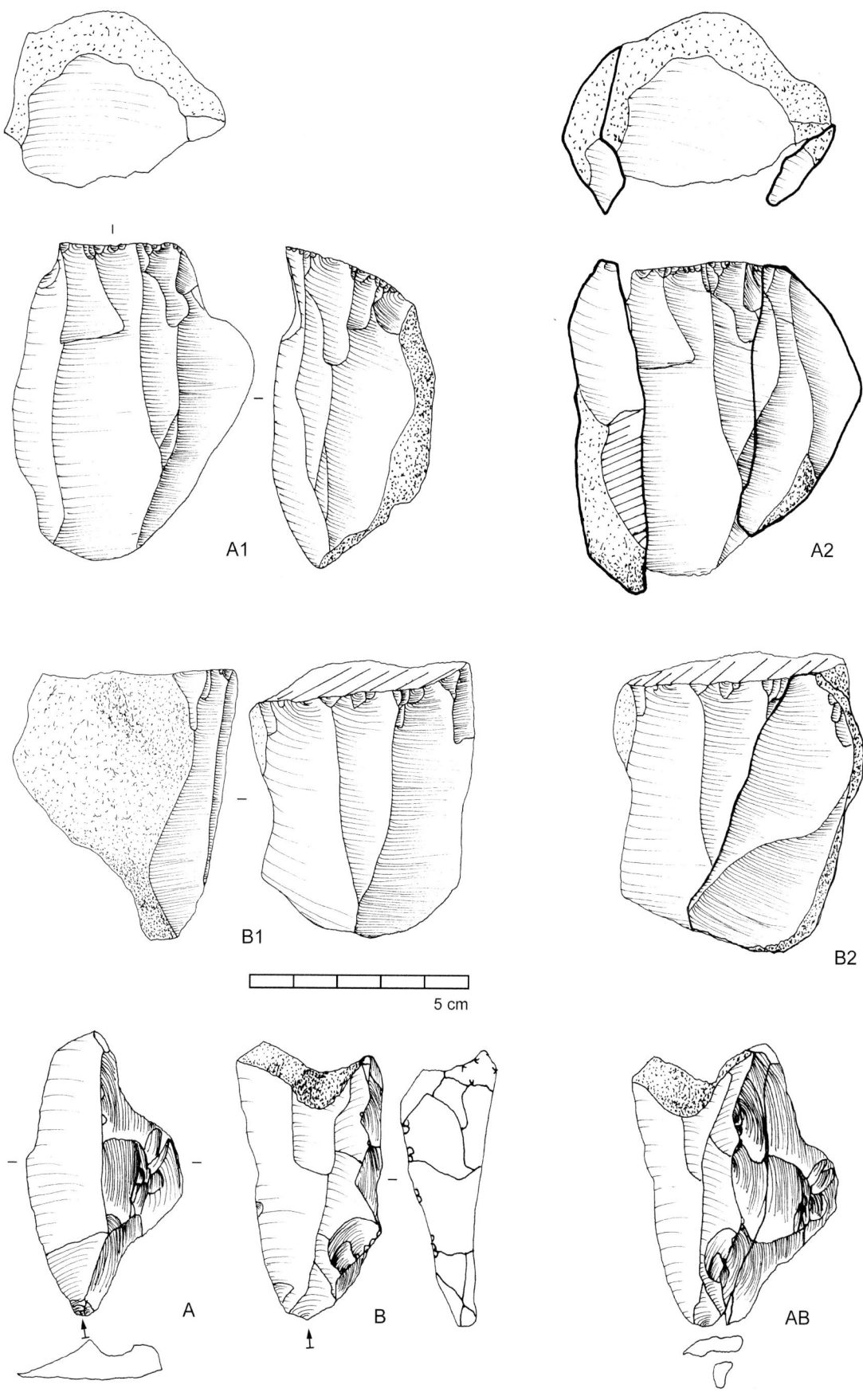

Figure 4.46.TH.34 refittings: (A1, A2) blade core with débordant refits, (B1, B2) blade core with thick lateral refit (illustrations by Y.H. Hilbert)

Table 4.20. Débitage metric data from TH.34.

Length (mm)	Max Length	Min Length	Avg Length	StDev Length	Count
Flake	77	15,23	39,16495614	10,96110828	228
Blade	104,86	24,59	51,64028986	14,08360801	69
Cortical flake	84,86	23,23	48,57903509	13,37323261	114
Cortical blade	90,08	29,14	57,23733333	15,12102303	30
Débordant flake	93,2	34,91	55,22960784	13,00801583	51
Débordant blade	97,79	33,03	61,7962963	13,51162615	81
Width (mm)	Max Widths	Min Widths	Avg Widths	StDev Widths	Count
Flake	73,04	14,06	31,61756364	9,890315891	275
Blade	42,19	11,17	20,38761905	5,670730944	84
Cortical flake	86,1	16,47	36,18592857	11,82335933	140
Cortical blade	42,78	10,3	23,75151515	7,61533737	33
Débordant flake	71,08	15,03	36,70305085	11,55683665	59
Débordant blade	40,59	12,28	24,94375	6,648593401	96
Thickness (mm)	Max Thickness	Min Thickness	Avg Thickness	StDev Thickness	Count
Flake	40,03	1,88	9,563032491	4,581594025	277
Blade	23,26	2,26	7,73202381	3,214390377	84
Cortical flake	34,62	4,24	12,75070423	6,20289759	142
Cortical blade	26,14	5	10,53090909	4,34793871	33
Débordant flake	38,05	5,6	16,10033898	7,088979783	59
Débordant blade	33,89	5,01	14,38479167	6,13947503	96
Weight (g)	Max Weight(g)	Min Weight(g)	Avg Weight(g)	StDev Weight(g)	Count
Flake	136	1	13,88888889	16,32709223	279
Blade	146	1	11,38554217	17,64682748	83
Cortical flake	244	2	30,23529412	34,96234153	153
Cortical blade	168	4	25,78787879	31,92349994	33
Débordant flake	213	2	41,6440678	42,22834589	59
Débordant blades	153	2	25,83333333	23,27260267	96

Summary of Upper and Late Palaeolithic Findings

The youngest of the assemblages presented here presented appears to be TH.34, collected on the terrace above Al-Hatab rockshelter. Technological and typological indications supporting this interpretation are the lack of bifacial production, the use of Wa'shah technique for blade and bladelet production and the presence of multiple and perpendicular platform cores, which are also known from the Khashabian assemblages excavated at Khumseen and Ghazal rockshelters dating between 9,500 and 7,000 BP (Hilbert *et al.* 2012; Hilbert 2013). The TH.262 and TH.143a Late Palaeolithic assemblages are technologically and typologically similar to the Late Palaeolithic horizon at Al-Hatab, which is bracketed between 14,000 and 11,000 years ago. These assemblages are characterized by a more conservative approach to blade production using either the core's narrow working surface or recurrent unidirectional blade cores with working surfaces arranged across the broad frontal face of chert nodules. This earlier phase of the Late Palaeolithic is also consistently associated with the manufacture of bifacial and trifacial tools using hard hammer percussion. The presence of bifacial preforms and fragments at TH.38 suggest temporal overlap with Al-Hatab.

Assemblage TH.68 stands in marked contrast to the Late Palaeolithic sites presented here. The suite of characteristics includes backed bladelets, bifacial and partly bifacial points, unifacial points, carinated pieces and a cresting technique. Together, these features fit comfortably within the Upper Palaeolithic between 35,000 and 20,000 years ago. The bifacial points hint at long distance connection with the Horn of Africa, where bifacial technology coupled with curated blade production systems and backed microliths are regionally distinctive features of the Late Stone Age (Brandt *et al.* 2012; Clark 1954). This observation is in accordance with genetic studies of mtDNA haplogroup R0a, which is thought to have originated in an ice age refugium within South Arabia, before dispersing into East Africa after the Last Glacial Maximum (Gandini *et al.* 2016; Platt *et al.* 2017). Further research is needed to verify this and other hypotheses.

While Upper Palaeolithic sites are exceedingly rare, the Late Palaeolithic is widespread across much of southern Arabia, with only minor regional and temporal variability. This archaeological trend matches the demographic scenario observed in the fluorescence of mtDNA R0a and related haplogroups HV1 and R2 during the Late Glacial around 12,000 years ago, each thought to have spread from South Arabia (Černý *et al.* 2011).

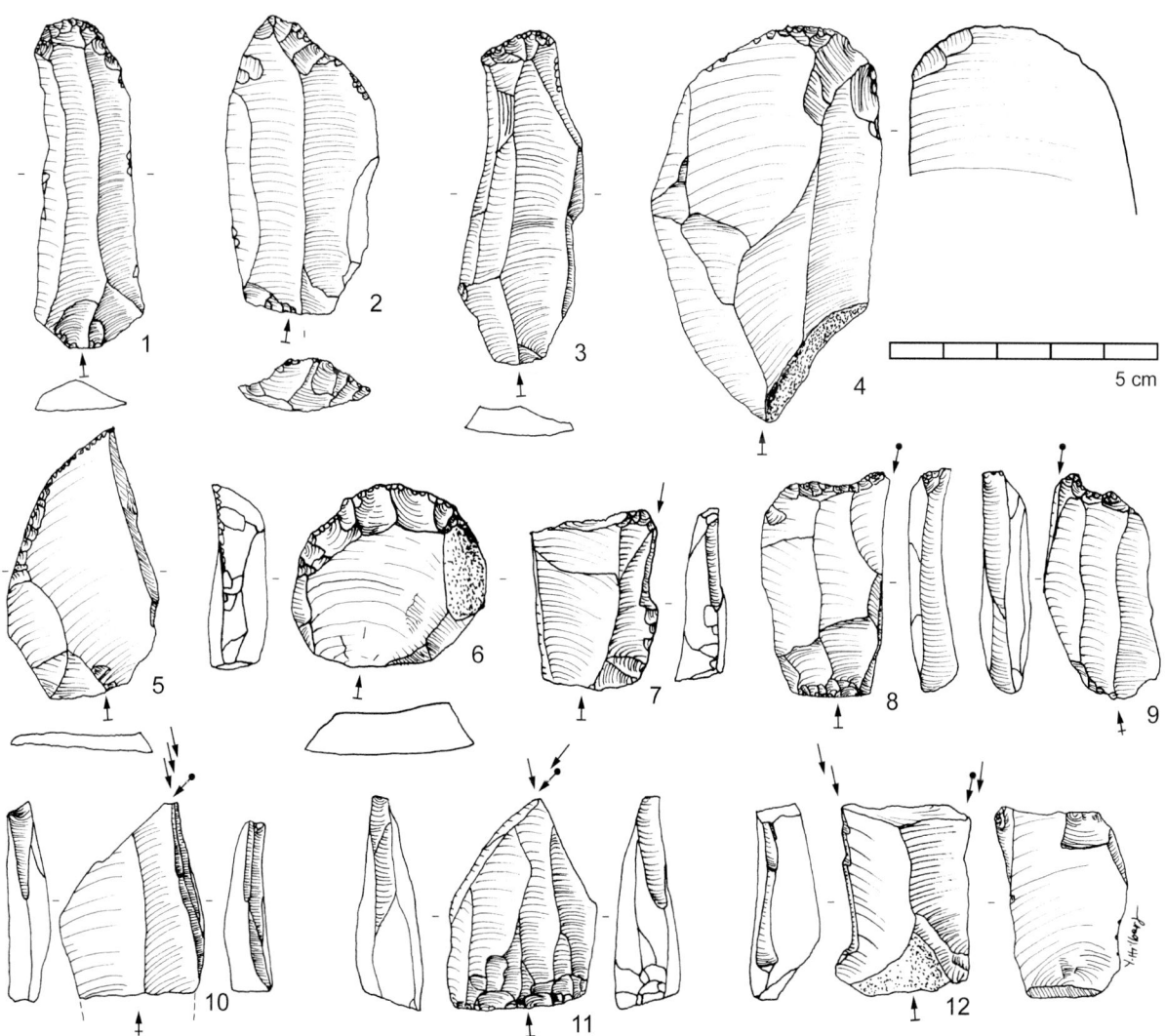

Figure 4.47. Tools from TH.34: (1-3,6) end scrapers, (4,5) retouched blanks, (7-9) burins on truncation, (10,11) dihedral burins, (12) burin on snap (illustrations by Y.H. Hilbert).

Chapter 5

Conclusions and avenues for future research

Palaeolithic Assemblage Types in Dhofar

There are countless lithic surface scatters littering the diverse landscape of the Nejd Plateau and southern Rub Al-Khali in Dhofar (Hilbert 2014; Hilbert *et al.* 2018; McClure 1994; Payne and Hawkins 1963; Pullar 1974; Rose and Hilbert 2014; Rose and Usik 2009; Whalen *et al.* 2002; Zarins 2001). These findspots occur in a variety of settings and comprise different types of occupations; they are single discarded cores or isolated points, specialized activity zones, habitation sites, or vast lithic workshops extending over several kilometers. Diverse lithic technologies are found together at these workshops, exhibiting significantly different surface weathering and spatial patterning.

Yet, there is a dearth of absolute dates with which to build a Palaeolithic chronology. From the Middle Palaeolithic period, we have a single set of OSL numeric age estimates from the Nubian Complex site of Aybut Al-Auwal, which brackets the burial of a Nubian Levallois core in secondary position between 116,000 and 97,000 years ago (Rose *et al.* 2011). Although there are no dated Upper Palaeolithic sites in Dhofar, Amirkhanov (1994, 2006) reports stratified Upper Palaeolithic sites in Mahra, the territory of Yemen bordering Dhofar to the west, with radiocarbon ages between 30,000 and 18,000 years ago. A series of rockshelters with stratified Late Palaeolithic deposits in the southern Nejd and Dhofar highlands cluster between 14,000 and 7,000 BP (Cremaschi *et al.* 2015; Cremaschi and Negrino 2002; Hilbert *et al.* 2012, 2015a, 2015b; Rose and Usik 2009).

These few data points provide temporal anchors to build a relative sequence of Palaeolithic assemblage types. During the 2013 field campaign, we carried out an experiment to test the correlation between spatial distribution, taphonomic weathering patterns and technological features at multi-component workshop sites. While some of the sites were inconclusive, a few workshops demonstrated clearly discernable clusters. These cultural units vary in resolution from technocomplex, to tradition, to industry, to facies, depending on the degree to which they are articulated in time and space. Based on these findings, we suggest the following broad lithic units:

Acheulean Complex

Acheulean diagnostic elements include handaxes, choppers, radial cores and flakes produced from these cores. The handaxes are typically between 10 and 15 cm in length, thick and range in shape from cordiform/sub-cordiform to ovate. Cleavers are notably absent. Radial cores vary from high-backed to discoidal, either exploiting a single working surface or both. Characteristic débitage associated with these assemblage types include large bifacial shaping flakes and flakes with radial scar patterns. The latter are often characterized by wide and deep striking platforms that are straight or dihedral faceted, with pronounced bulbs of percussion (Figure 5.1). Given the limited sample sizes, we cannot distinguish temporal variability among the Dhofar Acheulean assemblages. The one exception is TA.23 found on the Salalah coastal plain, which included a single handaxe (Figure 5.1: 1) in addition to large polyhedrons. The TA.23 assemblage may represent an early stage of the Acheulean, although more findspots of similar composition are required to test this speculation.

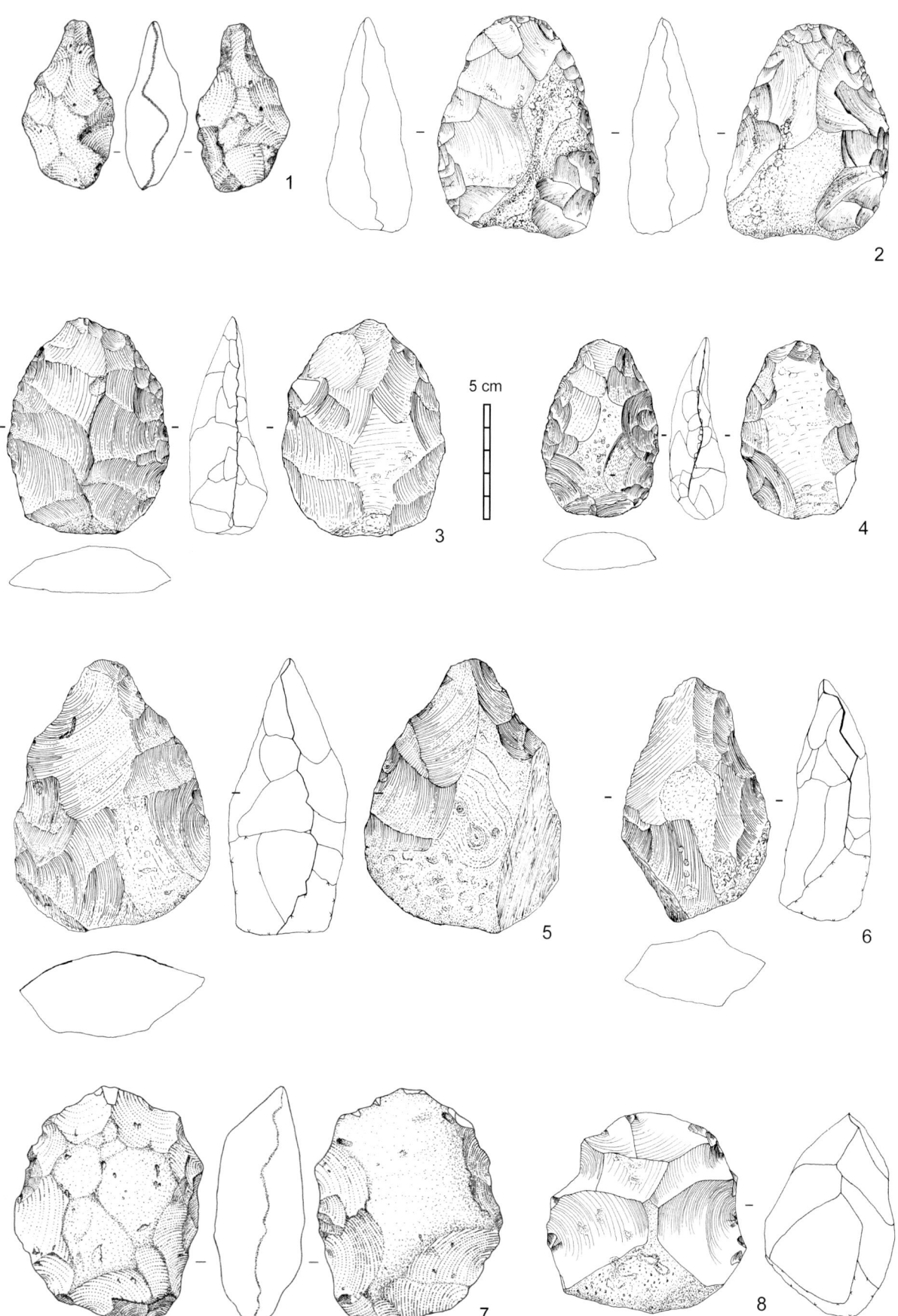

Figure 5.1. Acheulean artifacts from Dhofar: (1-6) handaxes from the Nejd Plateau and coastal plain, (7,8) Lower Palaeolithic cores (illustrations by A. Beshkani and Y.H. Hilbert).

Late Lower Palaeolithic Large Blade Group

Within the Lower Palaeolithic there is a second, evidently later assemblage type we call the "Large Blade" group, due to the distinctively massive laminar débitage, which typically range from 10 to 20 cm in length. The associated cores are also massive, showing both frontal and narrow working surfaces exploited by single platform, unidirectional reduction systems. The elongated blanks are significantly larger and thicker than Upper and Late Palaeolithic blade industries in Dhofar, with characteristically narrow and deep striking platforms and pronounced bulbs of percussion. Platforms are unfaceted and, in many cases, cortical.

Lingering questions abound as to the variability and dating of these assemblages. The Large Blade group was consistently found spatially and taphonomically between Acheulean and Nubian assemblages at multi-occupation workshop sites. We can now only surmise a timeframe between 400,000 and 150,000 BP based on the loose technological correlates in East Africa and the Levant. Whether the Large Blade assemblages are ever associated with bifacial manufacture and/or early Nubian Levallois technology is not yet known.

The Nubian Tradition

The Afro-Arabian Nubian Technocomplex was widely distributed across Northeast Africa and Arabia during MIS 5. In Dhofar, there are at least two distinct Nubian industry types that appear to be separated in time. The earlier Nubian phase is represented at Aybut Al-Auwal, dating sometime before 100,000 BP and is characterized by the overwhelming predominance of the Nubian Levallois method of core reduction, which produced elongated Levallois points, Nubian diagnostic débitage and Nubian Levallois cores (Figure 5.2). Following the definitions proposed in previous publications (e.g., Van Peer 1992; Crassard and Hilbert 2013; Usik *et al.* 2013), Nubian cores are recognized by the combined presence of these three morphological attributes: 1) triangular/sub-triangular shapes, 2) a steeply-angled median distal ridge formed by distal divergent removals, bilateral removals, or some combination of these organizational systems, and 3) faceted striking platforms, often chapeau de gendarme. The intended end product of the Nubian Levallois strategy was an elongated point with either triangular or pitched shape. The few retouched tools from earlier Nubian sites in Dhofar include retouched Levallois points, side scrapers and end scrapers.

The Mudayyan is a late Middle Palaeolithic industry derived from the earlier Nubian Complex. Mudayyan technology continued to rely on the Nubian Levallois method, albeit consistently producing categorically smaller Nubian cores (Rose and Marks 2014; Usik *et al.* 2013). This diminution of point production in the later stages of the Middle Palaeolithic coincides with the incorporation of additional reduction methods that allowed for the serial production of small, elongated points and blades with dihedral or facetted platforms (Figure 5.3). These were detached from flat recurrent bidirectional opposed platform cores, or struck from the narrow working surface of thin plaquettes. Albeit rare, evidence for cresting to prepare and maintain narrow working surface blade cores has been documented in some Mudayyan assemblages (Rose and Marks, 2014). Unlike the earlier Nubian assemblages, in which retouched tools are either rare or difficult to distinguish from edge damage, Mudayyan assemblages have sizable toolkits comprised primarily of end scrapers and burins, as well as small (<7 cm) Levallois points and flakes. With no end date for the earlier Nubian industry and no ages associated with the Mudayyan assemblages, we can only loosely place the Mudayyan between 100,000 and 40,000 BP. The Emiran of the southern Levant and the Taramsan of the Nile Valley are also regionally distinct industries derived from the Nubian Complex. Both are considered transitional between the Middle and Upper Palaeolithic and date between 60,000 and 45,000 BP (Marks 1983; Van Peer *et al.* 2010), suggesting a narrower Mudayyan timeframe from MIS 4 to early MIS 3.

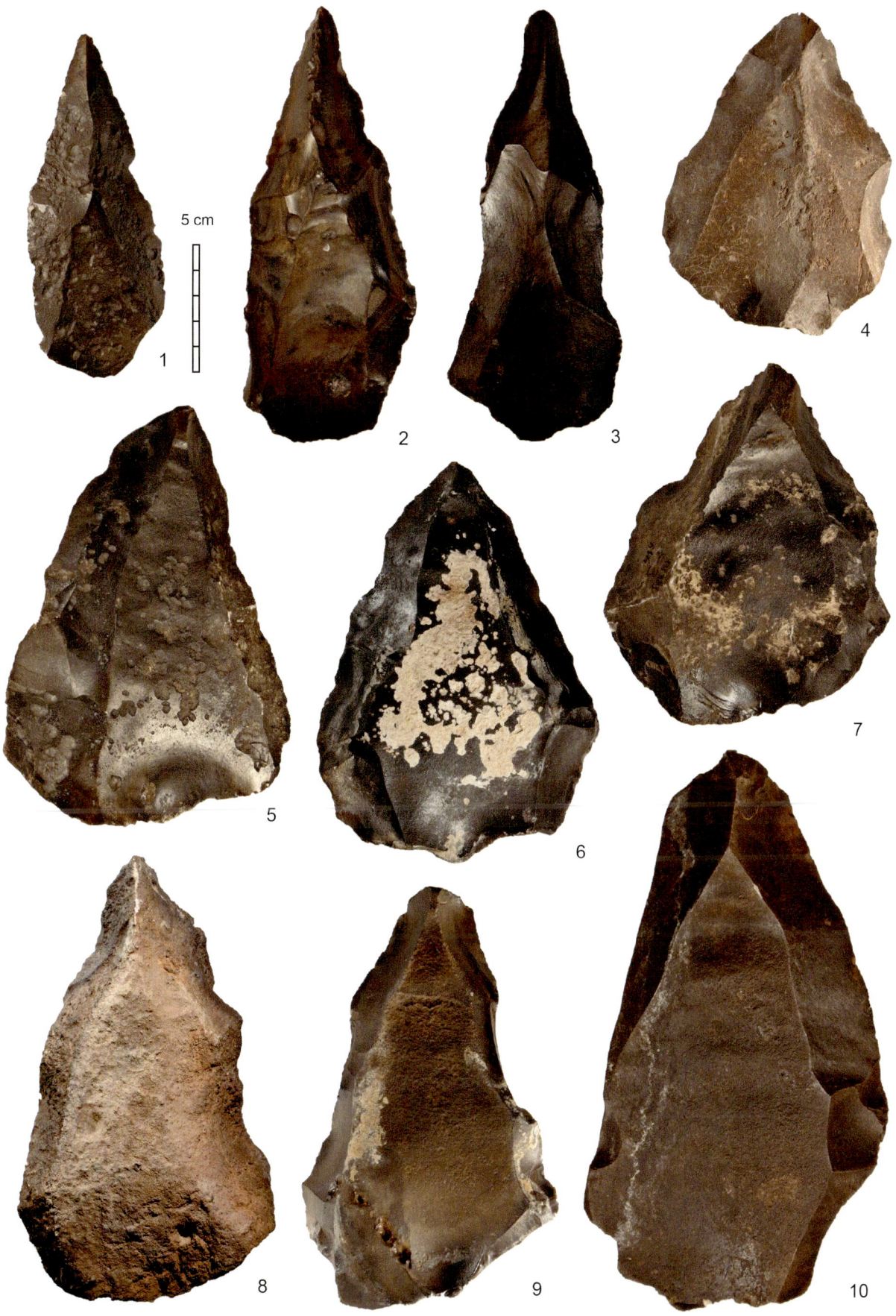

5 cm

Figure 5.2. Earlier Middle Palaeolithic artifacts from Dhofar: (1-3) Nubian Levallois points, (4-10) Nubian Levallois cores (photographs by Y.H. Hilbert).

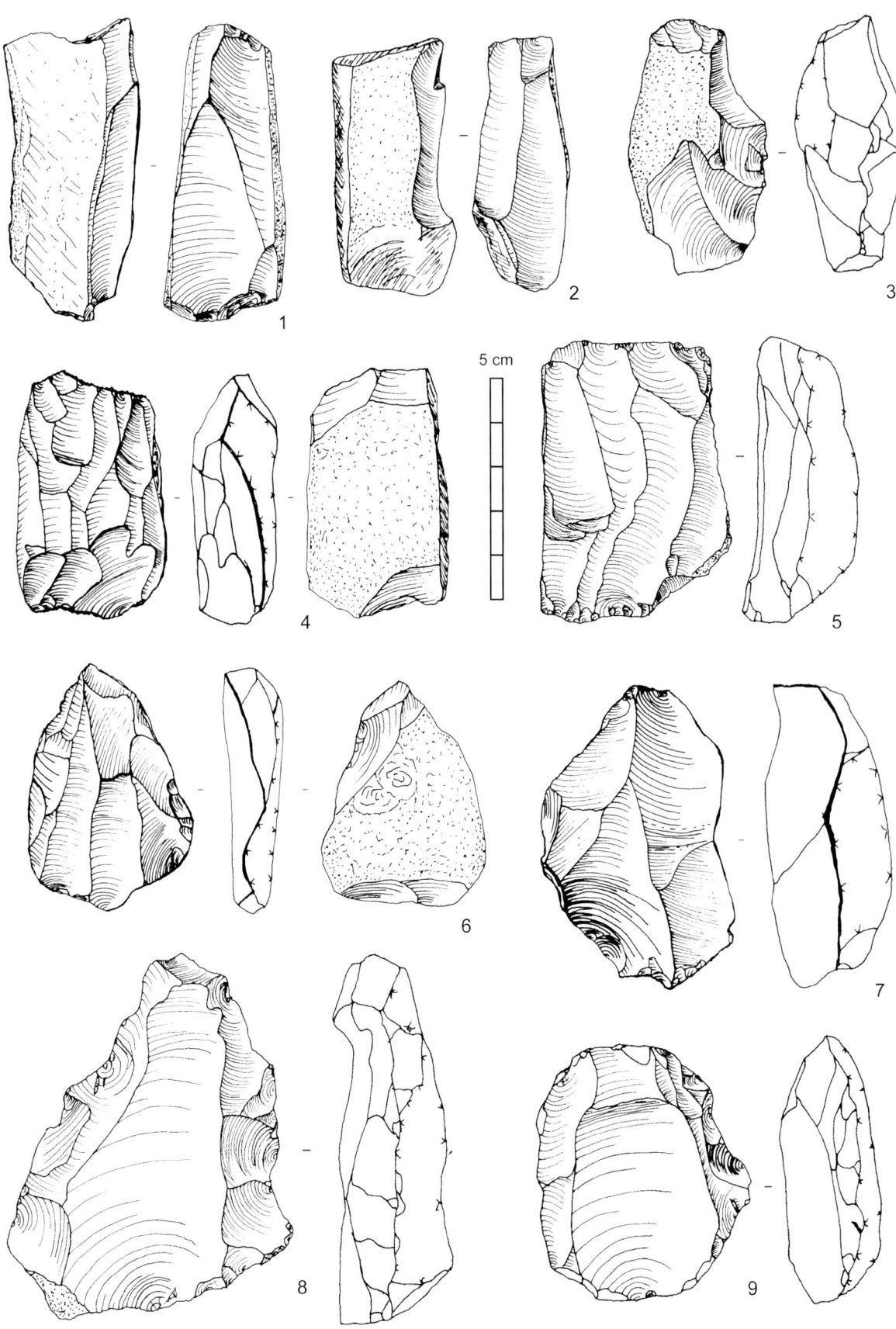

5 cm

Figure 5.3. Later Middle Palaeolithic artifacts from Dhofar: (1) bidirectional narrow surface core, (2) unidirectional narrow surface core, (3) unidirectional narrow surface core with ridge preparation, (4,5) bidirectional opposed blade cores, (6-8) Nubian Levallois cores, (9) Levallois preferential cores (illustrations by Y.H. Hilbert).

Upper Palaeolithic

Upper Palaeolithic findspots are the most rare in Dhofar and in all of Arabia for that matter. The Dhofar Archaeological Project mapped just seven findspots with Upper Palaeolithic diagnostic features, including backed tools and cresting technology. The only site that yielded a substantial assemblage for analysis was TH.68, located on the top of Jebel Kareem inselberg overlooking the Wadi Aybut floodplain. The technology recorded at TH.68 includes three distinct reduction strategies: 1) recurrent blades and bladelets produced from single and opposed platform cores, 2) bifacial points made from blanks, and 3) Kareem segments. This third technique is a core-on-flake method that detached small transverse segments along the longitudinal axis of thick elongated blanks. The products – Kareem segments – were almost all subsequently retouched with a burin blow. Other tools include convex, shouldered and nosed end scrapers, carinated pieces, dihedral burins and backed bladelets (Figure 5.4). It is the only instance of laminar technology where we observe punctiform striking platforms and a high frequency of platform edge abrasion. Unlike Lower and Late Palaeolithic bifacial technologies in Dhofar, the unifacial, partly-bifacial and bifacial points were all made on blanks. Although there are no observable taphonomic differences between the bifacial and laminar components of the TH.68 assemblage, we cannot be certain whether these reduction strategies are contemporary. Regardless if it represents one or recurring occupations, the bifacial points, carinated pieces, crested blades and backed bladelets are typical of the surrounding Upper Palaeolithic phases in Iran, South Asia, as well as the Late Stone Age in the Horn of Africa. Hence, we tentatively suggest a time frame for this type of Upper Palaeolithic assemblage in Dhofar between 30,000 and 20,000 BP, consistent with the numeric ages from Mahra, eastern Yemen (Amirkhanov 1994).

Late Palaeolithic

Late Palaeolithic findspots are the most common on the Nejd Plateau, stretching from the Jebel Qara highlands to the Rub Al-Khali desert. OSL numeric ages from Late Palaeolithic sites on the central-southern Nejd and Dhofar highlands indicate two chronological stages. The earlier is the Hatabian, bracketed between 14,000 and 11,000 BP. The only dated occurrence is Al-Hatab rockshelter, although there are numerous surface scatters throughout the Nejd bearing virtually identical techno-typological features (e.g., TH.23, TH.32, TH.124, TH.143a, TH.262): simple unidirectional hard hammer blade blanks struck from unmodified, single platform tournant and semi-tournant volumetric cores, burins on truncations, end scrapers, hard hammer thick bifacial foliates, trifacials and unifacial tanged points (Hilbert *et al.* 2015b).

The later phase of the Late Palaeolithic – the Khashabian – is known from dated occurrences at Ghazal and Khumseen rockshelters (Hilbert 2013; Hilbert *et al*, 2012), as well as rockshelters in the highlands south of the orographic barrier (Cremaschi *et al.* 2015; Cremaschi and Negrino 2005, 2002). Numeric ages for the Khashabian industry fall between 9,500 and 7,200 BP, correlating with peak rainfall conditions during the Holocene Climatic Optimum. The Khashabian exhibits subtle variations in blade reduction strategies. The Wa'shah method, first reported in Hadramawt (Crassard 2008b), has been documented at TH.34, TH.67, TH.524 and Ras Aïn Noor. It is an elaboration of the simple blade production method that enabled toolmakers to detach a pointed elongated end product. Rejuvenated blade cores with perpendicular or adjacent-opposed working surface are also more common in the Khashabian. There is no discernable difference in unifacial retouched tools such as side scrapers, end scrapers, denticulates, tanged points and burins on truncations (Figure 5.5).

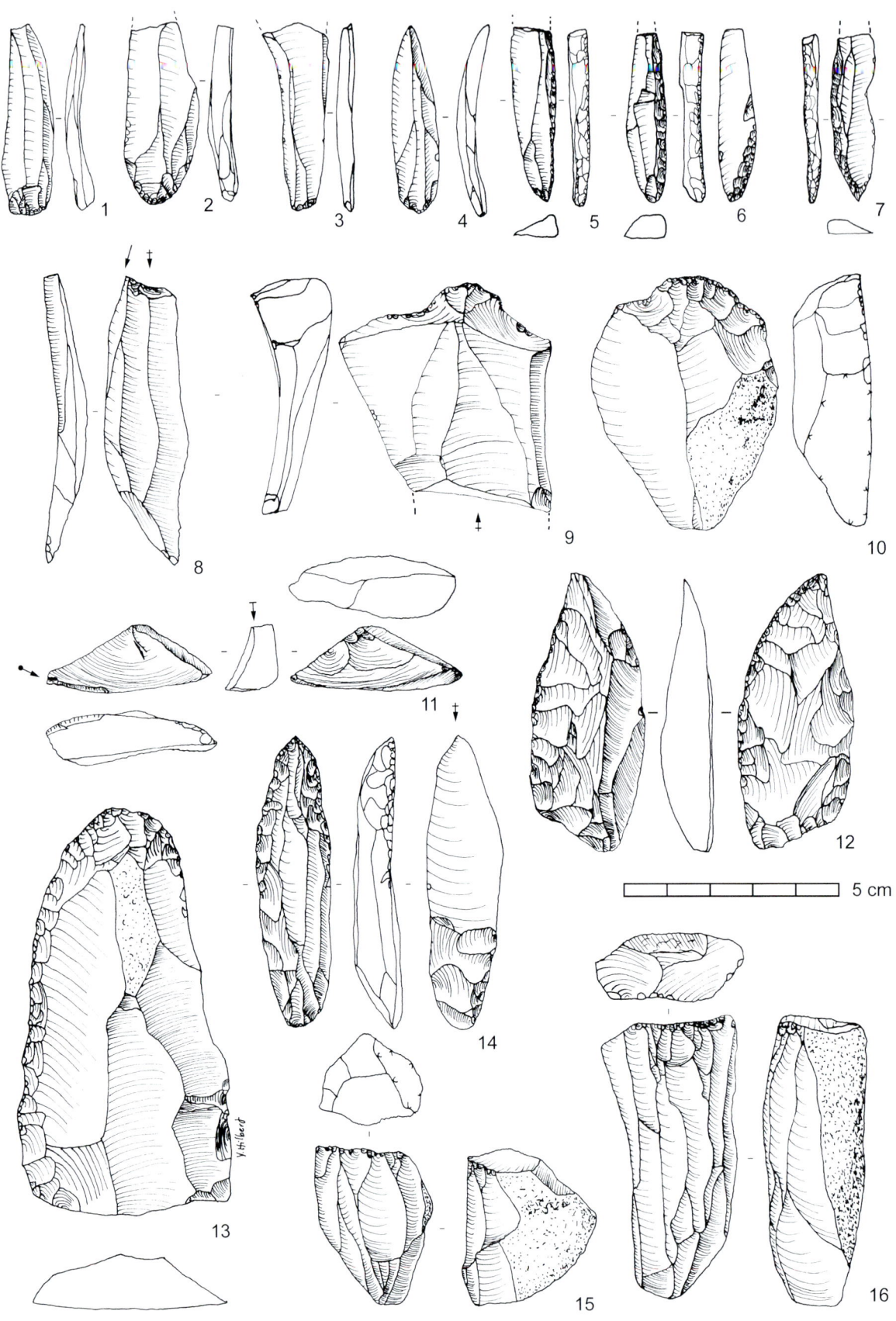

Figure 5.4. Upper Palaeolithic artifacts from TH.68: (1-4) bladelets, (5-7) backed bladelets, (8) burin on truncation, (9,10) shouldered end scrapers, (11) burin on segment, (12) bifacial plano-convex point, (13) end scraper with lateral retouch, (14) unifacial point (15,16) bladelet cores (illustrations by Y.H. Hilbert).

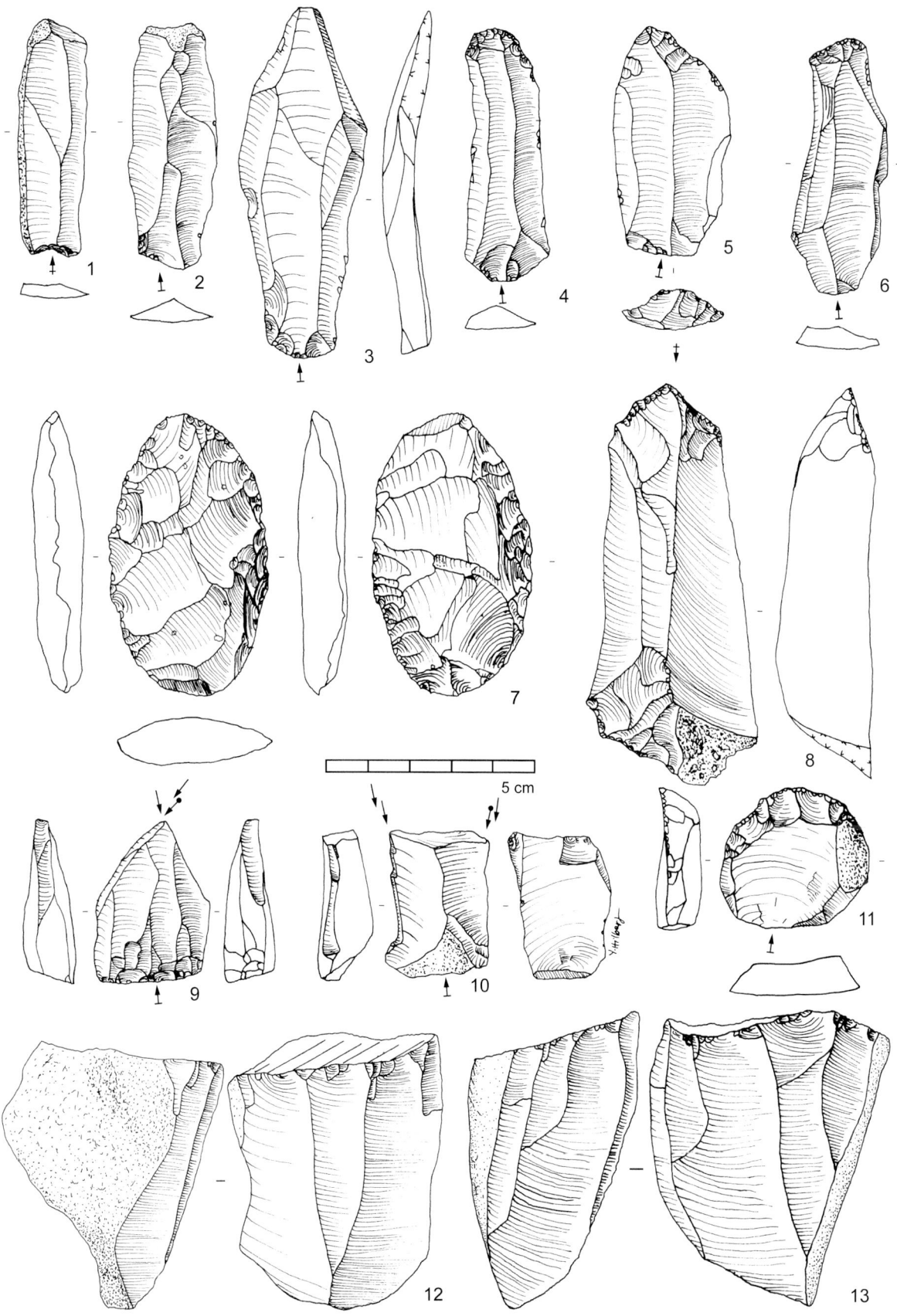

Figure 5.5. Late Palaeolithic artifacts from Dhofar: (1-3) blades and débordant blades, (4-6,8,11) end scrapers, (7) ovate biface, (9) dihedral burin, (10) burin on natural surface, (12) Wa'shah core, (13) unidirectional-parallel semi-tournant blade core (illustrations by Y.H. Hilbert).

However, bifacial tools are conspicuously absent in the Khashabian. This pattern hints at a change in raw material usage, which might have replaced stone knives with an alternative material. Given their propensity for carpentry (Hilbert *et al.* 2018), this potentially includes a number of workable substances available during the Climatic Optimum such as hard wood, horn, or bone.

Taphonomic Patterns

DAP is carrying out an ongoing study of spatial distribution, lithic taphonomy and technological patterning at several multi-occupation workshop sites on the Nejd, including findspots TH.76, TH.123, TH.143, TH.418, TH.419 and TH.501 presented in this book. This study is based on degrees of chemical dissolution, patination, edge damage and ridge rounding, which have been used to create discrete taphonomic weathering clusters.

The surfaces of Late Palaeolithic artifacts typically show the least amount of post-depositional modification (Figure 5.6: 9-12). Late Palaeolithic assemblages on Mudayy chert, have a light yellowish-brown patina, sharp ridges, minimal edge damage and smooth surfaces with no signs of chemical dissolution. Mudayyan artifacts are brown to dark brown in color and have a smooth, waxy veneer (Figure 5.6: 6-8). Artifact edges are sharp and some of the assemblages show moderate edge damage. The first signs of chemical dissolution are apparent on some artifacts, creating a pock-marked surface across small portions of the piece.

Specimens belonging to the Nubian Complex exhibit more varied weathering patterns, which is expected given its long duration at least throughout MIS 5, lasting over 50,000 years. Nubian Complex artifacts' surfaces often have a black manganese oxide coating or a dark brown or gray matte finish (Figure 5.6: 5). Artifact edges are often moderately worn and the ridges are somewhat rounded from aeolian abrasion (Figure 5.6: 3,4). Some Nubian Complex assemblages exhibit moderate to severe chemical dissolution on one or more surfaces, while others show only minor dissolution. Pieces exhibiting both weathering extremes have been refit together at the same site, indicating that these taphonomic processes are complex and not necessarily linear. We can be certain, however, that the Middle Palaeolithic occupation of Dhofar was prolonged and successive, based on the frequency of recycled Nubian cores exhibiting different stages of surface weathering.

The Large Blade assemblages are heavily weathered, with substantial chemical dissolution on both dorsal and ventral surfaces. In many cases, the blades and cores were so heavily weathered that original surfaces were completely removed. When found together with Nubian MP specimens at the same site, Large Blade artifacts have more advanced chemical dissolution that has removed portions of the manganese oxide varnish. Acheulean artifacts display the highest degree of surface decay and rounding. The specimens are dark brown and the original surfaces have been completed eradicated by dissolution (Figure 5.6: 1-2).

We surmise that the taphonomic weathering and spatial distribution recorded among the different assemblages at multi-component workshop sites is the product of landscape development, which has variably exposed the local chert outcrop over time as the scarp eroded. This erosion is primarily due to base level lowering and rock dip occurring over long periods of time, while short-term erosion rates are influenced by changes in climatic regime (Howard and Selby 2009). On the Nejd, these processes have gradually broken down the soft bioclastic matrix surrounding Mudayy chert nodules and slabs, episodically revealing new raw material exposures for over half a million years. We also cannot rule out anthropogenic erosion caused by quarrying chert nodules, as observed among Nubian Complex toolmakers in Egypt (Van Peer *et al.* 2010).

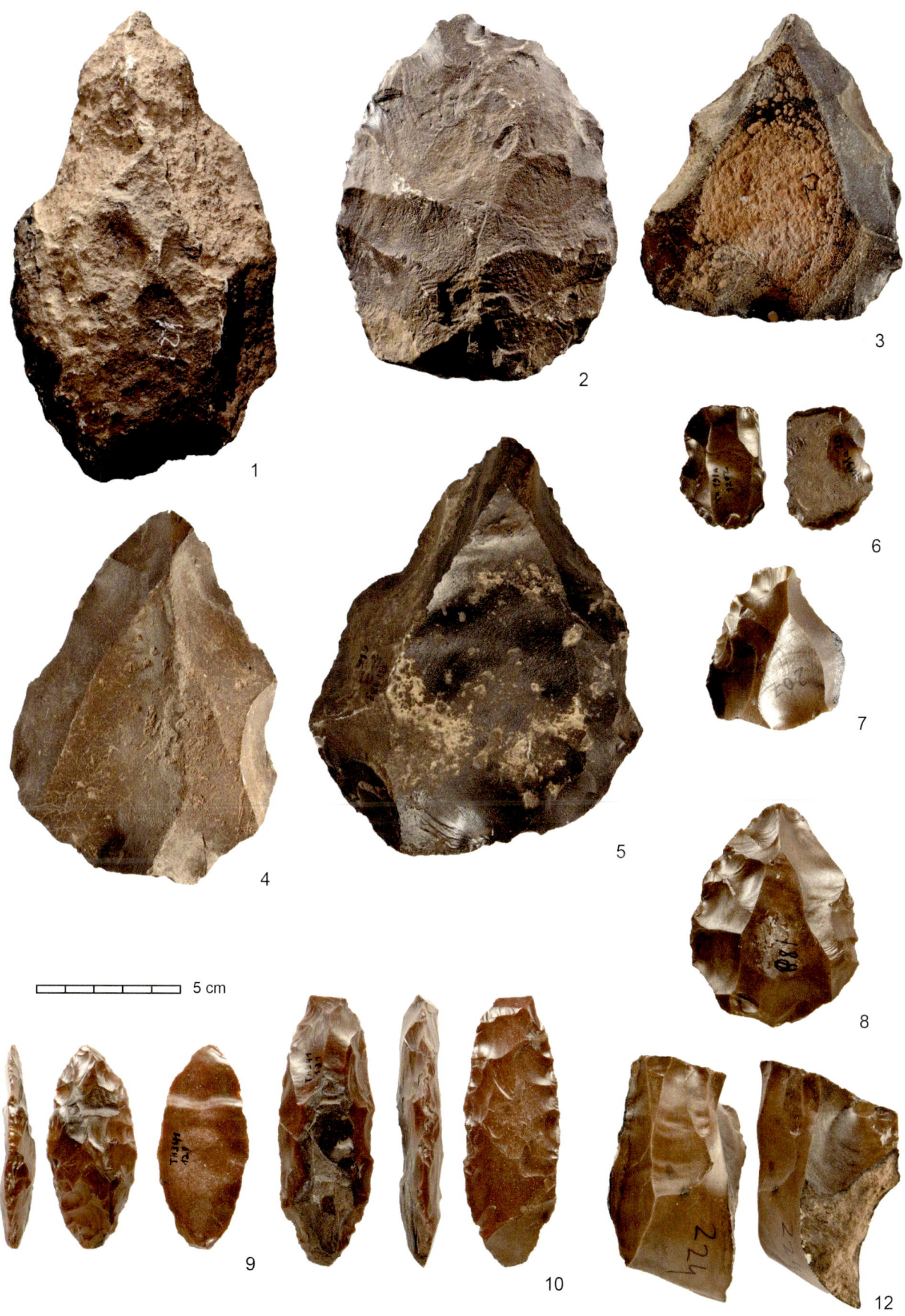

Figure 5.6. Palaeolithic artifacts showing different stages of weathering: (1,2) Lower Palaeolithic, (3-5) earlier Middle Palaeolithic, (6-8) later Middle Palaeolithic, (9-11) Late Palaeolithic (photographs by Y.H. Hilbert).

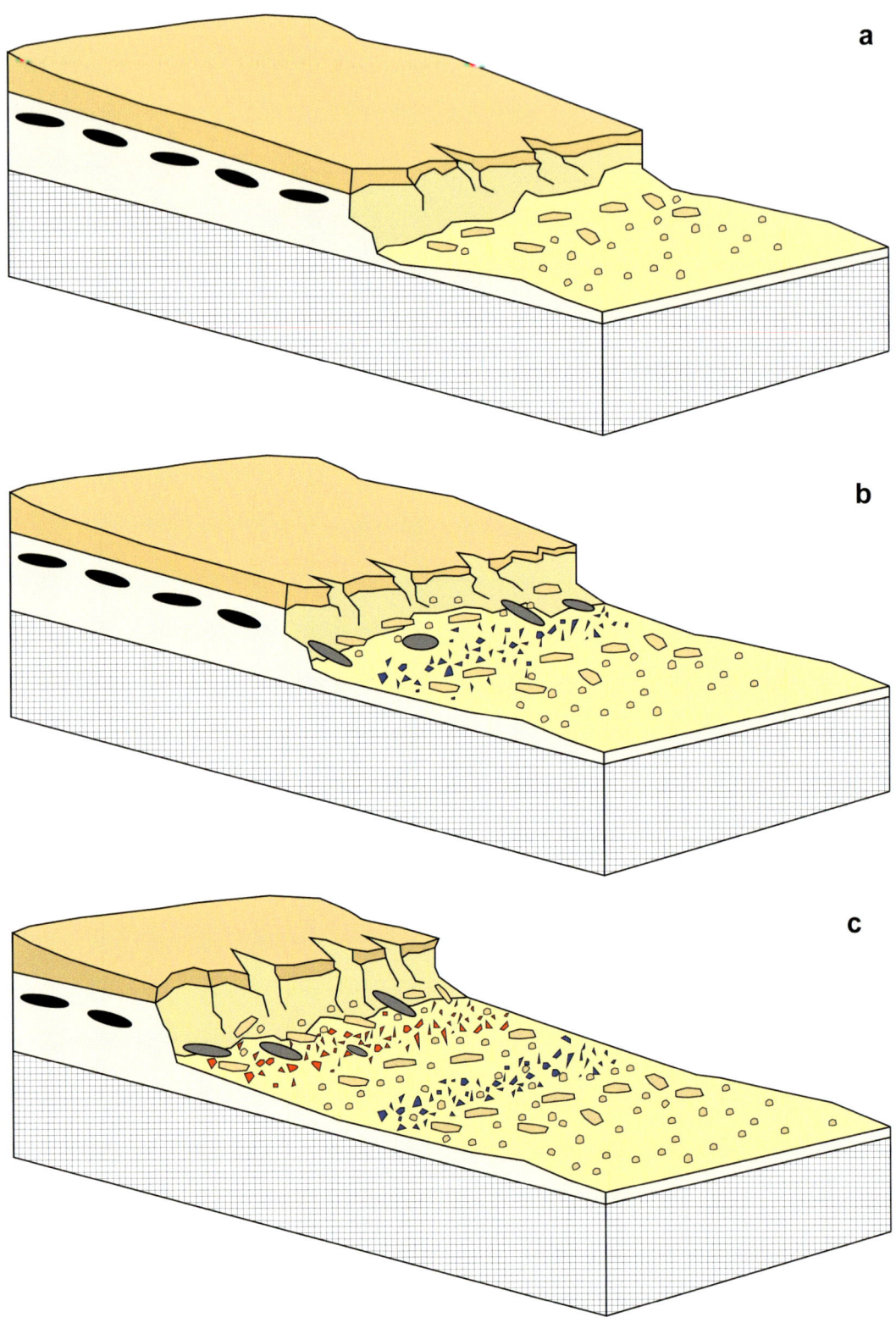

Figure 5.7. Schematic representation of multi-occupation site formation processes showing hypothetical retreat of the scarp doe to erosion: (a) Stage 1 shows a typical block section from the Nejd with chert nodules and slabs eroding within, (b) Stage 2 shows the advance of scarp erosion that exposes fresh chert nodules, which were used to produce Lower Palaeolithic stone tools by the initial hominid inhabitants of the Nejd Plateau, (c) Stage 3 shows continued erosion and retreat of the low scarp, which exposes new chert nodules, continuing throughout the Palaeolithic and Holocene. During subsequent stages, successive groups of toolmakers returned to exploit fresh chert nodules eroding from the edge of the scarp (illustration by Y.H. Hilbert).

DAP's "lateral stratigraphy" experiment is designed to assess whether spatial distribution and taphonomic weathering patterns are useful variables for relatively dating lithic assemblages at multi-component workshop sites on actively eroding chert quarries. Preliminary results suggest that in locations where there is a single, homogenous seam of raw material, we find older, more heavily weathered artifacts further from the present seam, while younger, less weathered specimens occur closer to the outcrop. This process is envisioned in Figure 5.7, where the first stage of exploitation leaves the chipping waste from Industry A around the original extent of the scarp. Sometime later, the scarp eroded back revealing fresh nodules, which were subsequently worked by Industry B, and so on. This model is predicated on the assumption that toolmakers were exploiting fresh chert exposures rather than weathered nodules.

The Dhofar Refugium?

There were two questions underpinning the Dhofar Archaeological Project: from where and when came the earliest anatomically modern humans in southern Arabia and was this region a demographic refugium during climatic downturns? We have had limited success answering both questions and in doing so have generated several new avenues of inquiry.

It is now certain that there were cultural connections between Africa and Arabia during MIS 5, associated with an early *Homo sapiens* population. We can be less certain of its locus of origin. Scholars currently trace the source of Nubian Complex technology to northern Sudan some 150,000 years ago, posited to have developed out of the Lupemban industry (Van Peer *et al.* 2003). Until the vast territories linking North Africa and Southwest Asia are more thoroughly explored, this question must remain open.

The Nubian tradition endured in Dhofar for sufficient time to develop into the derivative Mudayyan industry. The observed diminution of Levallois point technology may be associated with a shift in hunting practices. Scholars have proposed that toward the end of the Middle Palaeolithic, hunters required lower mass armatures to prey on small animals such as birds, rabbits and reptiles (Sisk and Shea 2009). If this explains the transition to smaller Mudayyan Levallois points, it follows that Mudayyan hunters had adapted to a landscape that no longer supported medium and large game. For now, the fate of the Mudayyan peoples of Dhofar remains unknown, although it is noteworthy that prepared core, bidirectional point production systems are reported from Jebel Faya AH II and Umm Taqa in the Gulf basin, the former bracketed between 40,000 and 10,000 BP (Bretzke *et al.* 2014).

While archaeologists have thus far failed to produce concrete evidence of Upper Palaeolithic human occupation in southern Arabia during MIS 2, geneticists have isolated the remains of deeply-rooted mtDNA haplogroups reaching back to the Terminal Pleistocene in Yemen and Dhofar (Al-Abri *et al.* 2012; Černý *et al.* 2011; Gandini *et al.* 2016). These studies point to a significant ice age refugium in South Arabia, highlighting the significance of the Upper Palaeolithic assemblage from TH.68. Were those western Nejd Plateau catchment systems outside the Dhofar Mountain rain shadow active during MIS 2, while the rest of the Peninsula languished in aridity and desiccation? Future research within these ancient river valleys will likely shed new light on Dhofar's ice age habitats.

Bibliography

Al-ABRI, A., E. Podgorná, J. I. Rose, L. Pereira, C. J. Mulligan, N. M. Silva, R. Bayoumi, P. Soares & V. Černý 2012. Pleistocene-Holocene boundary in Southern Arabia from the perspective of human mtDNA variation. *American Journal of Physical Anthropology* 149: 291-298. DOI: https://doi.org/10.1002/ajpa.22131

ALSHAREKH, A. 1995. *The Archaeology of Central Saudi Arabia: Investigations of lithic artefacts and stone structures in Northeast Riyadh* (Unpublished doctoral dissertation). Cambridge, University of Cambridge.

AMIRKHANOV, H. 1994. Research on the Palaeolithic and Neolithic of Hadramaut and Mahra. *Arabian Archaeology and Epigraphy* 5: 217-228.

AMIRKHANOV, H. 2006. *Stone Age of South Arabia*. Nauka, Moscow.

ANDERSON, D. E., A. S. Goudie & A. G. Parker 2007. *Global Environments through the Quaternary: Exploring environmental change*. Oxford, Oxford University Press.

ARMITAGE, S. J., S. A. Jasim, A. E. Marks, A. G. Parker, V. I. Usik & H.-P. Uerpmann 2011. The southern route "Out of Africa": evidence for an early expansion of modern humans into Arabia. *Science* 331: 453-456.

ARONSON, J., T. B. Aronson, A. Patzelt, S. G. Knees, G. P. Lewis, D. Lupton, H. Taifour, M. F. Gardner, H. Thompson, S. Al-Hatmi, S. & A. W. Al-Khulaidi 2017. Paleorelicts or archaeophytes: Enigmatic trees in the Middle East. *Journal of Arid Environments* 137: 69-82. DOI: https://doi.org/10.1016/j.jaridenv.2016.11.001

ATTWELL, L., K. Kovarovic and J. R. Kendal 2015. Fire in the Plio-Pleistocene: the functions of hominin fire use, and the mechanistic, developmental and evolutionary consequences. *Journal of Anthropological Science* 93: 1-20.

BAILEY, G. N., M. H. Devès, R. H. Inglis, M. G. Meredith-Williams, G. Momber, D. Sakellariou, A. G. M. Sinclair, G. Rousakis, S. Al-Ghamdi & A. M. Alsharekh 2015. Blue Arabia: Palaeolithic and underwater survey in SW Saudi Arabia and the role of coasts in Pleistocene dispersals. *Quaternary International* 382: 42-57.

BELLOMO, R. V. 1994. Methods of determining early hominid behavioral activities associated with the controlled use of fire at FxJj 20 Main, Koobi Fora, Kenva. *Journal of Human Evolution* 27: 173-195.

BESHKANI, A., T. Beuzen-Waller, S. Bonilauri & G. Gernez 2017a. Large Kombewa flake production in north Oman. *Arabian Archaeology and Epigraphy* 28: 125-137.

BESHKANI, A., T. Beuzen-Waller, S. Bonilauri & G. Gernez 2017b. The first evidence of Middle Palaeolithic Nubian technology in north-central Oman. *Antiquity*: 91.

BEYIN, A. 2013. A surface Middle Stone Age assemblage from the Red Sea coast of Eritrea: Implications for Upper Pleistocene human dispersals out of Africa. *Quaternary International* 300: 195-212.

BIAGI, P. 1994. An Early Palaeolithic site near Saiwan (Sultanate of Oman). *Arabian Archaeology and Epigraphy* 5: 81-88.

BLECHSCHMIDT, I., A. Matter, F. Preusser & D. Rieke-Zapp 2009. Monsoon triggered formation of Quaternary alluvial megafans in the interior of Oman. *Geomorphology* 110: 128-139. DOI: https://doi.org/10.1016/j.geomorph.2009.04.002

BOËDA, E., S. Bonilauri, J. Connan, D. Jarvie, N. Mercier, M. Tobey, H. Valladas, H. Al-Sakhel & S. Muhesen 2008. Middle Palaeolithic bitumen use at Umm el Tlel around 70,000 BP. *Antiquity* 82: 853-861.

BONILAURI, S., T. Beuzen-Waller, J. Giraur, M. Lemée, G. Gernez & E. Fouache 2015. Occupation during the Lower and Middle/Late Palaeolithic period in the Sufrat Valley (Adam region, Sultanate of Oman). *Proceedings of the Seminar for Arabian Studies* 45: 21-34.

BORDES, F. 1988. *Typologie du Paléolithique ancien et moyen.* Presses du CNRS.

BOUZOUGGAR, A., N. Barton, M. Vanhaeren, F. d'Errico, S. Collcutt, T. Higham, E. Hodge, S. Parfitt, E. Rhodes & J.-L. Schwenninger 2007. 82,000-year-old shell beads from North Africa and implications for the origins of modern human behavior. *Proceedings of the National Academy of Sciences* 104: 9964-9969.

BRANDT, S. A., E. C. Fisher, E. A. Hildebrand, R. Vogelsang, S. H. Ambrose, J. Lesur & H. Wang 2012. Early MIS 3 occupation of Mochena Borago Rockshelter, southwest Ethiopian highlands: Implications for Late Pleistocene archaeology, paleoenvironments and modern human dispersals. *Quaternary International* 274: 38-54. DOI: https://doi.org/10.1016/j.quaint.2012.03.047

BRÄUER, G. & M. J. Mehlman 1988. Hominid molars from a Middle Stone Age level at the Mumba rock shelter, Tanzania. *American Journal of Physical Anthropology* 75: 69-76.

BRAUN, D. R., T. Plummer, J. V. Ferraro, P. Ditchfield & L. C. Bishop 2009. Raw material quality and Oldowan hominin toolstone preferences: evidence from Kanjera South, Kenya. *Journal of Archaeological Science* 36: 1605-1614.

BRETZKE, K., N. J. Conard & H.-P. Uerpmann 2014. Excavations at Jebel Faya: the FAY-NE1 shelter sequence. *Proceedings of the Seminar for Arabian Studies* 44: 69-82.

BRETZKE, K., E. Yousif & S. Jasim S 2017. Filling in the gap – The Acheulean site Suhailah 1 from the central region of the Emirate of Sharjah, UAE. *Quaternary International 466.A: 23-32.*

CASANA, J., J. T. Herrmann & H. S. Qandil 2009. Settlement history in the eastern Rub al-Khali: Preliminary report of the Dubai Desert Survey (2006–2007). *Arabian Archaeology and Epigraphy* 20: 30-45.

ČERNÝ, V., C. J. Mulligan, V. Fernandes, N. M. Silva, F. Alshamali, A. Non, N. Harich, L. Cherni, A. B. A. El-Gaaied, A. Al-Meeri & L. Pereira 2011. Internal diversification of mitochondrial haplogroup R0a reveals post-Last Glacial Maximum demographic expansions in South Arabia. Molecular Biology and Evolution 28: 71-78.

CHARPENTIER, V., J.-F. Berger, R. Crassard, F. Borgi & P. Béarez 2016. Les premiers chasseurs-collecteurs maritimes d'Arabie (IXe-IVe millénaires avant notre ère). In C. Dupont & G. Marchand (Eds.), *Archéologie Des Chasseurs-Cueilleurs Maritimes. De La Fonction Des Habitats à l'organisation de l'espace Littoral.* Paris, Société préhistorique française, pp. 23-36.

CLARK, J. D. 1954. *Prehistory of the Horn of Africa*. Cambridge University Press, Cambridge.

CLARK, J. D. 1988. The Middle Stone Age of East Africa and the beginnings of regional identity. *Journal of World Prehistory* 2: 235-305.

CONARD, N. J. 2003. Palaeolithic ivory sculptures from southwestern Germany and the origins of figurative art. *Nature* 426: 830.

CORNWALL, P. B. 1946. A Lower Palaeolithic hand-axe from central Arabia. *Man* 46: 144.

CRASSARD, R. 2008a. La préhistoire du Yémen: diffusions et diversités locales, à travers l'étude d'industries lithiques du Hadramawt. BAR international series. Oxford, Archaeopress.

CRASSARD, R. 2008b. The "Washah method": an original laminar debitage from Hadramawt, Yemen. *Proceedings of the Seminar for Arabian Studies* 38: 3-14.

CRASSARD, R. and Y. H. Hilbert 2016. The prehistory of the region of Al-Kharj. In J. Schiettecatte & A. Alghazzi (Eds.), Al-Kharj I: Report on Two Excavation Seasons in the Oasis of Al-Kharj 2011 - 2012 Saudi Arabia. Riyadh, Saudi Commission for Tourism and National Heritage, pp. 51-80.

CRASSARD, R. & Y. H. Hilbert 2013. A Nubian Complex site from central Arabia: implications for Levallois taxonomy and human dispersals during the Upper Pleistocene. *PLoS One* 8, e69221.

CREMASCHI, M. & F. Negrino 2005. Evidence for an abrupt climatic change at 8700 14C yr B.P. in rockshelters and caves of Gebel Qara (Dhofar-Oman): Palaeoenvironmental implications. Geoarchaeology 20: 559-579. DOI: https://doi.org/10.1002/gea.20068

CREMASCHI, M. & F. Negrino 2002. The frankincense road of Sumhuram: Palaeoenvironmental and prehistorical background. In A. Avanzini (Ed.), Khor Rori Report 1. Pisa, Edizioni Plus, pp. 325-363.

CREMASCHI, M., A. Zerboni, V. Charpentier, R. Crassard, I. Isola, E. Regattieri & G. Zanchetta 2015. Early-Middle Holocene environmental changes and pre-Neolithic human occupations as recorded in the cavities of Jebel Qara (Dhofar, southern Sultanate of Oman). *Quaternary International* 382, 264-276. https://doi.org/10.1016/j.quaint.2014.12.058

DRECHOU, H., F. Hivernel & R. Karpoff 1968. Nouvelles stations préhistoriques dans les reliefs anciens de l'Arabie saoudite: Industries paléolithique et néolithique murets et gravures rupestres. *Bulletin Société Préhistorique Fr. Études Trav* 65: 817-832.

DRESCHLER, P. 2007. The Neolithic dispersal into Arabia. *Proceedings of the Seminar for Arabian Studies* 37: 93-109. DOI: https://doi.org/10.2307/41224060

EDENS, C. 2001. A bladelet industry in southwestern Saudi Arabia. *Arabian Archaeology and Epigraphy* 12: 137-142.

FEDELE, F. G. 2008. Wadi at-Tayyilah 3, a Neolithic and Pre-Neolithic occupation on the eastern Yemen Plateau, and its archaeofaunal information. *Proceedings of the Seminar for Arabian Studies* 38: 153-172.

FIELD, H. 1961. Palaeolithic implements from the Rub'al Khali. *Man* 61: 22-23.

FLEITMANN, D., S. J. Burns, A. Mangini, M. Mudelsee, J. Kramers, I. Villa, U. Neff, A. A. Al-Subbary, A. Buettner, D. Hippler & A. Matter 2007. Holocene ITCZ and Indian monsoon dynamics recorded in stalagmites from Oman and Yemen (Socotra). *Quaternary Science Reviews* 26: 170-188. DOI: https://doi.org/10.1016/j.quascirev.2006.04.012

GANDINI, F., A. Achilli, M. Pala, M. Bodner, S. Brandini, G. Huber, B. Egyed, L. Ferretti, A. Gomez-Carballa, A. Salas, R. Scozzari, F. Cruciani, A. Coppa, W. Parson, O. Semino, P. Soares, A. Torroni, M.B. Richards & A. Olivieri 2016. Mapping human dispersals into the Horn of Africa from Arabian Ice Age refugia using mitogenomes. *Scientific Reports* 6. DOI: https://doi.org/10.1038/srep25472

GARROD, D. A. E. 1934. Excavations at the Wady Al-Mughara, 1932-3. *Palestine Exploration Quarertly* 66: 85-89.

GIBBARD, P. L., M. J. Head & M. J. C. Walker 2010. Formal ratification of the Quaternary System/Period and the Pleistocene Series/Epoch with a base at 2.58 Ma. *Journal of Quaternary Science* 25: 96-102.

GLADIKH, M. I., N. L. Kornietz & O. Soffer 1984. Mammoth-bone dwellings on the Russian plain. *Scientific American* 251, 164-175.

GLENNIE, K. 2005. *The Desert of Southeast Arabia*. Manama, Gulf PetroLink.

GODER-GOLDBERGER, M., N. Gubenko & E. Hovers 2016. "Diffusion with modifications": Nubian assemblages in the central Negev highlands of Israel and their implications for Middle Paleolithic inter-regional interactions. *Quaternary International* 408: 121-139. DOI: https://doi.org/10.1016/j.quaint.2016.02.008

GOWLETT, J. A., J. W. Harris, D. Walton & B. A. Wood 1981. Early archaeological sites, hominid remains and traces of fire from Chesowanja, Kenya. *Nature* 294: 125.

GRÜNBERG, J. M. 2002. Middle Palaeolithic birch-bark pitch. *Antiquity* 76: 15-16.

GUICHARD, J. & G. Guichard. 1965. The Early and Middle Palaeolithic of Nubia: a preliminary report. In F. Wendorf (Ed.), *Contributions to the Prehistory of Nubia*, Dallas, Fort Burgwin and Southern Methodist University Press, pp. 57-116.

HADJOUIS, D. 2007. La faune des grands mammifères. In M.-L. Inizan & M. Rachad (Eds.), *Art Rupestre et Peuplements Préhistoriques Au Yémen*. Sanaa, Centre français d'archéologie et de sciences sociales. DOI: https://doi.org/10.4000/books.cefas.1591

HARMAND, S., J. E. Lewis, C. S. Feibel, C. J. Lepre, S. Prat, A. Lenoble, X. Boës, R. L. Quinn, M. Brenet & A. Arroyo 2015. 3.3-million-year-old stone tools from Lomekwi 3, West Turkana, Kenya. *Nature* 521: 310-315.

HARRIS, J. W. & G. Isaac. 1976. The Karari industry: Early Pleistocene archaeological evidence from the terrain east of Lake Turkana, Kenya. *Nature* 262: 102.

HENSHILWOOD, C. S., F. d'Errico & I. Watts 2009. Engraved ochres from the middle stone age levels at Blombos Cave, South Africa. *Journal of Human Evolution* 57: 27-47.

HERSHKOVITZ, I., G. W. Weber, R. Quam, M. Duval, *et al.* 2018. The earliest modern humans outside Africa. *Science* 359: 456-459. DOI: https://doi.org/10.1126/science.aap8369

HILBERT, Y. H. 2013. Khamseen rock shelter and the Late Palaeolithic-Neolithic transition in Dhofar. *Arabian Archaeology and Epigraphy* 24: 51-58.

HILBERT, Y. H. 2014. *Khashabian: a Late Paleolithic industry from Dhofar, southern Oman.* BAR International Series 2601. Oxford, Archeopress.

HILBERT, Y. H., J. I. Rose & R. G. Roberts 2012. Late Palaeolithic core reduction strategies in Dhofar, Oman. *Proceedings of the Seminar for Arabian Studies* 42: 101-118.

HILBERT, Y. H., A. Parton, M. W. Morley, L. P. Linnenlucke, Z. Jacobs, L. Clark-Balzan, R. G. Roberts, C. S. Galletti, J.-L. Schwenninger & J. I. Rose 2015a. Terminal Pleistocene and Early Holocene archaeology and stratigraphy of the southern Nejd, Oman. *Quaternary International* 382: 250-263.

HILBERT, Y. H., V. I. Usik, C. S. Galletti, M. W. Morley, A. Parton, L. Clark-Balzan, J.-L. Schwenninger, L. P. Linnenlucke, R. G. Roberts, Z. Jacobs & J. I. Rose 2015b. Archaeological evidence for indigenous human occupation of Southern Arabia at the Pleistocene/Holocene transition: The case of al-Hatab in Dhofar, Southern Oman. *Paléorient* 41: 31-49.

HILBERT, Y. H., R. Crassard, J. I. Rose, J. M. Geiling & V. I. Usik 2016. Technological homogeneity within the Arabian Nubian Complex: Comparing chert and quartzite assemblages from central and southern Arabia. *Journal of Lithic Studies* 3. DOI: https://doi.org/10.2218/jls.v3i2.1420

HILBERT, Y. H., R. Crassard, G. Charloux & R. Loreto 2017. Nubian technology in northern Arabia: Impact on interregional variability of Middle Paleolithic industries. *Quaternary International* 435: 77-93. DOI: https://doi.org/10.1016/j.quaint.2015.11.047

HILBERT, Y. H., I. Clemente-Conte, J. M. Geiling, J. Setin, E. Ruiz-Martinez, C. Lentfer, V. Rots & J. I. Rose 2018. Woodworking sites from the Late Paleolithic of South Arabia: functional and technological analysis of burins from Dhofar, Oman. *Journal of Archaeological Science: Reports* 20, 115-134.

HILDEBRANDT, A. & E. A. Eltahir 2006. Forest on the edge: seasonal cloud forest in Oman creates its own ecological niche. *Geophysical Research Letters* 33, L11401. DOI: 10.1029/2006GL026022.

HOORN, C. & M. Cremaschi 2004. Late Holocene palaeoenvironmental history of Khawr Rawri and Khawr Al Balid (Dhofar, Sultanate of Oman). *Palaeogeography, Palaeoclimatology, Palaeoecology* 213: 1-36. DOI: https://doi.org/10.1016/j.palaeo.2004.03.014

HUBLIN, J.-J., A. Ben-Ncer, S. E. Bailey, S. E. Freidline, S. Neubauer, M. M. Skinner, I. Bergmann, A. Le Cabec, S. Benazzi, K. Harvati & P. Gunz 2017. New fossils from Jebel Irhoud, Morocco and the pan-African origin of *Homo sapiens*. *Nature* 546: 289-292. DOI: https://doi.org/10.1038/nature22336

INGLIS, R., A. Sinclair, A. Shuttleworth, A. Alsharekh, M. Devès, S. Al-Ghamdi, M. Meredith-Williams & G. Bailey 2014. Investigating the Palaeolithic landscapes and archaeology of the Jizan and Asir regions, south-western Saudi Arabia. *Proceedings of the Seminar for Arabian Studies* 44: 193-211.

INIZAN, M.-L. & L. Ortlieb. 1987. Préhistoire dans la région de Shabwa au Yemen du Sud (R.D.P. Yemen). *Paléorient* 13: 5-22. DOI: https://doi.org/10.3406/paleo.1987.4414

JAGHER, R. 2009. The Central Oman Paleolithic Survey: Recent research in southern Arabia and reflection on the prehistoric evidence. In M. D. Petraglia & J. I. Rose (Eds.), *The Evolution of Human Populations in Arabia*. Dordrecht, Springer, pp. 139-150.

JAGHER, R. and C. Pümpin 2010. A new approach to central Omani prehistory. *Proceedings of the Seminar for Arabian Studies* 40: 185-200.

JENNINGS, R. P., C. Shipton, P. Breeze, P. Cuthbertson, M. A. Bernal, W. O. Wedage, N. A. Drake, T. S. White, H. Groucutt & A. Parton 2015. Multi-scale Acheulean landscape survey in the Arabian Desert. *Quaternary International* 382: 58-81.

KINDERMANN, K., P. Van Peer & F. Henselowsky 2017. At the lakeshore - an Early Nubian Complex site linked with lacustrine sediments (Eastern Desert, Egypt). *Quaternary International*. DOI: https://doi.org/10.1016/j.quaint.2017.11.006.

KLEIN, R. G. 2009. *The Human Career: Human biological and cultural origins*. Chicago, University of Chicago Press.

KURASHINA, H. 1987. *An Examination of Prehistoric Lithic Technology in East-Central Ethiopia*. (Unpublished doctoral dissertation), Berkeley, University of California.

LAMBECK, K. 1996. Shoreline reconstructions for the Persian Gulf since the last glacial maximum. *Earth and Planetary Science Letters* 142: 43-57.

LEAKEY, M. D. 1971. *Olduvai Gorge III: Excavations in Beds I and II, 1960-1963*. Cambridge, Cambridge University Press.

LEAKEY, M. G. & J. M. Harris. 1978. *Koobi Fora Research Project: the fossil hominids and an introduction to their context, 1968-1974*. Oxford, Oxford University Press.

LEPVRIER, C., M. Fournier, T. Bérard & J. Roger 2002. Cenozoic extension in coastal Dhofar (southern Oman): Implications on the oblique rifting of the Gulf of Aden. *Tectonophysics* 357: 279-293.

LÉZINE, A.-M. 2009. Climatic history of the African and Arabian deserts. *Comptes Rendus Geoscience* 341: 569-574. DOI: https://doi.org/10.1016/j.crte.2009.09.002

LÉZINE, A.-M., S. J. Ivory, P. Braconnot & O. Marti 2017. Timing of the southward retreat of the ITCZ at the end of the Holocene humid period in southern Arabia: Data-model comparison. *Quaternary Science Reviews* 164: 68-76. DOI: https://doi.org/10.1016/j.quascirev.2017.03.019

LISIECKI, L. & M. Raymo 2005. A Pliocene-Pleistocene stack of 57 globally distributed benthic δ18O records. *Paleoceanography* 20, PA1003. DOI: 10.1029/2004PA001071.

MACUMBER, P. 2011. A geomorphological and hydrological underpinning for archaeological research in northern Qatar. *Proceedings of the Seminar for Arabian Studies* 41: 187-200.

MAHER, L. A. 2009. The Late Pleistocene of Arabia in Relation to the Levant. In M. D. Petraglia & J. I. Rose (Eds.), *The Evolution of Human Populations in Arabia*. Dordrecht, Springer, pp. 187-204.

MANDAVILLE, J. P. 1990. *Flora of Eastern Saudi Arabia*. London Kegan Paul.

MARKS, A. E. 1968. The Mousterian industries of Nubia. In F. Wendorf (Ed.), *The Prehistory of Nubia, vol. 1*. Dallas, Fort Burgwin and Southern Methodist University Press, pp. 194-314.

MARKS, A. E. 1983. *Prehistory and Paleoenvironments of the Central Negev, Israel, vol. 3*. Dallas, Fort Burgwin and Southern Methodist University Press.

MATTER, A., E. Neubert, F. Preusser, T. Rosenberg & K. Al-Wagdani 2015. Palaeo-environmental implications derived from lake and sabkha deposits of the southern Rub Al-Khali, Saudi Arabia and Oman. *Quaternary International* 382: 120-131. DOI: https://doi.org/10.1016/j.quaint.2014.12.029

MAZZA, P. P. A., F. Martini, B. Sala, M. Magi, M. P. Colombini, G. Giachi, F. Landucci, C. Lemorini, F. Modugno & E. Ribechini 2006. A new Palaeolithic discovery: tar-hafted stone tools in a European Mid-Pleistocene bone-bearing bed. *Journal of Archaeological Science* 33: 1310-1318.

McBREARTY, S. & A. S. Brooks 2000. The revolution that wasn't: a new interpretation of the origin of modern human behavior. *Journal of Human Evolution* 39: 453-563.

McCLURE, H. A. 1976. Radiocarbon chronology of late Quaternary lakes in the Arabian Desert. *Nature* 263: 755.

McCLURE, H. A. 1994. A new Arabian stone tool assemblage and notes on the Aterian industry of North Africa. *Arabian Archaeology and Epigraphy* 5: 1-16.

McDERMOTT, F., C. Stringer, R. Grün, C. T. Williams, V. K. Din & C. J. Hawkesworth 1996. New Late-Pleistocene uranium-thorium and ESR dates for the Singa hominid (Sudan). *Journal of Human Evolution* 31: 507-516.

McDOUGALL, I., F. H. Brown & J. G. Fleagle 2005. Stratigraphic placement and age of modern humans from Kibish, Ethiopia. *Nature* 433: 733.

McPHERRON, S. P., Z. Alemseged, C. W. Marean, J. G. Wynn, D. Reed, D. Geraads, R. Bobe and H. A. Béarat 2010. Evidence for stone-tool-assisted consumption of animal tissues before 3.39 million years ago at Dikika, Ethiopia. *Nature* 466: 857-860. DOI: https://doi.org/10.1038/nature09248

MERCIER, N., H. Valladas, L. Froget, J.-L. Joron, P.-M. Vermeersch, P. Van Peer and J. Moeyersons. 1999. Thermoluminescence dating of a Middle Palaeolithic occupation at Sodmein Cave, Red Sea Mountains (Egypt). *Journal of Archaeological Science* 26: 1339-1345.

MILANKOVIČ, M. 1920. *Théorie mathématique des phénomènes thermiques produits par la radiation solaire*. Paris, Gauthier-Villars.

MILLER, A. G. & M. Morris. 1988. *The Plants of Dhofar*. Muscat, Office of the Advisor to His Majesty the Sultan for Cultural Affairs.

OLSZEWSKI, D. I., H. L. Dibble, S. P. McPherron, U. A. Schurmans, L. Chiotti & J. R. Smith 2010. Nubian Complex strategies in the Egyptian high desert. *Journal of Human Evolution* 59: 188-201.

OTVOS, E. G. 2015. The last interglacial stage: Definitions and marine highstand, North America and Eurasia. *Quaternary International* 383: 158-173.

PARKER, A. G., L. Eckersley, M. M. Smith, A. S. Goudie, S. Stokes, S. Ward, K. White & M. J. Hodson 2004. Holocene vegetation dynamics in the northeastern Rub Al-Khali desert, Arabian Peninsula: a phytolith, pollen and carbon isotope study. *Journal of Quaternary Science* 19: 665-676. DOI: https://doi.org/10.1002/jqs.880

PATZELT, A. 2011. The Themeda quadrivalvis tall-grass savannah of Oman at the crossroad between Africa and Asia. *Edinburgh Journal of Botany* 68, 301-319.

PAYNE, J. C. & S. Hawkins 1963. A Surface Collection of Flints from Habarut in Southern Arabia. *Man* 63: 185-188.

PETRAGLIA, M. D. 2003. The Lower Paleolithic of the Arabian Peninsula: occupations, adaptations, and dispersals. *Journal of World Prehistory* 17: 141-179.

PLATEL, J., J. Roger, T. Petters, I. Mercolli, J. Kramers & Le-Métour. 1992. *Geological map of Salalah, explanatory notes*. Muscat, Ministry of Petroleum and Minerals, Sultanate of Oman.

PLATEL, J.-P. & J. Roger. 1989. Evolution géodynamique du Dhofar (Sultanat d'Oman) pendant le Crétacé et le Tertiaire en relation avec l'ouverture du golfe d'Aden. *Bulletin de la Société Géologique de France*: 253-263.

PLATT, D. E., M. Haber, M. B. Dagher-Kharrat, B. Douaihy, G. Khazen, M. Ashrafian Bonab, A. Salloum, F. Mouzaya, D. Luiselli, C. Tyler-Smith, C. Renfrew, E. Matisoo-Smith & P. A. Zalloua 2017. Mapping Post-Glacial expansions: the peopling of Southwest Asia. *Scientific Reports* 7, 40338. DOI: https://doi.org/10.1038/srep40338

PRESTON, G. W., D. S. G. Thomas, A. S. Goudie, O. A. C. Atkinson, M. J. Leng, M. J. Hodson, H. Walkington, V. Charpentier, S. Méry, F. Borgi & A. G. Parker 2015. A multi-proxy analysis of the Holocene humid phase from the United Arab Emirates and its implications for southeast Arabia's Neolithic populations. *Quaternary International* 382: 277-292. DOI: https://doi.org/10.1016/j.quaint.2015.01.054

PREUSSER, F. 2009. Chronology of the impact of Quaternary climate change on continental environments in the Arabian Peninsula. Comptes *Rendus Geosciences* 341: 621-632. DOI: https://doi.org/10.1016/j.crte.2009.02.003

PULLAR, J. 1974. Harvard Archaeological Survey in Oman, 1973: I-Flint sites in Oman. *Proceedings of the Seminar for Arabian Studies* 4: 33-48.

RACHAD, M. 2007. *Chapitre VII Chronologie et styles de l'art rupestre. Art Rupestre Peoplements Préhistoriques Au Émen*. Sana'a, CEFAS Editions, pp. 73-82.

RADIES, D., S. T. Hasiotis, F. Preusser, E. Neubert & A. Matter 2005. Paleoclimatic significance of Early Holocene faunal assemblages in wet interdune deposits of the Wahiba Sand Sea, Sultanate of Oman. *Journal of Arid Environments* 62: 109-125. DOI: https://doi.org/10.1016/j.jaridenv.2004.09.021

RAFFAELLI, M. & M. Tardelli 2006. Phytogeographic zones of Dhofar (Southern Oman). *Bocconea* 19: 103-108.

RHOTERT, H. & F. M. T. Böhl. 1938. *Transjordanien: Vorgeschichtliche Forschungen*. Strecker und Schröder.

RICHTER, D., G. Tostevin & P. Škrdla 2008. Bohunician technology and thermoluminescence dating of the type locality of Brno-Bohunice (Czech Republic). *Journal of Human Evolution* 55: 871-885.

ROSE, J. I. 2006. *Among Arabian Sands: defining the Palaeolithic of Southern Arabia* (Unpublished doctoral dissertation). Dallas, Southern Methodist University.

ROSE, J. I. 2007. The Arabian Corridor Migration Model: archaeological evidence for hominin dispersals into Oman during the Middle and Upper Pleistocene. *Proceedings of the Seminar for Arabian Studies* 37: 219-237.

ROSE, J. I. 2010. New light on human prehistory in the Arabo-Persian Gulf oasis. *Current Anthropology* 51: 849-883.

ROSE, J. I. & Y. H. Hilbert 2014. New prehistoric sites in the southern Rub'al-Khali desert, Oman. *Antiquity* 88: Project Gallery.

ROSE, J. I. & V. I. Usik 2009. The "Upper Paleolithic" of South Arabia. In M. D. Petraglia & J. I. Rose (Eds.), *The Evolution of Human Populations in Arabia*. Dordrecht, Springer, pp. 169-185.

ROSE, J. I. & A. E. Marks 2014. "Out of Arabia" and the Middle-Upper Palaeolithic transition in the southern Levant. *Quartär* 61: 49-85.

ROSE, J. I., V. I. Usik, A. E. Marks, Y. H. Hilbert, C. S. Galletti, A. Parton, J. M. Geiling, V Černý, M. W. Morley & R. G. Roberts 2011. The Nubian Complex of Dhofar, Oman: an African Middle Stone Age Industry in southern Arabia. *PLoS One* 6, e28239. DOI: https://doi.org/10.1371/journal.pone.0028239

ROSENBERG, T. M., F. Preusser, I. Blechschmidt, D. Fleitmann, R. Jagher & A. Matter 2012. Late Pleistocene palaeolake in the interior of Oman: a potential key area for the dispersal of anatomically modern humans out-of-Africa? *Journal of Quaternary Science* 27: 13-16. DOI: https://doi.org/10.1002/jqs.1560

ROTS, V., P. Van Peer & P. M. Vermeersch 2011. Aspects of tool production, use, and hafting in Palaeolithic assemblages from Northeast Africa. *Journal of Human Evolution* 60: 637-664.

RUST, A. 1938. Beitrag zur erkenntnis der Abwicklung der vorgeschichtlichen Kultur-perioden in Syrien. *Prähistorische Zeitschrift*: 205-218.

SCERRI, E. M., P. S. Breeze, A. Parton, H. S. Groucutt, T. S. White, C. Stimpson, L. Clark-Balzan, R. Jennings, A. Alsharekh & M. D. Petraglia 2015. Middle to late Pleistocene human habitation in the western Nefud desert, Saudi Arabia. *Quaternary International* 382: 200-214.

SCHMIDT, C., K. Kindermann, P. Van Peer & O. Bubenzer 2015. Multi-emission luminescence dating of heated chert from the Middle Stone Age sequence at Sodmein Cave (Red Sea Mountains, Egypt). *Journal of Archaeological Science* 63: 94-103. DOI: https://doi.org/10.1016/j.jas.2015.08.016

SEMAW, S. 2000. The world's oldest stone artefacts from Gona, Ethiopia: their implications for understanding stone technology and patterns of human evolution between 2· 6–1· 5 million years ago. *Journal of Archaeological Science* 27: 1197-1214.

SEMAW, S., M. Rogers & D. Stout 2009. The Oldowan-Acheulian transition: is there a "Developed Oldowan" artifact tradition?. In *Sourcebook of Paleolithic Transitions*. Dordrecht, Springer, pp. 173-193.

SHACKLETON, N. J., M. F. Sánchez-Goñi, D. Pailler and Y. Lancelot 2003. Marine isotope substage 5e and the Eemian interglacial. *Global Planetary Change* 36: 151-155.

SHIMELMITZ, R., R. Barkai & A. Gopher 2016. Regional variability in late Lower Paleolithic Amudian blade technology: Analyzing new data from Qesem, Tabun and Yabrud I. *Quaternary International* 398: 37-60.

SHIMELMITZ, R., R. Barkai & A. Gopher, A. 2011. Systematic blade production at late lower Paleolithic (400–200 kyr) Qesem Cave, Israel. *Journal of Human Evolution* 61: 458-479.

SHIPTON, C., A. Parton, P. Breeze, R. Jennings, H. S. Groucutt, T. S. White, N. Drake, R. Crassard, A. Alsharekh & M. D. Petraglia 2014. Large Flake Acheulean in the Nefud desert of northern Arabia. *PaleoAnthropology* 2014: 446-462.

SISK, M. L. & J. J. Shea 2009. Experimental use and quantitative performance analysis of triangular flakes (Levallois points) used as arrowheads. *Journal of Archaeological Science* 36: 2039-2047.

SMITH, J. R., A. L. Hawkins, Y. Asmerom, V. Polyak & R. Giegengack 2007. New age constraints on the Middle Stone Age occupations of Kharga Oasis, Western Desert, Egypt. *Journal of Human Evolution* 52: 690-701.

STEKELIS, M. & L. Picard. 1938. Jisr Banat Ya'qub. Quarterly of the Palestine *Antiquities Department* 6: 214-215.

STEKELIS, M., L. Picard, N. Schulman & G. Haas. 1960. Villafranchian Deposits near 'Ubeidiya'in the Central Jordan Valley (Preliminary Report). *Bulletin of the Israel Research Council* 9: 175-184.

STEWART, M., J. Louys, G. J. Price, N. A. Drake, H. S. Groucutt & M. D. Petraglia 2017. Middle and Late Pleistocene mammal fossils of Arabia and surrounding regions: Implications for biogeography and hominin dispersals. *Quaternary International*. DOI: https://doi.org/10.1016/j.quaint.2017.11.052

STOUT, D. J. Quade, S. Semaw, M. J. Rogers & N. E. Levin 2005. Raw material selectivity of the earliest stone toolmakers at Gona, Afar, Ethiopia. *Journal of Human Evolution* 48: 365-380.

STOUT, D. S. Semaw, M. J. Rogers & D. Cauche 2010. Technological variation in the earliest Oldowan from Gona, Afar, Ethiopia. *Journal of Human Evolution* 58: 474-491.

THIEME, H. 2007. Die Schöninger Speere. *Mensch Jagd Vor* 400: 1-247.

TOMSKY, J. 1982. *Das Altpaläolithikum im Vorderen Orient*. Stuttgart, Reichert Verlag.

TOTH, N. 1985. The Oldowan reassessed: a close look at early stone artifacts. *Journal of Archaeological Science* 12: 101-120.

UERPMANN, H.-P., D. T. Potts & M. Uerpmann 2009. Holocene (re-)occupation of eastern Arabia. In M. D. Petraglia & J. I. Rose (Eds.), *The Evolution of Human Populations in Arabia*. Dordrecht, Springer, pp. 205-214.

UERPMANN, H.-P., M. Uerpmann, A. Kutterer & S. A. Jasim 2013. The Neolithic period in the central region of the Emirate of Sharjah (UAE). *Arabian Archaeology and Epigraphy* 24: 102-108.

UERPMANN, M. 1992. Structuring the late stone age of southeastern Arabia. *Arabian Archaeology and Epigraphy* 3: 65-109.

USIK, V. I., J. I. Rose, Y. H. Hilbert, V. Van Peer & A. E. Marks 2013. Nubian Complex reduction strategies in Dhofar, southern Oman. *Quaternary International* 300: 244-266.

VAN PEER, P. 1992. *The Levallois Reduction Strategy, Monographs in World Archaeology*. Madison, Prehistory Press.

VAN PEER, P., R. Fullagar, S. Stokes, R. M. Bailey, J. Moeyersons, F. Steenhoudt, A. Geerts, T. Vanderbeken, M. De Dapper & F. Geus 2003. The Early to Middle Stone Age transition and the emergence of modern human behaviour at site 8-B-11, Sai Island, Sudan. *Journal of Human Evolution* 45: 187-193.

VAN PEER, P. & P. Vermeersch 2007. The place of northeast Africa in the early history of modern humans: new data and interpretations on the Middle Stone Age. In P. Mellars, K. Boyle, O. Bar-Yosef & C. Stringer (Eds.), *Rethinking the Human Revolution*. Cambridge, McDonald Institute for Archaeological Research, pp. 187-198.

Van Peer, P., P. M. Vermeersch, J. Moeyersons & W. Van Neer. 1996. Palaeolithic sequence of Sodmein cave site, Red Sea Mountains, Egypt. In G. Pwiti & R. Soper, (Eds.), *Aspects of African Archaeology*. Harare, University of Zimbabwe Publications, pp. 149-156.

VAN PEER, P., P. M. Vermeersch & E. Paulissen 2010. *Chert quarrying, lithic technology and a modern human burial at the palaeolithic site of Taramsa 1, Upper Egypt*. Leuven, Leuven University Press.

VERMEERSCH, P. M., E. Paulissen, P. Van Peer, S. Stokes, C. Charlier, C. Stringer & W. Lindsay. 1998. A Middle Palaeolithic burial of a modern human at Taramsa Hill, Egypt. *Antiquity* 72: 475-484.

VILLA, P. & F. d'Errico 2001. Bone and ivory points in the Lower and Middle Paleolithic of Europe. *Journal of Human Evolution* 41: 69-112.

WAELBROECK, C., L. Labeyrie, E. Michel, J. Duplessy, J. McManus, K. Lambeck, E. Balbon & M. Labracherie 2002. Sea-level and deep water temperature changes derived from benthic foraminifera isotopic records. *Quaternary Science Reviews* 21: 295-305. DOI: https://doi.org/10.1016/S0277-3791(01)00101-9

WAHIDA, G., W. Y. Al-Tikriti & M. Beech 2008. Barakah: a Middle Palaeolithic site in Abu Dhabi Emirate. *Proceedings of the Seminar for Arabian Studies* 38: 55-64.

WALKER, M. J., M. Berkelhammer, S. Björck, L. C. Cwynar, D. A. Fisher, A. J. Long, J. J. Lowe, R. M. Newnham, S. O. Rasmussen & H. Weiss 2012. Formal subdivision of the Holocene Series/Epoch: a discussion paper by a working group of INTIMATE (Integration of ice-core, marine and terrestrial records) and the subcommission on Quaternary Stratigraphy (International Commission on Stratigraphy). *Journal of Quaternary Science* 27: 649-659.

WENDORF, F. & R. Schild 1980. *Prehistory of the Eastern Sahara*. Dallas, Fort Burgwin and Southern Methodist University Press.

WHALEN, N. M., A. Killick, N. James, G. Morsi & M. Kamal 1981. The Comprehensive Archaeological Survey Program. Saudi Arabian Archaeological Reconnaissance 1980. Preliminary Report on the Western Province Survey. *Atlal* 5: 43-58.

WHALEN, N. M. & D. W. Pease 1991. Archaeological survey in southwest Yemen, 1990. *Paléorient* 17: 127-131.

WHALEN, N. M. & K. E. Schatte 1997. Pleistocene sites in southern Yemen. *Arabian Archaeology and Epigraphy* 8: 1-10.

WHALEN, N. M., M. Zoboroski & K. Schubert 2002. The Lower Palaeolithic in Southwestern Oman. *Adumatu* 5: 27-34.

YANG, M. A. & Q. Fu 2018. Insights into Modern Human Prehistory Using Ancient Genomes. *Trends in Evolutionary Genetics* 34: 184-196. DOI: https://doi.org/10.1016/j.tig.2017.11.008

ZARINS, J. 2001. *The Land of Incense: Archaeological work in the Governorate of Dhofar, Sultanate of Oman, 1990 - 1995*. Muscat, Sultan Qaboos University Publications.

Index

http://mhc.gov.om

Ministry of Heritage and Culture

@mhc_gov

mhcgov

تراث وثقافة